The HIDDEN TREASURE of DUTCH BUFFALO CREEK

BY JACKSON BADGENOONE

 FriesenPress

Suite 300 - 990 Fort St
Victoria, BC, Canada, V8V 3K2
www. friesenpress. com

ISBN
978-1-4602-6734-9 (Hardcover)
978-1-4602-6735-6 (Paperback)
978-1-4602-6736-3 (eBook)

1. Fiction, Historical

Distributed to the trade by The Ingram Book Company

Table of Contents

Chapter I. Beacon for Tadpoles 1
Chapter II. Sifting East and West of Dixie 12
Chapter III. Sifting Through Sands of Time .15
Chapter IV. Aftermath of a Live Round 19
Chapter V. Let The Marbles Roll 26
Chapter VI. Truth Sometimes Floats On Water 30

[Book 2] The Book of The Never Born
Preface to The Book of The Neverborn 34
Chapter VII. It Is A Wonderful Life 37
Definitions of the High Water Markers 41

[Book 2] The Book of The Never Born
Chapter X. The Original Badgenoone 52

[Book 3] The High Water Markers of Jackson's Observee
Preface to The High Water Markers of Jackson's Observee 70
Chapter I. Around A Georgia Campfire 74

[Book 4] The High Water Markers of Anna's Observee
About the Author 80
Preface to the High Water Markers of Anna's Observee 82
Chapter I. Born For The Journey 88
Chapter II. Fifty-six Steps 96
Chapter III. A Golden Cross And Silver Streams 98
Chapter IV. The Altruist 102
Chapter V. What's In A Color? 112
Chapter VI. A New Family Emerges 119
Chapter VII. A Chance Encounter 123
Chapter X. A Warm Fuzzy 125

Chapter XI. What's In An Imprint? *131*

Chapter XXI. Super Bowl Reducere *137*

[Book 5] The High Water Markers of Bernadette's Observee

Preface to The High Water Markers of Bernadette's Observee . . . *154*

Chapter II. The Tracks From Transfer Station *157*

Chapter III. A New Order Emerges. *159*

Chapter V. The Last Supper *163*

Chapter XII. Rails To And From A Windy City *164*

Chapter XXVII. Rings of Smoke. *168*

[Book 6] The High Water Markers of Christopher's Observee

Preface to The High Water Markers of Christopher's Observee. . *180*

Chapter VII. Print Shop Prelude *183*

Chapter VIII. The World is a Big Round Sphere *185*

Chapter IX. Champion for a Cause *189*

Chapter XI. Cascade, The War Bride Returns Home *191*

Chapter XV. Just an Hour Away from an Open Lock *196*

Chapter XXI. Thimbles for NuNu *198*

Chapter XXV. Quotes of the Day *200*

[Book 7] The High Water Markers of Daniel's Observee

Chapter I. Streets Paved With Gold *204*

Chapter V. A Small Price to Pay *208*

Chapter XI. Less Fortunate Women *210*

Chapter XV. M&Ms, This One's for You *212*

Chapter XXIV. Treasure Every Canvas *216*

[Book 8] The High Water Markers of Elizabeth's Observee

Preface to The High Water Markers of Elizabeth's Observee *220*

Chapter XII. A Year of Reckoning *222*

Chapter XXIX. Count Every Stroke *227*

Chapter XXX. Not Just Another Day at the Beach. *231*

Chapter XXXIX. The Last Lincoln Mercury Grand Marquis . . . *232*

[Book 9] The High Water Markers of Frederick's Observee

Preface to the High Water Markers of Frederick's Observee 236

Chapter II. Enjoy Yourself—It's Later Than You Think 238

Chapter VII. Just Right 240

Chapter VIII. A Fateful Duel 244

Chapter XI. What's In a Name? 249

Chapter XV. An Empty Nest 256

Chapter XIX. More Ripples 261

Chapter XXIII. Honor Twenty-four Young Men,
Seventy Times Seven Times 265

Chapter XXV. Not a Line In The Sky 268

[Book 10] The High Water Markers of George's Observee

About the Author 272

Chapter II. A Headstone Without Flowers 273

Chapter III. Count The Cost 274

Chapter IV. Notes Also Tell a Story 275

Chapter V. The Green Wave 276

Chapter XIV. Seats 3A and 3B Connect
at Thirty-thousand Feet 279

[Book 11] The High Water Markers of Henry's Observee

Chapter I. The Surprise Baby 284

Chapter III. Another Striking Resemblance 285

Chapter VIII. A Northern Bell 287

Chapter X. Merryall 289

Chapter XIV. The Pilot 292

[Book 12] The High Water Markers of Israel's Observee

Preface to The High Water Markers of Israel's Observee 296

Chapter III. Connecting Waters 297

Chapter IV. Under The Gun 299

Chapter VI. View From The Top 302

Chapter X. Pan For Gold 306

[Book 1] The Hidden Treasure of Dutch Buffalo Creek

Chapter LXXIII. Back To The Den *310*

Selected Notes *320*

Bibliography *321*

About Jackson Badgenoone *332*

CHAPTER I
Beacon for Tadpoles

The creek bed was nearly dry, a rivulet with barely a stir. Thirty feet beneath the western ridge, ten feet east of where the cool water kissed the muddy western bank, a glint of silver reflected skyward from a shallow, slow-swirling cranny.

It was a warm summer day in 2014, Anno Domini, A.D., a year of reflection and reconciliation. At high noon, a beacon of sunlight danced through the leaves of a sweet gum tree. A focused ray silhouetted an object in the water below. Up closer, it appeared more like gold; perhaps it *was* gold.

Just a few miles to the southeast, gold was discovered in another rocky creek bed. That find led to the formation of the first commercial gold mine in the United States. The mine produced enough ore to prompt the establishment of a mint in the neighboring city of Charlotte, North Carolina.

It was not long after the founding of the new country, and not long before a conflict that would test the foundation of that republic. To this day, children at heart from near and far continue to sift with metal pans for nuggets of gold at the Reed Gold Mine.

Two books, *Golden Promise in the Piedmont: The Story of John Reed's Mine* and *The Carolina Gold Rush*, describe in some detail how the mine came into being. They also consider the impact it had on the local economy and the emergence of a growing national obsession.

The object shimmering in the water demanded attention.

A rope was anchored to a maple tree, wound three times around the trunk. It stretched another fifty feet, more than sufficient to lower to the edge below, and halfway to the eastern bank. Dust plumes rose as boot-clad feet pressed into the parched brown mud and dull orange clay; the feet then made a cautious descent to the water.

Above the surface, a cylindrical object stood guard; it was about three inches high, with a diameter not much greater than that of a Roman Denarius. It was not gold, nor silver, but it *was* some sort of metal. Beneath the surface, ten tadpoles circled about their temporary aquatic home.

With a gentle tug, the submerged portion of the object began to appear, releasing a cloud of silt. The amphibians scattered to each of four points on a compass. They would assume terrestrial bodies on land based north, southeast, southwest and west of the creek.

It was a bayonet. Lifted gently, the blade glistened inch by inch, with nearly another twenty added to the three above the surface. It slowly rose from the watery grave that held it captive for so long. Intense curiosity overcame disappointment when an old man named James was reminded *that all that glitters is not gold.*

How long it had been there—or how it got there—was anyone's speculation. Most likely it hailed from the War of Northern Aggression or the War of Southern Secession. The color of the uniform labeled the cause. Future historians would refer to it as the Civil War.

The bayonet might have been manufactured in North Carolina. A USA or CSA label could have been engraved in the blade, incidental to the year it was forged.

It might have been crafted in England and left in the mud by a soldier in the service of King George III two generations earlier. Perhaps it had been polished in Germany, Italy or Japan and surrendered to time by a veteran returning to his home a century later. Years and corrosion had wiped clean any evidence of origin.

There might be gold hidden in the rock bed, he thought, recalling his father's words when they visited a California gold mine and ghost town. That was almost six decades prior to the descent into

Jackson Badgenoone

this creek. Often, when you find gold, a whip, sword or bayonet may be nearby.

The moment that the tip of the bayonet touched the summer air, a forceful gust of wind caught the uppermost boughs of a strand of southern pine. It filtered through seven hundred and fifty thousand green pine-scented needles, then through fifty-five thousand bitter-nut hickory leaves.

Gaining additional voice as it travelled along the forest floor, it then became a gentle wisp that drifted to the west. She brought moist refreshment to the parched path, revealing her name in the echo of the breeze.

Jackson's apparition whispered. *The national origin of this glittering iron has no more meaning. It was once a source of pride, possibly an instrument of death. Now it is a low water marker, destined for den, country auction, Craigslist or eBay.*

James brushed aside her voice, wiped off the mud, and brought the blade back to his den.

Within days, rains returned, and the creek rose to a new level. It spilled into the recently-harvested corn fields. Dry brown stalks disappeared beneath the rising blue tide. Neighbors bragged that they acquired lakefront property several times each year when Dutch Buffalo Creek satisfied her flood plain. They marked the high water with wooden or plastic stakes and wondered if the next rise would threaten their homes.

The bayonet claimed a different kind of wonderment. Perhaps the bones of two soldiers, one the victor, the other vanquished, rested with each other in a peaceful meadow near a meandering creek, covered with clover, scented with wild flowers. Songbirds would provide a perfect serenade under a Carolina blue sky.

The metal yielded no flesh, no bone. Water and time had also washed away any blood from this blade. Maybe this bayonet wasn't used to kill a soldier.

Bayonets were originally fashioned for hunting, not war. Perhaps it staved off a black bear, a panther or a wolf. Perhaps it served as a convenient metal rod to measure the melt of snow in decades long ago.

It was wishful thinking on his part. The heart of man was bent on conflict. He confirmed that notion by placing the blade alongside an illustrated documentary work. *Battle, A Visual Journey Through 5000 Years of Combat* was literally and figuratively the heaviest book in the den overlooking Dutch Buffalo Creek.

James sat in his favorite chair and ran his hand through pepper gray hair. His mind conjured fanciful possibilities. He imagined that the bayonet was placed in a crevice formed by the displacement of a gold-laden rock. Maybe it was positioned as a pointer to a hidden treasure. Anger knotted in his throat. He had not taken the time to record the direction of the socket base.

He was certain that the tip of the blade pointed downward into the mud, giving him a sinking suspicion that this artifact harbored broader wealth.

Nuggets of truth, any relevance for the dead or living, would require sifting through a screen of events. Sifting for the truth and relevance of the bayonet would prove more arduous than sifting for precious metal. He chose the easier search: a return to the creek as soon as the water receded.

On his next trek through the woods, Jackson made her presence felt once again. She encouraged him to postpone another descent in search for gold. He marked the high water and the place where he had heard her voice for the second time.

He agreed. There would be time enough to search for any precious metal sheltered in the bottom water. He paused to consider the high water markers. They were anchored shallow and deep, narrow and wide. They were a measure of change for oceans, rivers, streams, creeks and civilizations. He would first seek their meaning.

Throughout time, they served as reminders of the possible, of what was and what might be again. This creek would ebb and crest with the same regularity that visits the rise and fall of people, men and women, industries, nations, and empires.

Jackson's voice emanated from a million fallen leaves and for a third time met him at the eastern end of the path. He sometimes thought of it as his little Appian Way. Perhaps this time her voice would shed some light on the value of this marker.

Instead, her spirit surrendered deeper wisdom. She would help define the markers of some of the living and others who had passed. Those markers are the prisms of each life. When properly aligned, they capture and amplify light from interlocking lives, past, present and future.

Now lodged in his inner ear, Jackson whispered to him farther up the path, through the woods, the backyard, up the wooden deck, and into the house. It was nestled on the fringe of an early twenty-first century housing development.

They entered the home through the rear door. The environment was immediately transformed by one counterclockwise turn of a key. Country, woods, creek, and field teeming with Canadian geese framed the view to the east.

Jackson escorted him into his other world. She attached herself to his mind and soul. Impervious to a raging wind, the structure was no barrier to the new breeze borne by her spirit.

The door closed behind them and she joined him on a new journey. It began with a few measured steps through the kitchen and into the dining room. Long before that moment, her name and very existence were linked to several personalities, some long since vanished.

Now she could participate again in the fabric of a living soul. Through his pen and keyboard she could reach a new circle of family, friends, and strangers, even those who had not yet drawn breath.

He pulled back the curtains and opened the window. A westward glance outlined tidy houses in a suburban setting. They surrounded a neatly-manicured play-land for neighborhood children. It also provided a sanctuary for birds of every feather. Metaphorically, Jackson stood once more on terra firma. She delighted in the sights and sounds that passed through the screen above the windowsill. They entered into her mind's eye and ear.

A robin fed her young in a newly-established nest. It was hidden from predators and most of the world by an ornamental bush planted in front of the brick house. Robins nested in front of nearly every home in the neighborhood. Jackson acknowledged the maternal tenacity of the loving little bird with a smile.

Such was this community called Golden Meadow Estates. It included road name reminders of the Germans who settled this part of the country: Oberhaus Road, Rhineland Street, and Alish Court.

The development was connected to the downtown main street intersection by a mile of sidewalk shaded by mulberry bushes and magnolia trees. The little town had withstood the vagaries of time. A post office, pharmacy, library, museums, several houses of worship, two banks, and a number of restaurants provided meeting places for local residents.

A middle school and an elementary school were within walking distance. The high school was just down the road. The volunteer fire department maintained a shiny fleet of equipment. The County Fairgrounds was a stone's throw away.

On the fourth Saturday of each summer month, in this peaceful southern town, proud owners of vintage automobiles lined the main street during a Cruise-in event. Many of the cars participated in annual parades attuned to various holidays.

They joined the local high school marching band, along with a bevy of beauty queens and an occasional princess. Local men and women were festooned with appropriate dress or uniform from several periods in American history. Equestrians displayed their skills to the delight of the roadside audience.

Fire engines and police car sirens announced the beginning and end of each event. Young children tossed candy from horse-drawn floats to the younger children lining the parade route. The American flag waved from every home.

Mont Amoena was established in 1848, a year of reflection and revolution(s). By 2014, it was a growing village on the outskirts of Charlotte. Somewhere along the way it was designated as a bird sanctuary. The designation provided a measure of protection for another little brown bird nested with four baby blue eggs.

It also protected, to some extent, the Northern Cardinal, Eastern Blue Bird, Yellow-Billed Cuckoo, Downy Woodpecker, Red-Headed Woodpecker, Yellow-Throated Vireo, Blue Jay, Winter Wren, Ruby-Throated Hummingbird and Mourning Dove. Jackson encouraged him to enjoy them all in the appropriate time.

James observed a few at the feeders. Binocular lens brought into focus those nesting in the nearby woods and meadow. They all inspired him to frequent a birdwatcher's field guide. He'd received the book from his first-born granddaughter and looked forward to a time when he could share the findings with his other grandchildren.

High water markers made from plastic vanity lamps with no remaining light outlined the most recent crest of the creek behind Alpine Lane. In the garden, hickory stake markers stood as testaments to the vegetables and fruit that would grace the dinner table in the coming months.

All manner of deer, squirrel, rabbit, raccoon, and other small mammals roamed the garden and woods. They provided hours of viewing enjoyment. Raised tunnels signaled an active world beneath the soil. Voles and moles were busy at work.

Red-tailed Hawks stood guard over the meadow and viewed the activity with marked interest. Black snakes lurked behind the stone wall, ready for the next meal. Turkey buzzards circled overhead keeping a vigilant eye for any lifeless form.

Owls, usually hidden during daylight hours, made their presence felt in the woods when they pierced the evening mist with shrill and hoot. During the summer months they seemed to momentarily silence the chirp of crickets and the barking canine several houses down the lane.

The Golden Retriever thought of the high water markers as so many play toys. He would fetch and then bury them alongside a treasure chest of meatless bones.

Indoors, up the stairs, into the den were markers of a different kind. Photos, maps, letters, yearbooks, cassette audio recordings,

CDs, DVDs, VHS tapes, record albums, magazines and books lined the eastern, southern and western walls.

They represented a lifetime of some of the markers that defined life before and beyond the neighborhood, the yard, the woods, and meadow. It was a life developed long before the house was built above the creek.

Other artifacts were aligned along the northern wall. At the center of that wall, a similar blade hung parallel over the entrance door to the den. It was not as wide or long. The two bayonets were close enough in shape, form and function to mount in cross-swords manner. He determined to keep this relic.

A laptop computer and a blinking modem shed some light in the parlor. The balcony hall that overlooked the living area on the floor below connected the rooms. Surely the most expedient way to learn about this bayonet was a quick search on the Internet.

In recent years, the World Wide Web seemed to consume the whole of human knowledge. Jackson whispered, *It offers knowledge, but not understanding; images of objects, but not objects; memories of people, but not people.*

Even so, he thought, *perhaps the net can help establish the exact measure of this particular weapon. It might deliver the date when it was honed, the place where it rendered service, even the time if and when it first drew blood.*

He assumed the net couldn't reveal the meaning of the bayonet in his life or the lives of the people who touched his life. The artifacts in the den would be no more productive. She disagreed.

Jackson beckoned again: *Circle the blade. Return to the den. Sift through the artifacts. The net can't contain them. Search your highlighted books—another reading might reveal a golden nugget that escaped first sift through that sluice box.*

Some of the covers provided a hint of the treasure-filled pages. Other titles were less ubiquitous. She didn't dictate where to begin the search. He knew from his earlier readings that the bayonet had a limited run in the timeline of war.

He had already discovered a website that provided visual clues. It featured a blade that bore a striking resemblance to the metal from the creek.

Armed with that image and mindful of the discovery site, he assumed it served in a North American land conflict, probably the War for Independence. She forced him to suspend the web search and relinquish an image of *the* blade, to carve instead the image of *a* blade.

That blade of imagery might somehow have made a way to the Tar Heel State from a distant war, delivered to the creek bed by some circuitous route. Broadening the scope of the image would bring into the truth-sifter the War of 1812, the Mexican American War, The Boer War, and The Crimean War. Possible were any number of the many conflicts that featured the bayonet as a highly visible instrument of war around the globe through several centuries.

The den housed an entire section dedicated to the period between 1860, a year of reflection and compromise, and 1865, a year of reflection and reunification. One shelf was lined with titles that spoke to the cause or consequence, imagined or real. Some examined the roots of the conflict. Others depicted images in blue and gray, black and white.

They told but a few of the hundreds of thousands of stories that touched the lives of so many souls during those years. They would redefine the struggle of a nation and millions of citizens.

In a search for a broader image, it seemed reasonable to begin by looking through those several thousand pages. Titles on the top shelf considered the viewpoints of Jefferson Davis and Robert E. Lee, Abraham Lincoln and Ulysses S. Grant.

He started with those and then continued reading from books on the other shelves, among them:

The Causes of the American Civil War; Mathew Brady: Historian with a Camera; They Lie Forgotten; and The South Was Right.

The pictures, line drawings, words, sentences and paragraphs circled the image of the bayonet just as the tadpoles had teased the actual blade in the creek. They were not able to define it, nor could they justify the weapon—they merely made one aware that the bayonet existed.

One notable observation was buried deep within the pages of a book on the third shelf. The bayonet was a most perfect weapon of war when it was not employed.

Paraphrased, it was better to frighten the enemy from across a meadow with the glitter of steel but kill him from afar with a ball of lead. Using the bayonet up close in hand-to-hand combat might just as easily result in a mortal wound inflicted to your side of the line. There were times when there was no other choice.

At one critical engagement in July of 1863, a year of reflection and redefinition, a blue line had nearly exhausted all bullets for rifle and revolver. A former college professor from Maine became an officer in the Union Army. He seized the moment and ordered a fateful bayonet charge.

It changed the course of that conflict and the war. This bayonet may have seen service at that time and place in a little crossroads town of Gettysburg, Pennsylvania, just two states north of Dutch Buffalo Creek. That Civil War did seem to provide a high water mark for the bayonet in battle.

These books shed some light on the reason for using the weapon. They yielded visions of battles and campaigns. No book or number of books could really capture the horror of that war or any war.

They couldn't adequately describe the thoughts of a man as he plunged sterile steel into the body of another human being. Nor could they capture the final image and thoughts of a dying soldier as the blade entered his heart. Despite hours of sifting, the books yielded no secret for this weapon.

In a gentle reprimand, she whispered again, *Insightful books, insufficient search. Those books might shed some light on the blade, but not on the men who suffered on either end of the metal or the other lives affected by their actions. Look beyond your books; there are other markers available to illuminate the truth.*

At this he grew agitated. What was this voice that spoke to him? He challenged her at that moment.

"I have heard *of* voices like you before," he said.

Her immediate retort was to the point. "You have heard *from* voices like mine. My name is Jackson Badgenoone from the universe of the Neverborn. You'll learn more about me in due time; please continue your investigation."

"That's fine," he replied. "I can wait to learn more about you. Since you've finally introduced yourself, let me return the courtesy: my name is James; when I was a young boy, my friends called me the Wannabe Cisco Kid; my dad called me Trav; later, my co-workers and colleagues called me Point Man and Nav. You can't imagine the frustration a person feels when one aspect of his personality defines his identity."

"I've known your names for a long time now," she said, "and I will call you by the appropriate name during the course of your exploration. I fully appreciate the conflict that defines identity. I have no form, yet I cast a shadow. I have no voice, yet you hear my message. Listen carefully."

Her voice tormented him. He brought his hands up to cover his ears. He had just swallowed another Vicodin in response to severe arthritis pain. Surely he heard the hydrocodone. Even as he tried to silence her voice, she said, "Provoke, not torment."

CHAPTER II

Sifting East and West of Dixie

Perchance there was a map of the Reluctant State of North Carolina, the county, Mont Amoena, or Dutch Buffalo Creek. It might trace a movement of troops through the Carolina Piedmont in the mid 1860s. No such map existed in the artifacts of the den.

The only map there was published in Washington, DC during July, 1944, a year of reflection and anticipation. It was a red-lined copy of a map of Germany and its approaches with International Boundaries as of September 1, 1939, the day Germany invaded Poland in that year of reflection and reckoning.

A different shade of red highlighted the boundaries that were recognized on January 1, 1938, a year of reflection and appeasement, before Germany seized Austria and Czechoslovakia.

Compiled and drawn in the cartographic section of the National Geographic Society for *National Geographic* magazine, Gilbert Grosvenor, editor, posted a note: *This edition for use by War and Navy Department Agencies.*

Additional red lines articulated the zones of occupation that would define post-WWII Germany in 1945, a year of reflection and rebuilding. Fragmentation outlined the British Zone, the French Zone, the Russian Zone, and the US Zone.

Drawn in 1944, a full year before the end of the war, it certainly was not a map of the high water mark of the Third Reich. It marked rather the shape of a divided nation that would be central to a Cold War.

Some of the early post-WWII US Baby Boomers drew first breath in Germany. They were the children of servicemen entrusted with carving a peace from the ruins of that most ruinous of wars.

That Cold War would dominate international politics for Boomers on both sides of the Iron Curtain for decades.

James thought it presumptuous of the mapmakers to define the boundaries at a time when the outcome of the conflict was not at all certain. Then he realized that they were just doing a job assigned by the strategists who would dictate the peace.

Other strategists in other wars had similar maps constructed by the cartographers of their day. Some had to imagine a Mexico sans California or Arizona in the aftermath of the Mexican War. Others visualized a redefined Soviet Union.

Jackson whispered some clues to help focus his search. His mother was a war bride born and raised in Brussels, Belgium; his father was a captain in the US Army of occupation. His certificates of birth and baptism were issued in the German language. His declaration of citizenship was printed in English, stamped US citizen, born to an American parent in the occupied US zone.

She continued to help him gently shift the knowledge sluice box. Did this have anything to do with the division of the United States almost a century before his birth near a river in Frankfurt? Were the men who fought at the point of a bayonet there just a few years earlier any different from those who fought in other zones of Germany in the Second World War?

Were they different than distant cousins who fought for ground in World War I, the Franco-Prussian War, the Napoleonic wars or any war fought throughout the ages? She encouraged him to search Genesis for the earliest clues of conflict, the gospels for a measure of conflict resolution. Dutch Buffalo Creek was linked by water and blood and spirit to a much larger universe.

Jackson, still without discernible form, fell silent. James imagined that he saw her shadow reflected upon glass that preserved a picture.

It hung near the hall banister that joined the parlor and the den. It was a photo of the US Army Transport, Edmund B. Alexander.

A single-stack troop transport vessel, the ship ferried servicemen and their families from Europe when the army of occupation was recalled back to the United States following WWII. In 1947, a year of reflection and realignment, the Statue of Liberty greeted weary but hopeful passengers en route to Governors Island. Among them was the captain's family.

In 2014, James reflected on the men who fought during the Civil War. They arrived almost a century before he arrived at that place of salt and freshwater confluence.

Those men would have entered the country on ships of sail in that very harbor. It was possible that they came from Ireland, Scotland, Germany, or England. They might have been neighbors before the war.

Maybe, maybe, groaned the voice. Her groan lingered on the wind in his mind's ear. It morphed into the drone of an airplane engine, then another, and then two more. He heard the strain of those engines as the Sabena DC-7C aircraft rolled down the runway at Idlewild. He closed his eyes, pushed back the brown recliner chair, and drifted into a deep sleep.

CHAPTER III
Sifting Through Sands of Time

This sleep was not quite as deep as the one that lulled him during the flight decades before. When he awoke from that earlier slumber in 1958, a year of reflection and renewal, his plane had just landed in Brussels. The propellers feathered into silence. A mobile staircase greeted the open door. One by one the passengers walked down the metal stairs.

He had returned just a decade and a year after his parents waved a farewell to the European Continent. His mother wanted her children to visit the sites of a newly-reconstructed Europe. She also wanted to introduce them to their other family.

This first stop would bond them with the parents, brothers, sisters, nephews and nieces she had left behind in the years immediately following the Second World War. Along with his sister and younger brother, James was introduced to aunts, uncles, cousins, and grandparents. All had stories to share of family and friends, trial and tribulation, sorrow and joy. They would help him understand the significance of the brick and mortar in his line of sight.

Each newly-found relative greeted him with a kiss on each cheek, and a third for good measure. Nearly five decades later, in 2007—a year of reflection and resignation—several remained. Older but still young in spirit, they gathered in a Belgian countryside restaurant to reminisce and pose for a photo.

In 1958, cathedrals and castles inspired awe. Horse-drawn carts announced their travel along cobblestone streets. The aroma of French fry potatoes, fresh baked bread, and steamed mussels welcomed him to every neighborhood. He was curious about the attention given to a statue of a little boy urinating into a fountain.

On the other side of the city, the Atomium symbolized promise for the peaceful use of the atom. It marked the progress of nations exemplified at the World's Fair of 1958, the first such gathering of nations since the end of the Second World War. Thirteen years prior to the fair, two atomic bombs melted ten thousand bayonets and vaporized twenty times that number of breathing souls. So many voices were extinguished within one beat of a heart.

That August in 1945, Jackson was drawn from the winds. She emerged into the whirlwind that mushroomed to the top of the clouds and witnessed the aftermath. Only twisted metal remained near ground zero.

A mile away, a pale blue bicycle and a bright red wagon, recently drawn by a young child, surfaced from the smoldering rubble. Jackson whispered into the consciousness of a local photographer who survived the carnage, "Capture those images."

The war in Europe had come to an end a few months earlier; the challenge of that conflict was still fresh in the minds of his family in 1958. Their immediate neighborhood had been spared. Elsewhere on the European Continent, entire cities were gone. They could only imagine the consequence of an atomic weapon in the hands of the Nazi regime.

Mounted atop V2 rockets or nuclear-armed descendants they could snuff out the lights of Brussels, London, Paris, and New York. Cousins on both sides of the Atlantic would cease to exist.

Unlike the bayonet that took one life at a time, these new weapons erased entire populations within the blink of an eye. They also obliterated the architecture, art, and artifacts that defined those people. Sheets of music, paintings, sculptures, and collections of every sort would be consumed by the inferno. So much was already lost during that war. The A-bombs were never dropped in Europe or North America. People and collections there managed to survive.

His aunt was only too eager to bequeath to his new and growing stamp collection an entire album assembled during the Nazi occupation. It included a prominent section that bore the image of a former WWI German corporal. Other pages featured the likeness of a Belgian king—not her favorite.

Until then, his albums contained images of wildlife, fowl, and flower of every stripe and color. From that time forward, James would collect images that featured nations, dignitaries, and events.

He carefully mounted perforated pieces of gum-backed paper that bore the likeness of emperors, kings, queens, presidents, and military leaders. Occasionally an inventor, industrialist, artist, poet, author, or composer peered from the pages.

His aunt's generosity spoke volumes about her feelings of that war. She provided no hint of the tragedy that nearly destroyed her family. There was no mention from her older siblings or his grandparents about the previous war that had savaged the country and the family a generation earlier. At war were some of the same nation states, different leaders, and different bayonets.

His cousin was too young to remember the Second World War. He was consumed with life, fishing in creeks and streams, rafting rivers, shooting rapids, traversing falls, hiking mountains, exploring villages, towns, cities, and battlefields.

Cousin's most treasured possessions included a fishing pole, a rubber raft, and a Belgian walking cane. Made of a sturdy timber, it featured a curved handle and a pointed iron tip. The staff was adorned with metallic decals. They depicted the places he had explored from one end of the country to the other.

Cousin George gifted to him a wooden cane bejeweled with decals from some of the sites they had walked and hiked together. Among them were Jalhay, SPA, Septon, Durbuy, Coo, Dinant, Anseremme, Mery, Brussels, and Waterloo.

The house of his mother's youngest brother stood quiet and warm off a trolley line that ran near the Grand Place. Around the corner, the Manneken Pis fountain reminded onlookers that water in life passes into the drain and returns to the ocean.

His uncle enjoyed smoking a Meerschaum pipe. He brought music to life through the strings on his violin and loved to recant tales about a Europe that was no more.

He also elaborated on a new and unified continental power. Uncle hoped that it would emerge in his lifetime. He imagined that Brussels would be at the center of it all.

Uncle's home was rich with artifacts. The most comforting was a single golden rose. On the fireplace mantle, it seemed to add life to a waterless vase placed beneath the family portrait. It kept alive the memory of his missing children.

An ash-covered brush, a firewood-tarnished shovel, and a rusty bayonet hung alongside the fireplace hearth. The blade might have been a relic from Verdun or Bastogne—or maybe it was just an ornamental poker to stir a dying flame.

CHAPTER IV
Aftermath of a Live Round

Another month evaporated before Jackson returned to the den overlooking Dutch Buffalo Creek. It was 2014, and it was her fourth appearance. At Jackson's urging, James had passed up the opportunity for a second scale down to the creek bed. Instead he focused his energy on cultivating a garden at the edge of the woods.

The garden yielded cucumbers, squash, beets, carrots, green beans, and peppers. Tomatoes, strawberries, and corn didn't provide much at harvest, unable to tolerate relentless summer rains. The rains replenished Dutch Buffalo Creek.

The creek spawned her lake once more. Neighbors dubbed it Lake Winihawhaw. Just as quickly, Winihawhaw surrendered her water to cornfields and meadow.

Plastic lamps positioned to mark the last high water ridge were carried away by the new ebb and flow. Battery-depleted solar lamps that could no longer provide a lighted path along the stone wall were pressed into service as replacement markers.

Five decades and six years after his cousin's farewell, the Belgian walking cane cast a shadow on the most recent high water markers of Dutch Buffalo Creek.

This time, Jackson encouraged him to document the event as a video. It joined a growing digital collection housed on Tumblr, Vimeo, and YouTube. He considered ways to preserve all the source material along with the computer external hard drive where he stored his digital archives.

Perhaps a cedar chest would protect them from the capricious nature of technology platform evolution and nefarious elements of time. Jackson assured him that she would help post it and all the other digital artifacts in her cloud, a more lasting record, assuming the hosting servers would survive into some distant future.

Still, she couldn't guarantee that the source materials would survive. She was intrigued by the notion of an airtight container, almost a diminutive version of Noah's ark.

RJ-11 phone jacks and cable outlets in every room were already obsolete by the time of Jackson's fifth visit. It was just twelve years after the foundation stones were laid for the house on Alpine Lane.

How long would it be before some new energy delivery system sent the electrical sockets to the proverbial dust bin? The sockets had extinguished the flame from gas light fixtures a century in the past.

Baby-proof plugs covered every aperture. They were designed to protect visiting young ones. His offspring were well along with their lives. Now even his children's children no longer required plastic to shield them from innocent mischief. The covers did serve to further insulate the house, to keep it slightly warmer in the winter and cooler during the southern summer months. Jackson bypassed them all.

"Backward compatibility" was a euphemism often employed by twentieth-century technologists eager to protect previous hardware and software investments. By the turn of the next century and following a Y2K speed bump, data from the previous millennia poured into the net.

Jackson reminded him, *Data, but not knowledge; information, but not understanding; opinions, but not necessarily truth.*

Perhaps the only reservoir of truth in the future would be sheltered in hermitically-sealed environments, complete with author's intent. It assumed that future generations would be able to read and interpret the treasures.

Songbirds greeted the rising sun as cool air and the spirit of Jackson drifted through the window. She noticed that the squirrels had returned to the bird feeders. Evening rain had washed away the cayenne pepper placed on them to repel the perpetually-hungry gray furry critters.

The hummingbird feeder was still topped off with red sugar water. A continent away, the winter habitat of those birds was destroyed. Jackson could only observe. She wasn't able to shed the tears that would have come had she ever been born.

Eventually, a new family of hummingbirds made the migration to the north. They signaled resilience in the force of nature. Jackson could smile again.

Once in the house, her presence seemed to reflect upon the protecting glass of another photo. It displayed an image of the USS General W.M. Mitchell. During WWII, this two-stack troop transport carried soldiers into what was incongruously described as the Pacific theater of war. After the war, she ferried military and dependents into the newly-occupied lands of the former Japanese empire.

Following victory in Europe, VE day, a number of US soldiers stayed on as an army of occupation in Europe. A significant force remained there well throughout the duration of the Cold War and into the twenty-first century.

Some troops were shifted to the Pacific following victory in Japan, VJ day. A few were still there a handful of years later, ready but not anxious to support the next military action in that part of the world. It was a not so cold a war in Korea.

The captain, now a major, was one of those caught up in the shift. Following a brief stateside tour, he deployed to Okinawa. Soon his war bride and two children climbed up the gangplank of the USS Mitchell to join him in 1952, a year of reflection and revision. The children were old enough to sense that this was a different sort of earth.

Dense forest sprang from deep swamp bogs. During the rainy season, charcoal-black mud seemed to dominate every inch of the island. It provided a somewhat favorable environment for cultivating rice gardens.

Reminders of the war surfaced from the receding waters of flooded fields and along a strand-line, the high water mark of a recent typhoon. One relic stood at almost the height of a paper US ten-dollar bill.

The object was an unexpended heavy caliber machine-gun round. The gleaming metal jacket with pointed tip was an inviting toy for a young lad fond of driving nails into wooden planks. The major grasped the hammer from his hand a second before James could slam the shell into a block of oak. Hours later, the metal casing was rendered harmless. Eventually it joined the artifacts in the den overlooking Dutch Buffalo Creek.

Other children were not as fortunate. This island harbored some of the most horrific battles in the final days of the war. Left behind were unexploded bombs, concealed land mines, and discarded ordinance that took a civilian toll for years.

Relics of bravado, emblem of the Rising Sun, the Samurai Sword, and the field bayonet also littered the landscape. They posed a danger to the mind and soul as much as to the body of the little ones who sifted them from murky hiding places.

In 2014, Jackson's mist seemed to linger on another shelf that housed books about that war. She passed slowly over *Okinawa, the last battle of WWII; World War II: A Photographic History.*

Several titles emerged on the next shelf. They included *Eisenhower's Own Story of the war: The Complete Report by the Supreme Commander on the War in Europe from Day of Invasion to the Day of Victory* and *General Marshall's Report: The Winning of the War in Europe and the Pacific.* Others considered expanded periods of time, books like *The Century* and *We Interrupt This Broadcast.*

Less readily-available works were protected by plastic cover on an adjoining shelf. They included a collection of documents published six years after the war by the Department of the Army: *Historical Study No.20-201; Military Improvisations During the Russian Campaign; No. 20-292 Warfare in the Far North; No.20-233 German Defense Tactics against Russian Breakthroughs.*

On the same shelf were field manuals published by the War Department during or soon after the global conflict. Among them were *FM 21-26 Advance Map and Aerial Photograph Reading*; *FM 5-15 Field Fortifications*; and *FM 30-5 Combat Intelligence*.

Periodicals about the time leading up to the war, the conflict, and the aftermath lined the shelf below. Arranged chronologically, the first was a magazine, *News-Week Vol. IV, No. 25, December 22, 1934*. It featured a headline that said, "Don't Block Italian Expansion." The message was reinforced by a photo of a dictator astride a tank.

Another *News-Week Vol. II No. 12, March 21, 1936* headline read, "Hands Across the Alps." The cover photo portrayed that dictator clasping the right glove arm of his German protégé, ruler of the Third Reich.

The July 31, 1939 issue of Newsweek could be purchased for a price of ten cents. It displayed a picture of a helmeted soldier with a rifle on his shoulder, a bugle pressed to his lips. He was mounted on a white horse, its eyes cast down while the soldier gazed upward. The caption read, "Poland's biggest army wants no appeasement."

Two months later, German tanks breached the border, and soon most of Europe was involved. Subsequent issues chronicled the changing political boundaries.

On December 14, 1942, *Newsweek* published a cover story titled "America at War; The First Year." It featured a photo of a determined and optimistic US president pointing to a map of the Pacific as it appeared a year and a week after the attack on Pearl Harbor.

One year later—July 19, 1943—*Newsweek's* headline announced, "Beachhead! Invasion comes to Fortress Europe."

The August 28, 1944 issue proclaimed more good news: "Triple Play for Paris, Monty to Bradley to Patton." A picture of three victorious allied generals graced that cover.

By May of the following year it was finished in that theater of war. There was no headline, just the photo of a German soldier. His arms reached skyward in a gesture of surrender. He appeared on the May 7, 1945 issue of *Newsweek*.

More weeks and months of searching yielded no golden nugget about the artifact. James pored through postcards and letters written from the major to his wife. In one correspondence, the major described an encounter with a naval officer.

Long before the war, they were best of buddies. They recalled a time in the first quarter of the century when they ruled the Fifth Street neighborhood. Back then, cobblestone had just replaced dirt roads and a Model T replaced at least one horse on the tree-lined street.

At this meeting in the second half of the century, they compared notes about the old gang and the respective journey of each friend and brother before, during, and following the war. For a split second, neither man cared about rank.

The years melted away for Tony, the lieutenant commander, and Jimmy, the major. Jimmy was the first to describe the paths of his brothers during the war.

Albert served in North Africa, Sicily, and the boot of Italy. He was able to visit briefly with aunts, uncles, and cousins in Naples before he went on to Rome. Dominic was assigned to duty in Southeast Asia where he foraged through the Burma jungle with Vinegar Joe. Dick returned to the Transfer Station after a brief tour in India.

Gennaro was too old for military service. He did his part for the war effort as a foreman at a civilian plant in downtown Rochester. Al and Dominic joined Gerry in civilian life after the war.

Jimmy's tour took him to Europe from D-Day plus three to the Rhine River crossings. He stayed in uniform in the aftermath of war. Despite government warnings about fraternization, he married a Belgian girl and started a family. Now here he was sharing stories with an old friend at an officer's club in Okinawa.

Anthony, more commonly known as Tony, picked up the conversation. He managed to spend the first years of the war on the mainland before picking up an assignment at the island base of Midway. His brother, Sal, was the only one of the original Transfer Station buddies who never made it back home.

Tony released the anger he still carried long after news that his brother perished at the thrust of a bayonet. For the sake of a gold pocket watch, it was administered without compassion during the Bataan Death March in 1942, a year of reflection and retrenchment.

A repentant former Japanese prisoner of war sought out Tony soon after the war and returned the watch he had appropriated from his brother. He asked to be forgiven. He had already asked for and said that he had received forgiveness from his Savior.

Tony was no longer angry with this warrior; he was angry with war. He gave the gold watch to Jim, sure that it belonged back in his family. For the lieutenant commander it was a way to release the anger. For the major it was just another reminder of why he hated war and why he still wore the uniform.

Correspondence with his wife didn't dwell on the exchange. He went on instead to describe the happy times they shared at Naha and how much he looked forward to greeting her again at the dock in California. Temporary living quarters awaited them near the Presidio, just below the Golden Gate Bridge.

CHAPTER V
Let The Marbles Roll

It wasn't the most flattering label; nonetheless, "military brats" constituted a significant segment of the US post-WWII Baby Boomer generation. A number of them were on the USS Mitchell as she steamed back to San Francisco in 1953, a year of reflection and repair. Now in 2014, Jackson continued to help James to reflect.

His parents could provide memories of the voyage across the Atlantic. The major had been assigned duty as transport commander and saved several ship newsletters. Those reinforced the oral stories and clippings from the *Stars and Stripes* newspapers that he'd saved over the years. The Liberation Issue made it to the den overlooking Dutch Buffalo Creek.

As the major's first-born son, James was old enough to remember the passage on this Pacific return voyage to the United States. He enjoyed the whiff of navy gray deck paint overwhelmed by the scent of salty sea air. He thrilled as the ship rose and fell with every mountain of water.

Whales far ahead of the bow wave captured his attentive gaze. Had they planned to construct a navigational path through the brine? Would they lead the ship all the way to American waters? Cumulus clouds on the horizon touched white-capped peaks. They magnified the vastness of this ocean.

The sea concealed thousands of sunken vessels. In the not-too-distant future, it would absorb the heat and radiation of atomic tests.

Years later, it would hide hazards to fish and fowl posed by hundreds of millions of plastic containers.

The Pacific, for now, was almost as pristine as in the day of Ahab's leg and the hunt for Moby Dick. Pure water of connected oceans hearkened all the way back to the day of Jonah.

No salted sea could entirely separate him from his dad. Between duty assignments, his mother, sister, and James remained in touch with the major. Serving in a nominal peace time army, he was promoted later that year to lieutenant colonel, usually just referred to as "the colonel."

Husband and wife continued to carry on a long-distance relationship. They kept the trunks packed, ready for the next rendezvous. Voice-O-Graph recordings and two-digit place-identifier phone calls that required operator assistance kept them connected. Postal-borne letters that didn't reference zip codes (a system that came into being in the early 1960s) provided written back-up. An air mail stamp could carry a letter across the country for six cents.

The next base was far removed from the jungles of Okinawa. It was a desert post, a perfect place to test metal for heat and friction that would stress armored vehicles on similar terrain in some distant war. It would also test the resolve of soldiers and their families. It would arouse the curiosity of young children.

The family would follow the colonel down the California west coast highways. They enjoyed side trips back in time within the walls of every Spanish mission along the way. They savored relics from the gold rush of 1849, a year of reflection and discovery.

They paused to marvel at the cities and suburbs that increasingly consumed orange groves, meadows, creeks, and farmland. Migrant farm workers waved to them as they motored down the highway. Within a few days the car entered a valley and veered east to a sleepy little town just north of the Arizona/Mexico border.

Less than half a century earlier, Arizona was still a territory. It wouldn't gain statehood until several years following the birth of the colonel on Mulberry Street in far-away New York City during the first decade of the new century.

At the time of his birth, FDR's distant cousin, Teddy Roosevelt, presided over the country. Edmund Morris documented the life of *that* colonel in *The Rise of Theodore Roosevelt*. He would usher in a new American century.

Howard Taft, Teddy's hand-picked successor, occupied the presidential office at the time of Arizona statehood. Yankee bayonets from California kept southern sympathizers from adding Arizona to the Stars and Bars a half century earlier.

Jackson stirred when a metal object the circumference of a musket ball fell to the floor of the den overlooking Dutch Buffalo Creek. It had made a fifty-seven-year journey through forty-five states. It was designed to serve as a tank ball bearing. The young brats thought it was the ultimate marble in a game defined by glass.

They called them "steels." Launched by a thumb and guided by a pointer finger, the relatively heavy metal round balls would scatter but not shatter the glass marbles. Those round pieces of reformulated sand were lined up in several row formations. Some were embedded with multi-colored flowers; a few were crystal-clear. Steels were available in just one shade of solid metallic gray.

Armed with steels, they were able to add hundreds of glass marbles to their collections. At the end of any day, they would have accumulated a remarkable assortment of marbles. Only the metal marble survived the decades.

Desert sands at the Yuma Test Station, later renamed Yuma Proving Ground, yielded steels of several sizes. The purpose of their design was to make more mobile the weapons of war that would render the bayonet irrelevant. The friends had found a way to bring them to these games of youth.

A half-century later, that metal would be tested in the sands of Iraq. A new generation of brats would remain stateside, connected to military parents by smartphones and email, Facebook, and Tweets. Marbles, the Voice-O-Gram, and the bayonet spoke to high water markers from a distant past.

Dependants in off-base housing participated in a broader civilian world. Those who remained on base experienced a different order. It was one that they could recognize: Base School, Base Commissary, PX, Base Chapel and kindred spirits.

CHAPTER VI

Truth Sometimes Floats On Water

Jackson had finally established permanent residence in the den overlooking the Dutch Buffalo Creek. James now required Percocet to mask the physical pain that racked his bones. Relentless rain was punctuated by a thunderous clap and a flash of lightning. It was very early in the morning that early autumn day in 2014. She raced past the door, across the deck, down the stairs, and through the woods. Winihawhaw had returned.

The maple tree that had stood firm and tall when it anchored the journey to the almost-dry creek bed now floated prostrate across the raging waters. The rope that had secured his descent two seasons ago remained wrapped around the trunk and drifted southward with the flow.

An airtight, waterproof hope chest lodged in branches on the north side of the fallen Crimson King Maple; the Belgian walking cane was just long enough.

It enabled him to guide the box toward the western bank. A gentle nudge with the stick rescued the container from a journey downstream. Once it reached the western shore, he placed it on a wheeled cart. He pulled it up through the woods and along the path.

He set it to rest, dry under the wooden deck. With a one-finger push on the button lock, the cover slowly swung open. The cedar-lined receptacle revealed one more than a score of books.

They were partitioned into three sections. The uppermost contained two titles: *The Book of the Neverborn* and *Definitions of the High Water Marker.*

The first book was just under a thousand pages; the second, not quite yet a book, contained a few more than twelve.

A second section was nestled under a place card that read, "Family and Friends." It contained nine titles focused on immediate family and one book about a distant relative. A third section was labeled "The Multitudes."

Jackson offered assistance and agreed to help sift through selected chapters from each book. She would encourage him and her Neverborn colleagues to skip over sections that were irrelevant to the search or inappropriate for young readers.

James removed the two works from the uppermost section and eleven additional books. Ten titles came from the "Family and Friends" section, another from "The Multitudes" section. James affixed a yellow sticky label to each book as a way to organize them on shelves in his den. Jackson encouraged him to begin the labeling process with the number 3. She informed him that number 1 was already assigned to *The Hidden Treasure of Dutch Buffalo Creek*; and number 2 would identify *The Book of The Neverborn.*

Book 3.*The High Water Markers of Jackson's Observee*

Book4. *The High Water Markers of Anna's Observee*

Book 5. *The High Water Markers of Bernadette's Observee*

Book 6.*The High Water Markers of Christopher's Observee*

Book 7.*The High Water Markers of Daniel's Observee*

Book 8.*The High Water Markers of Elizabeth's Observee*

Book 9.*The High Water Markers of Frederick's Observee*

Book 10.*The High Water Markers of George's Observee*

Book 11. *The High Water Markers of Henry's Observee*

Book 12. *The High Water Markers of Israel's Observee*

He resealed and locked the chest to preserve the other titles. When they arrived at the den, they started to read from book two.

Jackson knew that it would expose her identity.

[Book 2]

The Book of The Never Born

Copyright © 2015 by Jackson Badgenoone

Preface to *The Book of The Neverborn:*

A contemporary search on the web circa early 2014 would yield any number of interpretations of the Neverborn. Several sites invented characters that took physical form, sometimes finding representation in collectable icons. Another site suggested that everyone is Neverborn, and that all life is an illusion.

This book contemplates souls that were "never born" of flesh. Some were a consequence of abortion. Others were stillborn. Many came into existence through miscarriage. That scenario was respectfully considered in an article published in *Time* magazine: "Someone I Loved Was Never Born."1. Whatever the cause, these entities never knew the breath of air or the tug on the heart.

An attempt to reconcile salvation for such as these provoked dialog dating back to the early days of Christendom. Catholic tradition long ago invented a place for some like them and called it "limbo."

A similar tradition attempts to describe the difference between angelic beings and humans with free will and the capacity to internalize Christ. Even though they are without human form and are unable to experience salvation, at least three angels are identified by name in scripture; on occasion they are highly visible.

The Neverborn are not angels, and they can't participate in the human condition. They brandish no surname but are identified on a first-name basis. They don't protect or defend or alter. They have no voice but they can be heard. They have no form but can be imagined. They have purpose inasmuch as they provide a witness to events.

Their living counterparts, by contrast, have a purpose that shapes events and reflects salvation. They are recognized by God from before the time they are established in flesh:

> For he was yet in the loins of his father, when Melchisedec met him. (Hebrews 7:10)

[Jackson understood that the concept might be too much for James to digest. She could only rely again on scripture to help him to discern the mystery of it all.]

> As you do not know the path of the wind, or how the body is formed in a mother's womb, so you cannot understand the work of God, the Maker of all things. (Ecclesiastes 11:5)

A prophet provides another example that supports the importance of first-name recognition in the development of a story. Isaiah 43:1–3 writes:

> But now, this is what the LORD says—
> he who created you, Jacob, he who formed you, Israel:
> Do not fear, for I have redeemed you;
> I have **summoned you by name**; you are mine.
> When you pass through the waters, I will be with you;
> and when you pass through the rivers, they will not
> sweep over you.
> When you walk through the fire, you will not be burned;
> the flames will not set you ablaze.
> For I am the LORD your God,
> the Holy One of Israel, **your Savior**; I give Egypt for
> your ransom,
> Cush and Seba in your stead.

The Neverborn in this book are also identified by first name. Their names are reflective of a life or number of lives that they are destined to observe. The day, year and place of their creation are recorded in the book.

In a strictly literary sense, they are the ultimate of ghostwriters. Since they have no form they are incapable of holding a pen, and yet they guide those who are so able.

Neverborn often help stitch to each other the binding secrets of a single work. At times, they connect threads that bind together different titles.

By way of example, the author incorporates a segment from the *Hidden Treasure of Dutch Buffalo Creek* into *The Book of The Neverborn* preface.

References are always *italicized*, a leaning perspective from work to work.

The following is a chapter from *The Hidden Treasure of Dutch Buffalo Creek,* incorporated into the "Preface to The Book of The Neverborn":

CHAPTER VII

It Is A Wonderful Life

In 2014, James continued the search in a teeter-totter fashion. He consumed the books, letters and artifacts about the Civil War, then WWII. In pendulum motion he tapped into books about The Revolutionary War, then WWI, The War of 1812, then The Mexican American War, The War of The Regulation, The Spanish American War, prelude to the Great War, the time between the world wars . . .

Some of the books on those shelves had collected a portion of dust. Other titles were relatively new. Among them were **The Passing of the Armies, Hiroshima Nagasaki, The Real Story of the Atomic Bombings and Their Aftermath, 1776, The First World War, The Civil War of 1812, American Citizens, British Subjects, Irish Rebels & Indian Allies, North Carolina in the Mexican War, 1846 – 1848, The War of the Regulation and the Battle of Alamance May 16, 1771, The Spanish War, an American Epic 1898, July 14 Countdown to War, Paris 1919, Six Months That Changed The World.**

James expanded his search beyond the books, letters and artifacts in the den overlooking Dutch Buffalo Creek. It also housed a modest video collection.

It contained one VHS format and one DVD format of a classic movie that enriched film collections in homes across the land and around the globe. Released in 1946, a year of reflection and reconstruction, it received a modest initial reception but was viewed more widely the following year. Audiences at the time were still coming to grips with the end of WWII. It was a climate dominated by the Berlin Air Lift, an emerging Cold War, inflation and all manner of shortage.

Jackson encouraged him to watch the movie to learn more about the characters and some of the actors who portrayed them. She was eager to reveal the voices that haunted his memories. Search for the meaning of the bayonet was temporarily suspended.

The lead character in the film, George Bailey, was portrayed by an actor with so many real-life high water markers. He was born in an all-American community in western Pennsylvania. The year was 1908, a year of reflection and transition. Jimmy Stewart never broke the bonds of his hometown roots.

Those roots nourished Stewart as he built an award-winning body of cinematic work. One film portrayed the first man to fly solo across the Atlantic in 1927, a year of reflection and exuberance. Another chronicled the life of an orchestra leader who provided high water markers for the big band sound.

Jimmy's hometown roots, and a family rich with military accomplishments spanning at least five wars, provided strength of purpose. During WWII, he commanded a formation of B24 liberator bomber planes over Nazi-controlled Germany.

In a life parallel to his work on film, those missions led to his rise through the officer ranks of the Army Air Corps and US Air Force. He ultimately received recognition as a major general on the retired list.

The invented George Bailey never broke the bond to the imaginary small town of his birth. It was thought by some to have been modeled after a community in the Finger Lakes region of New York. George never did leave that place. Instead he dreamed of travel and adventure, mesmerized by the sound of anchor chains, plane engines, and train whistles.

Classified 4F during the war, he could only experience a military life vicariously through the service rendered by his younger brother. Following a calamitous financial event, he decided to end his seemingly-meaningless existence by plunging into a swirling ice laden creek swelled to river-like proportions.

The filmmaker provided a convenient alternative to suicide. George leapt from a bridge to save a hapless old man thought to have fallen into the raging current. It turned out that Clarence, his guardian angel, didn't fall—he jumped. He knew that George would follow to save him.

Clarence pointed out the tragedy of throwing away the precious gift of life. George agreed and wished that he had never been born. The angel granted the wish and George was given the opportunity to witness the consequences of his neverborn status.

In the film rendition, George was able to return to the land of flesh and blood. Once again he was able to savor the blessings of life.

The Neverborn in this book of the Neverborn have no such path available. They were never born. They could never be born. They couldn't change life for gain or loss, good or evil. Their time had come and gone. They could, however, shed light on the lives of those who drew breath.

One could be quick to point out that no single idea or thought is new. Generations have marveled at the same sunrise and retreat. They have heard the sound of the same songbird. They bear witness to the miracle of life, the sorrow of death.

They share countless markers of time and progress; how ideas are ordered and combined define what makes each story compelling unique and worth the read.

The placement of artifacts, the assemblage of memories, and the formation of relationships all lead to billions of stories. The Neverborn provide insights into the markers of each life. They remind people of the ones they knew and reveal others that are hidden.

It was not just where they had been or whom they had met along the way. What they learned and cherished defined the journey of their lives. They live on by the memories they leave behind, even on hearts they had never known.

Jackson punctuated the information.

What we are = Never Born. Who we are = Neverborn

Chapters in the first half of *The Book of the Neverborn* bring a measure of life to ten nontraditional life forms. Remaining chapters survey another seventy-nine.

Jackson urged him to set the book aside and pick up the uncompleted work still silent on the next table. He began to read the pages.

Definitions of the High Water Markers

**Reviewed by CBadgenoonecc,
CBadgenoonec and JBadgenoonej**

High Water Markers provide tangible evidence of the advance and retreat of creeks, streams, rivers, and oceans. Metaphorically they also provide a measuring stick for citizens, nations, enterprise and empire.

The denomination of a coin, its actual worth, a graduation ceremony, and an alma mater are some examples. Others are represented by a trophy with inscription, a military rank, a medal, or a prefix before a name.

Civilian title after a name, the number of boxes under a box on an organization chart, a corporation balance sheet represented others. GNP, Gross National Product, the size of an army, a navy or air force represents more broadly-based examples of those milestones.

Include the size of a house or lot, a zip code, the speed and make of a car, the type of aircraft or boat that a person might own. Some carry more weight, the ability to walk again after losing both legs, the moment when someone sets aside the bayonet and picks up the pen.

A few are life-changing events, a birth, a spiritual epiphany, a wedding, a divorce, a death. Telling additional examples in a random depth progression include:

- the first time you appreciate the scent of a desert cactus flower
- enjoying a cup of tea for the first time
- a night when you see all the stars and not the void
- your first hug

- beating your dad at arm wrestling
- wishing he could have won instead
- being named editor-in-chief of your school newspaper
- managing your own newspaper chain
- delivering the class valedictory speech
- appreciating the gravitas of the moment
- selling the first glass of lemonade at your home-made stand
- starting your own business
- selling the business
- sharing that first frosty mug of beer with your dad on your twenty-first birthday
- drinking your first glass of wine
- sipping your first glass of premium wine
- savoring wine from a sediment bottom gallon made by your grandfather
- smoking your first pipe, cigar, or cigarette
- smoking your last
- the first rung on the corporate ladder
- your first president's club recognition
- your first Golden Apple trip
- the final rung
- being elected president of your college fraternity
- being elected president of your college sorority
- your first good set of golf clubs that you want to protect with name and address identification labels (three in your golf foursome are reassured with the knowledge that eventually your favorite lob wedge might return; also, affixing one of those labels later in life to your cane, another to your walker, a third to your wheelchair. You are the envy of many in the Rehabilitation Center, because you still have a home address beyond those walls.)
- your first golf birdie
- viewing the stone bridge at Old Course Saint Andrews
- your first golf Eagle
- becoming an Eagle Scout

- your first true love
- your first tennis love
- your first chess match
- your first check and mate
- the gold watch with leather band and golden apple that you earned for ten years of service
- the moment when, thirty years later, a "Dora the Explorer" bandage (gifted from your granddaughter) is placed over the golden apple.
- buying a new car with factory-installed XM Radio.
- that moment a few years later when you are disappointed when "40s on 4" is replaced by a contemporary performer.
- then, the satisfaction you feel when you learn that, by popular demand, the station brought back the 40s.
- finding friends on LinkedIn
- finding them again on Facebook
- listing your work accomplishments on Facebook
- hiding the references, as they distract the social media mission
- a million likes
- a thousand followers
- a hundred friends
- one best friend
- fifty significant pins
- the first plane ride
- the first time you were the pilot, solo
- your first commercial real estate deal
- the first soap box derby car you built from a wooden plank and fruit box
- the first time you drove a real car
- your first Detroit car
- your first Italian, Japanese, or German automobile
- the first time your dad discovered that you didn't buy American
- the first time someone else drove you
- a transcendental meditation
- an existential moment

- when you first found religion
- the moment you first found Jesus

Jackson acknowledged that this list was modest. It was compiled to reflect life story vignettes of the community of souls woven together by the books in this treasure chest.

A more comprehensive view of their stories was penned by ten of the Neverborn. Each book title begins with the same series header:

The High Water Markers of . . .

She was open to the idea of recognizing high water markers that reflected lives beyond these works. Jackson would accept additional entries at her secondary email address, JBadgenoone@gmail.com. Originally intended to serve as a bookmark, the "Definitions" page expanded to nearly a sixteen-page signature.

Down deep, she realized that a more comprehensive list of the definitions would give birth to a reference-style manual with twenty or more signatures of sixteen. The list would be limited only by the number of people who found the path to inclusion by way of this book.

Jackson agreed to offer random prize rewards to those who chose to participate. Winners would be determined by a panel of Neverborn judges. Once every six months they would vote on the best entries.

Entrants would acknowledge that they agreed to have their definition published in the final version of the book. They could elect to reflect or hide their identity in print. Markers could not predate the year 1758, a year of reflection and formation. They would be required to provide a statement regarding their qualifications to submit an entry.

She imagined a few that might make the list. They included:

- developing a musical career to create listening enjoyment for the ear

- picking up a paint brush later in life to create inspiration for the eye
- forming a career to make people laugh
- a phonograph album to let them know that you can sing
- a Nobel Peace Prize
- a Pulitzer Prize
- a Golden Globe
- an Emmy award
- a beauty pageant tiara
- a green golf jacket
- a football Super Bowl ring
- a baseball World Series record
- a Triple Crown
- a NASCAR Trophy
- a World Cup Trophy

Jackson reviewed both lists. She realized that by and large they recognized the high water markers of individuals or teams of individuals. During the first two centuries of her existence, she witnessed the expansion of a different kind of persona, the corporation. She wasn't sure how they came upon their names. She remembered when Teddy Roosevelt gave some of them a run for the money.

Formed by and comprised of individuals, those organizations seemed to assume a life apart from them. She agreed to accept entries into a business classification. Again she thought of some possible candidates, especially those that had impacted the circle of lives reflected in the ten books. She began a modest list.

A few of those companies were small mom-and-pop shops. Some were privately held and accountable to immediate investors; others offered shares that were traded in the public marketplace. Management for those companies kept a sharp eye on quarterly earnings and sought inventive ways to satisfy shareholders. Jackson began to identify a handful of initial candidates:

- American Book Company
- Cogito Learning Media

- Compaq Computer Corporation
- D.C. Heath and Company
- Litchfield Companion Products
- Mohawk Airlines
- Pan American Airlines
- Rossotti Lithograph Corporation
- Sunburst Technology

A number of the companies ceased to exist by the beginning of the twenty-first century. Jackson thought it sad that some of them hadn't been granted a place in the ranks of the Neverborn. She was also sure that they wouldn't find rest with those born to flesh who returned to dust and spirit. Only stock certificates, papers of incorporation, and faded press releases remained to record their existence. She reflected that maybe some other legacy did survive.

Publishing companies left behind books, some of them classic works. Acquiring companies, a few larger publishers, others with no real interest in publishing, inherited the imprints. Modest rebranding and a new distribution channel might extend the shelf life of those titles.

Acquisitions, mergers, spin-offs, divestitures and restructuring were not unique to the publishing industry. Airline, automobile, manufacturing and technology icons melted like so much snowfall into the creeks, streams and rivers of capitalism.

Jackson viewed with detachment when US-based companies pursued an inversion strategy to avoid paying taxes. She was uncertain about others that had gone global. She wasn't always able to ascertain the motives that drove those organizations. They professed to care about stockholders.

On occasion, they paid lip service to the national priorities of one country or another. In the early twenty-first century, people still drew borders in the sand. They were superimposed over the recognizable lines Jackson encountered in her early years. The contrived borders were not visible to viewers circling the globe.

A few royal figures still wore crowns and lived in castles made of stone. Remnants of empires still dotted the globe. Republics were more prolific. Real democracy was beyond the reach of many. JBadgenoone would be glad to record the high water markers of those nations and political creations.

She agreed to accept entries, again starting with those that impacted the lives in the circle of the high water marker books:

- Argentina
- Austria
- Belgium
- Brazil
- Cambodia
- Chile
- China
- England
- Egypt
- France
- Germany
- Holland
- India
- Ireland
- Iran
- Iraq
- Israel
- Italy
- Japan
- Laos
- Palestine
- Russia
- South Africa
- Spain
- Thailand
- United States of America
- Viet Nam

Jackson tightened contest entry rules applied to countries. Contributions to arts, science, and literature would make the list. Consideration would be given to geography, politics, military strength, economic influence, and technological achievement.

Submissions could reflect only high water markers associated with a tangible impact on humanity. Extra points would be awarded for entries with acceptable supporting hyperlink anchors.

Markers could reflect the political reality of the time associated with the event. For example, a Russian contributor could speak to the achievement of the first earth-orbiting satellite, even though it was launched under governance by the USSR.

JBadgenoone realized that she had opened quite a challenge. She amused herself with the possibility of taking the list to greater horizons in the not-too-distant future. High water markers of planet Earth, an Earth moon colony, the planet Mars . . .

James thanked Jackson for her insights and put aside these pages. They planned to resume reading *The Book of The Neverborn* on the following day. Jackson had assured him that the book would provide additional clues in his search for hidden treasure, and the relevance of the bayonet.

A spectacular North Carolina sunrise greeted them the next morning.

Jackson encouraged him to open the window to accept the cool, crisp morning air. When it met his face, he couldn't contain the joy and began to sing a refrain from the Broadway Musical and film, *Oklahoma:*

"Oh what a beautiful morning, oh what a beautiful day . . ."

Before he could complete the lyrics of the song, a strong wind blew in from the south, southwest.

The Book of the Neverborn is arranged alphabetically by each Neverborn subject. He had planned to continue his reading starting at Chapter 1, corresponding to the letter A. The gust of wind pounced on the unopened book and unfurled the pages. The wind died at the letter *J*.

The citation leapt from the page: Jackson was never born on May 29, 1758.

[Book 2]

The Book of The Never Born

Copyright © 2015 by Jackson Badgenoone

CHAPTER X

The Original Badgenoone

Jackson was never born on May 29, 1758 in the wilderness of Virginia, to a woman destined to become a bride of the Cherokee nation. A soldier under the command of one Captain Nathaniel Terry would have been her father.

The soldier was one of many assigned to garrison Terry's Fort. It was a link in the chain of forts that protected the frontier. Few today remember Captain Terry. No one remembers the soldier.

Jackson's would-have-been mother, Amathlaah, met him on March 15, 1757, a year of reflection and foment. By early spring of the following year she had fallen in love with that soldier. These two young people put aside the differences of culture, skin color, language, tradition, and religion.

During the final week in May they consummated their relationship. There was no wedding ring, no ceremony, just an embrace that lasted through the evening hours.

Their first romantic encounter bore no fruit. The embryo that would have been Jackson was lost. Two months later Amathlaah conceived, and in proper time gave birth to a robust, blond-haired, bronze skinned, blue-eyed boy. They named him Erik.

Soon after the birth, the boy's father perished, not from the fever of war but from a war with fever. Shortly after his passing, she followed the Great Wagon Road that ran from the Maggoty Gap, down through the Blue Ridge. Centuries ago it had originated as the Great Warrior Path carved through the woods by the Iroquois.

Ceded to whites in 1744, a year of reflection and perihelion, it became one of the most heavily-traveled roads in Colonial America. She was reasonably sure that some of her roots were with them and that Mohawk blood coursed through her veins.

Her sister and brother had shared several versions of the same story that reflected their journey to Virginia. The stories rendered points of collaboration in several upstate New York locations.

She continued her life journey in North Carolina. Twelve months after the passing of her soldier she fell in love again, this time with a Cherokee Indian planter.

There was never mention of her first love. Her new love never questioned her past. He accepted Erik as a son, and eventually she carried eight more children to term. The daughters and sons of a farmer would join the son of a soldier. In 1772, a year of reflection and partition, the family migrated farther south.

They purchased several hundred acres and built a comfortable house. She managed the new home in the northwest part of Georgia. They assumed a life patterned after those of their Caucasian neighbors.

In the next century, approaching her ninth decade, she seemed to enjoy all the benefits of a nominally-blended society. They had a prosperous farm, a substantial expanded home, and a growing extended family.

She recalled the day when her husband greeted her at the front porch, eager to share good news. Gold was found just up the road. He was certain that they might discover some on their farm. Why not?

This find in Georgia prompted a second gold rush. The first had taken place in North Carolina not many years before.

She held her husband's hand and released a plaintive cry. "Remember Hernando de Soto?" That conquistador's obsession for gold more than two centuries before had deleterious consequences for their people. "This will not be good for us," she said.

In the following weeks, they received reports of an influx of new settlers into their community. They hadn't come to farm but they wanted the land. She opened the window overlooking the rolling hills and meandering stream.

A gust of wind blew in from the west northwest.

Several months passed. They were told to vacate their property and join thousands of other indigenous people on a journey to a better place beyond the Mississippi.

They received no gold for their home or farm. They carried what they could and began the slow and arduous trek to Oklahoma. This was a world totally removed from the Oklahoma portrayed in the twentieth-century play and film.

The very young and the very old seemed to perish first. She refused to ride in the provisions wagon. She relinquished her space to a young woman nursing a child.

With indomitable spirit, she trudged over stone-covered paths that ripped into her shoes and tore apart her weary feet. Then an ice-and-snow-laden rain forced her into mud-covered roads.

On the fifth day of the second month she saw the eastern bank. De Soto had named it "Rio de Espiritu Santo"—River of the Holy Spirit; she referred to it as the Great River. In the eleventh hour she heard the voice of her neverborn daughter. She knew then that she would never see the western bank.

Soon after, her husband kissed her head, buried her lifeless body, and continued the journey. On the other side of the river, he, along with several of their offspring, would surrender their lives.

Historians would chronicle this journey as the Trail of Tears. Three of her children, two brothers and a sister, managed to escape the forced migration. Another Jackson played a significant role in that journey. Years later, an observer would identify his image on the US twenty-dollar bill. JBadgenoone owed her first name in part to him. It was a name that would be vilified by many in her tribe.

She—Jackson—first encountered the young boy named Andrew a carriage ride away from the first modest piedmont home of

Amathlaah. There was at first no explanation for the linking of his last name to her first.

Andrew was prone to anger but exhibited firmness of purpose. He could forgive but would rarely forget an injustice. She watched him grow into a young man dedicated to a cause. Soon after his thirteenth birthday, he enlisted in the local militia and served as a courier in the war for American Independence.

Captured by the British, the teenager was reminded of his Scotts-Irish impertinence by the swipe of an officer's blade against his head. He remembered that slash when he gave the order to fire upon British ranks during the waning days of the next war.

She documented his progress in law and politics. She was with him in Salisbury, North Carolina when he studied for the bar. In the following years, she observed his election to the House of Representatives, then to the US Senate.

He was the first popularly-elected president and ushered in an era that would be defined by his last name. Many years later, more about him was recorded in Jon Meacham's Pulitzer-prize-winning book *Andrew Jackson in the White House, American Lion.*

When Andrew Jackson enforced the Indian Removal Act, Jackson Badgenoone began to understand the attachment of his name to hers. His life would be recorded and remembered in the history books. Memory of her family was her responsibility.

In the den overlooking Dutch Buffalo Creek, the story of Andrew's life was flanked on one side by another book: *A Country of Vast Designs: James K. Polk, the Mexican War and the conquest of the American Continent.*

Polk was introduced to the world of the living in Mecklenburg County. Fifteen years before Polk's birth, LORD Cornwallis described the center of the county as a Hornet's Nest. Perhaps the legacy of that environment influenced Polk's one-term tenure as president. It would redefine American expansionism, at least for a time.

Eight years after his birth, a US land acquisition from France was purchased with gold. Polk's additional real estate would be wrestled from Mexico with blood.

This new president owed some of his mission and a large dose of his success to his North Carolina protégé, a predecessor in the White House. The neverborn Jackson could only view the emergence of a new nation and several wars that followed from a vaporous point of view.

She couldn't affect the events that would lead to the destruction of her family or countless other families sacrificed on the foundations of nation building and nation restoration. Nor could she celebrate the constructive forces in and of their lives.

Jackson Badgenoone was there when her surviving first-born sister, Sarah, celebrated her seventeenth birthday. It was at the time when Georgia joined twelve other colonies on a path to rebellion against the British Empire.

In keeping with the naming tradition begun with her older half brother, her parents had also given to her a Judeo-Christian name. They instilled in her appreciation for the honored place of women in their society and a respect for their native language and roots. More about those roots was recorded in the book *Voices of Cherokee Women*.

During her formative years, Sarah acquired a mastery of the language, customs, and belief structure of English soldiers who occupied the country at the time.

Her mother had already impressed upon her an understanding of the colonial vocabulary and Scotts-Irish mores of her older brother. In her late teen years she acquired the Germanic lexicon of the Hessian soldiers sent to assist their British comrades-in-arms.

Jackson viewed with concern the journey of Sarah's younger brother, Samuel, and his offspring. He also escaped the Trail, unsure of the instruction he would provide to his sons. First-born Erik married within the nation and fathered four children.

The second-born released three slaves, sold his land, and joined several Cherokee compatriots on a journey to Texas shortly before the frail bones of his grandmother returned to the earth. Her tribe believed that her spirit returned to the stars in the Milky Way; her clan was sure that her soul returned to Paradise.

Erik had three sons and named the second-born Joshua. The first-born headed north and would settle in the Finger Lakes region of New York State. That boy played his part during the construction of a canal that would link the Great Lakes to the Atlantic. The youngest picked up the plow in western Tennessee. One of his descendants would captain a steamboat from Saint Louis to New Orleans.

Joshua enlisted in and then joined the American army moving on Mexico. Joshua was assigned to an artillery brigade commanded by a vibrant first lieutenant. Within days of his arrival on the field of battle, Joshua was stricken, but not fatally.

The wound was sufficient to keep him from his duty before a final and fateful cannonade. When the smoke cleared, a tangled mass of lifeless mothers and children lay prostrate on blood-soaked ground. He saw in them a striking resemblance to the faces of his Cherokee aunts and cousins.

At that moment, Jackson Badgenoone realized that her identity was drawn from at least one other Jackson. Several years later, Joshua's son went on to serve under the same officer that had commanded Joshua during the siege of Veracruz. This time, those men wore uniforms of gray. His son was felled at the First Battle of Bull Run (First Manassas), serving in the Stonewall Brigade.

His commander, Thomas Jackson, had made a telling observation about the bayonet during a crucial turning point in that battle. JBadgenoone was a witness to it all. More about that Jackson was recorded in the book *Such Troops as These: The Genius and Leadership of Confederate General Stonewall Jackson*.

Had she had flesh and bone, Jackson speculated, she might have been able to alter the events. She would have saved her loved ones and provided counsel to their adversaries. She lamented moreover that she had not been there to participate in the joyful tidings of life.

She could observe the birth of brothers and sisters, and she could absorb the melodic notes chanted by her mother in an early evening song shared with her would-have-been siblings. But she couldn't participate in any meaningful manner.

Andrew and Thomas Jonathan Jackson were the first of ten living souls that shared a name with JBadgenoone. Any number of books had been written about Andrew and Thomas.

Films were scripted about various aspects of the lives of these two iconic figures. More would surface when old wounds healed. Readers and viewers would be able to observe and appreciate the human joy, strength, and vulnerability of these men.

They would witness the life that attended each Jackson in and out of uniform. They would learn about the challenges and rewards before, during, and apart from the military service of both men.

Jackson Badgenoone began to appreciate the contribution of these men in her identity development. Andrew set in motion the journey of her Cherokee family. Thomas reminded her of the difficult travel undertaken by her Scots-Irish relatives. He would be vindicated by that clan.

She was eager to reveal more about the other eight namesake originators. The third of ten would go on to chronicle a journey by Sarah's distant cousins.

The story was captured by Louis Jackson in 1885, a year of reflection and exploitation. It was amplified in a novel, *Mohawks on the Nile: Journey of the Warrior Spirit*, published more than a century later. The remaining seven originators would appear during that twentieth century. Chapters surfaced about each of them in her section of *The Book of The Neverborn*. For the present moment, she decided to postpone reading about their stories.

She could sense that James displayed a growing curiosity about her full name.

He understood the importance of her first name but was eager to learn more about her Badgenoone identity. Before reading further, she would describe the genesis of her twenty-first-century reinvention. She would also describe the enlistment of her writing confederates.

James listened carefully as she delivered a third-party narrative of the development.

In the late eighteenth-century world, writing was fashioned by feathered pen and inkwell. An author needed only a first name. On occasion, that name could belong to another person, with or without form. With no last name, Jackson sought some way to expand her contribution to the storyline in the new millennium.

Jackson noticed that in the modern twenty-first century world, workers were sometimes referred to by a badge number. While she didn't toil, she considered herself a worker; her job was observing. She toyed with the idea of applying for a number that could facilitate an extended identity.

It would give her an opportunity to trump the angels. She could also separate herself from the faceless masses of the other neverborn. Since it was her idea, she assumed it reasonable enough to apply for "Badge Number One."

Jackson sought permission. The answer came swiftly and without fanfare: she could claim "badgenoone." It served as a painful reminder that *she was no one.*

She was determined to enter a digital world that required only an email address attached to a first and last name. With a formalized identity, Jackson Badgenoone could now help to amass and catalog countless digital artifacts.

Jackson proceeded to secure several email identities. They would take form as "badgenoone@ . . ." or alternately, "jbadgenoone@ . . ." The email addresses enabled her to open online storage accounts. With email and storage accounts secured, she could help preserve those artifacts in a virtual Hope Chest.

She could deposit copies of photos, videos, letters, magazines, artwork, and music. JBadgenoone found homes for the growing collection in Facebook, Pinterest, Historypin, Tumblr, Instagram, Vimeo, YouTube, and others.

A Twitter account also enabled her to collaborate more efficiently with a Neverborn cohort. She would be able to reference digital data from innumerable sources. JBadgenoone could map an electronic route for the digital representations of artifacts.

Jackson had already whispered into the ear of a local lithograph-printing proprietor. He agreed to print and bind twenty-one hardcover books in his modest building on the upper banks of Dutch Buffalo Creek. It was situated upstream just south of the Route 73 Bridge.

The printer promised to store them in a safe environment, a sealed box in a lean-to on the creek side of his building. He joked that only a major flood or act of God could dislodge the container from the granite north wall.

Now James began to understand. JBadgenoone sensed it and discontinued her discourse. He had taken another pill. It was time for him to rest in the brown recliner chair to consider the full meaning of what he had just heard.

On the following day they returned to the den.

She began to carefully parse through the opening pages of books written by nine of her neverborn colleagues. Jackson would help to set the stage for what they were about to read.

The books defined the high water markers of many lives that impacted the authorship of *The Hidden Treasure of Dutch Buffalo Creek*. Markers in each book shed dispassionate light on markers in all of the other books.

In the search for treasure, Jackson would relish the role of author's guide. She would also ghostwrite a tenth story. It described the journey of a young Hessian soldier employed in service to the British Crown. That soldier had an early role to play in the collection of markers that bound these families together.

These lives flourished against a backdrop of global change. It spanned just a few years more than three centuries, not that long when measured against all time.

She went on to explain that the young Hessian soldier had shed his uniform and had begun to farm a patch of land. In a few more than ten years, that patch of land would map to a new county. By 1798, a year of reflection and prediction, not long after North Carolina became a state, he added fifty acres to the original fifty.

Some of those acres touched upon the eastern bank of Dutch Buffalo Creek. The soldier farmer was unaware of and would have been unconcerned by the predictions made by Thomas Robert Malthus that same year.

At that time, evening light was provided by the moon, stars, and a candle. Whale-oil lamps eventually replaced wicker and wax. The population of living souls worldwide had not yet reached 800 million.

As author and author's guide, she continued to unlock truth about her own identity. She bore witness to the high water markers that stood as a backdrop to this collection of souls.

Jackson also felt obliged to provide a foundation layer of instruction for the young grandchildren. She knew they would first read the book in the year of reflection and reconciliation.

She began to paint the background canvas that would support seven generations. Kerosene replaced whale oil, and then electric bulbs replaced kerosene during the journey of these souls. Sailing ships were powered by wind during the time of Sarah and Samuel. Some vessels carried human contraband. Others were awash with the blood, blubber, and oil of the largest creatures from the depths of the sea.

Navies redeployed to protect coal when steam replaced the ocean breeze. They were reassigned to protect black gold when diesel engines powered screws. In the span of less than three centuries, Jackson observed at least three Orwellian civilizations that seemed to constantly challenge each other. They at times also strived internally against their own constituents.

Europe harbored numerous examples. Religion separated Orange from Green Ireland. Germany emerged from a thousand principalities that still commanded loyalty through a period of nineteenth-century unification and twentieth-century dismemberment and reunification.

Balkanization became a pejorative when a handful of states upended order and tradition. Italy was defined by dialect. Even little

Belgium was divided by language. One of those languages had a similar impact on Canada.

States rights drove a wedge into the heart of a union on the other side of the pond in the mid-nineteenth century. Those states had turned red and blue at the advent of the new millennium.

In other corners of the globe, colonialism gave way to nationalism. The political map was routinely redrawn. Viet Nam was fractured by north-south friction then reunited. Korea remained divided by economy and politics. Mainland China absorbed remnants of the British Empire. The subcontinent jewel of that empire was dissected. Sunni and Shiite contested boundaries in dozens of countries. Religions, empires, politics, and philosophy magnified differentiae.

It seemed that, almost everywhere, agriculture made room for an industrial revolution. Industry remade itself with the introduction of each new modern technology. On the Outer Banks of North Carolina in 1903, a year of reflection and fulfillment, two brothers flew the first motorized airplane. In 1927, a man would fly solo across the Atlantic. 1969 years after the birth of Christ, an astronaut would plant his feet and an American flag on the moon.

In the year of reflection and reconciliation, Jackson and her Neverborn compatriots had chronicled the lives of ten living souls. By 2014, the planet supported over seven billion people.

JBadgenoone took seriously her obligations as author's guide. Jackson wanted to provide guidance to her Neverborn colleagues as they crafted their work. She paid close attention to stories that considered the contributions of multiple supporting characters.

Jackson especially enjoyed reading about the implications of those interacting relationships over an extended period of time.

The first book to capture her attention was *The Adams Chronicles: Four Generations of Greatness*. It traced the accomplishments of this remarkable family from the formative years of the republic through the early days of the twentieth century.

She believed that Amy S. Greenberg provided a road map of sorts with the content and title of a book, *A Wicked War: Polk, Clay, Lincoln, and the 1846 US Invasion of Mexico*. JBadgenoone was also

certain that GJA O'Toole did a masterful job presenting the protago-
nists, antagonists, participants, and spectators in his portrayal of *The
Spanish American War.*

The inside jacket of that book captured Jackson's attention:

> Here is the color and drama of this turning point in
> American history. Through the wide-angle lens of his
> exhaustive research, G.J.A. O'Toole projects the sweep-
> ing panorama of peace and war, the epic human story of
> America crossing the threshold of the twentieth century.
> Marching across the pages are Theodore Roosevelt, Mark
> Twain, Clara Barton and Stephen Crane, sometimes
> unexpectedly joined by Queen Victoria, Kaiser Wilhelm,
> Winston Churchill, and William Randolph Hearst.

Jackson was intrigued by the links presented in the book. Many
of the same notables directly influenced her tribe of souls. O'Toole
also captured a handful of people unknown to the history books.
There was a level of scrutiny about those average citizens that she
hadn't observed in her earlier readings. She struggled to find ways to
replicate the formula in her work.

She recalled reading an account of the ordinary men and women
who fought America's wars, *Those Who Have Borne The Battle: A
History of America's Wars and Those Who Fought Them.* She imagined
writing a book where the ordinary folks were central to the plot.
Better-known figures would assume the role of supporting characters. The gesso was dry; she began to envision the colors.

Other stories chronicled the journey of unknown persons over a
period of decades or centuries. *How the West Was Won,* delivered to
the big screen in 1962, a year of reflection and challenge, provided
such an epic tale. It portrayed a migration of ordinary families that
helped to transform a continent. JBadgenoone's family was not
among them.

This template seemed closer to the mark that she was trying to
establish. Up until then, she had read about extraordinary people
shaping extraordinary events. She had also read about ordinary

people rising to meet the challenges of those events. Jackson anticipated an incremental step.

She kept repeating to herself, *Ordinary people and ordered events,
ordinary people and ordered events, ordinary people and* . . .

The storyline was set against some of the same backdrops that
affected the family bound together by *The Hidden Treasure of Dutch
Buffalo Creek* and the ten *High Water Markers* books attributed to
their journey. It was not her call to make, but she thought it appropriate to subtitle all ten titles as *How the West Was One Again.*

Jackson encouraged James to read for a third time the *Decline and
Fall of the Roman Empire.* The roots of many of his ancestors were
planted firmly in the pastures gone to seed during that period of time.

The section labeled "Family and Friends" contained ten titles.
They were arranged by Neverborn ghostwriters from A to J. Jackson
had established the surname assignment precedent for this small
band of observers.

They would each be known as a variation of Badgenoone. Only
the first initial of their first name would set them apart. Over time
they became like adopted siblings, prone to brother and sister ban-
tering, but respectful of each other.

Abadgenoone, Bbadgenoone, Cbadgenoone . . .

There were countless A's and B's and C's in the universe of the
Neverborn. These privileged few were the only ones permitted to
carry the Badgenoone credentials. Their assignment was to observe
ten interlocking lives in this community of souls who spanned
several centuries and three continents.

Each life touched the sinew of 200 or so more. They in turn were
touched by an equal or greater number of souls. Collectively, this
tribe provided a portal into the human condition that was unavailable when viewed through just one life.

Different assemblages of living souls were formed during the
same timeline. Others formed in different centuries or millennia. It
would fall upon other A's and B's and C's to tell those stories.

Jackson could imagine that their naming credentials would befit the time and circumstance. She mused about surnames attached to a coat-of-arms.

These ten firefly-like entities brightened the night. Jackson was the first to arrive to the story. Her observations began in the late eighteenth century. She continued to observe her namesake wards well into the twenty-first.

Like Jackson, the first name of each Neverborn was ordained by a particular tie to the object(s) of her/his observation. The other nine were all never born in the nineteenth or twentieth century.

Jackson confided that she was somewhat relieved by the manageable number of Neverborn assigned to her story. The naming convention was limited on the first pass by the number of letters in the English alphabet.

She conceded that more than one Anna or Fred might be called upon to reflect on a story. Jackson was adroit and knew that there was a manageable if somewhat limited solution to the challenge.

In those instances, a second iteration of the first letter would be added to the tail of the Badgenoone name. The same convention would apply to anyone who happened to share the same first initial of the Neverborn first name.

For example, if Neverborn Jeremy was asked to participate in this adventure, his surname would be BadgenooneJ. He might be alternately identified as Jeremy Badgenoonej. A subsequent Neverborn J would prompt a second iteration of the last letter. For example, Jessica would become Jessica Badgenoonejj.

As a concession to crafting their stories in a twenty-first century format, and in the interest of efficiency, Jackson agreed to store all of their digital artifacts in her cloud. She agreed to host weekly meetings for the Badgenoone ghostwriters. Jackson would also provide a performance review associated with the submission of selected chapters from each work.

JBadgenoone instructed her colleagues to consider a central guiding point in the construction of their tales. They would have achieved a measure of success at that point in the story when the observee recognized the observer. They would also realize that every year contained twelve months of reflection for someone. They shared responsibility for assigning a secondary calendar description.

She would lead the search for treasure with observations from the book that she had authored. She shared several concerns before allowing James to open the book.

Jackson confided that she was overwhelmed by the challenge to write about Frederick, but she took comfort in the role of author's guide. From that vantage point, she could observe the currents of history without serious commentary.

As a writer, she felt obliged to critique her observations. She came into being during the later part of the eighteenth century and was influenced by the authors of that time. She emulated some of the foundations of their storytelling style.

Jackson had become an avid reader by the second part of the nineteenth century. She loved stories of the sea. *Moby Dick*, Melville's tale of a great white whale, was her favorite. It seemed to garner new interpretations with each decade.

She devoured a body of works formed before, during, and following the American Civil War. Her favorite period author was Samuel Clemens. Jackson was amazed by his ability to parse complicated geopolitical commentary through the parochial voice of a character named Huck, brought to life in *The Adventures of Huckleberry Finn*. Mark Twain would have understood the vernacular of the young boy and the backdrop of events that shaped his life.

JBadgenoone wanted to set the stage for the story of a Hessian farm boy. She confided to James that, for the first time, she experienced the emotion of fear—fear that her writing style lacked contemporary flair. Jackson was quite certain that, as a Neverborn, she wasn't supposed to feel any emotion at all.

Yet she did.

Jackson was then quick to realize that this wasn't the first emotion that rustled her spirit. As an observer, she had encountered anger, remorse, sorrow, and joy. James promised to help her to sort through those feelings. He suggested that she join him on his daily walk to the center of town as it could help her to formulate her thoughts.

The walk from his home to a local restaurant just west of the downtown intersection could be done in fewer than twenty minutes. She didn't interrupt his stride. He had affixed ear buds to his iPhone and enjoyed listening to the movements of the Brandenburg Concerto.

The orchestra seemed to anticipate every new flower, each leaf on every tree along the stroll. They crossed the street at the traffic light equipped with a recently-installed pedestrian signal. Within a few short steps they arrived at the restaurant. Jackson noticed a cross that hung in the window facing the bank across the street.

An exterior section of the eatery was painted deep red. The establishment provided some of the best food in town. His favorite dinner was the meatloaf special offered up each Wednesday evening.

Prime rib was the special on the first Sunday of every month. He also enjoyed a chicken-fried steak or a pulled-pork sandwich. On this morning, he ordered his usual breakfast: a cup of coffee, two eggs over easy, bacon, and grits.

He was saddened to learn that one of his favorite waitresses had just passed following a brave battle with cancer. At a very young age she left behind a host of friends, family, and children who knew and loved her.

His wife Mimi and he had come to think of her as a daughter. They could only imagine the high water markers that awaited her had she been granted extra years. Her children, family, and friends were added to their prayer list. They promised to find a way to keep her memory alive.

Jackson and James listened attentively to a conversation at the next table. Another patron was sharing a tale about his ancestor, a Hessian who fought on the British side of the American War for Independence. James silently whispered to her nervous spirit, *Be still—these fellows will help you craft the preface to your book.*

The restaurant patron began to reveal his tale. How fortuitous—the story of her Frederick seemed to unfold from the casual conversation at the next table. Jackson wanted to record it word for word but was unfamiliar with the country cadence of the speaker and listener.

Now she experienced the emotion of jealousy. Why couldn't she construct what she heard in the local lingo, just as Mark Twain had done more than a century before?

He suggested that she put aside that impossible bar. *Tell the story the way you heard it,* he said. *Make it happen in your own voice.* Jackson took his advice and began to frame the conversation for eventual publication.

The patrons continued to share. JBadgenoone recorded. A week later they began to read.

[Book 3]

The High Water Markers of Jackson's Observee

Preface to The High Water Markers of Jackson's Observee

His ancestor, a soldier named Frederick, came to the county just months following the arrival of his friend and fellow conscript. Assigned to military duty in what became the state of Georgia both had deserted the British cause. They moved north to Mecklenburg County, North Carolina, the first place to declare independence from the crown.

The friend shed his uniform and his German name. Johannes Reith assumed a new identity as John Reed. He encouraged Frederick to join him. Within months Frederick also migrated to the north.

Still at his post before making that fateful decision, he confided his intentions to another soldier who was also disenchanted with the entire colonial adventure. As they continued to read, Jackson whispered to him, *I was there when that conversation took place.*

Frederick was confiding his intentions to Joseph. He was also determined to leave the futile struggle. His path would lead him back to his native Germany. He planned to return there within the year, with his soon-to-be war bride, Sarah. Jackson whispered again, *She would have been my sister.*

These Hessian soldiers didn't fit the stereotype image portrayed by artists and historians. They were just young men eager for adventure but looking forward to the prospect of long life. Frederick wished Joseph well.

As a wedding gift for the bride-to-be, Frederick gave Joseph a gold ring that had been in his family for generations.

Joseph presented the ring to Sarah as a token of the love that bound them together. She in turn would pass it on to her offspring. It would find a way back to American soil more than a century later.

Soon after he had given the ring to Joseph, Frederick shed his uniform for civilian attire and headed north. He tarried a while with his friend, John Reed. Unlike Joseph, these men would never return to the Hesse region of Germany.

They preferred to settle in this new country. Farmers at heart, they were thankful for the bounty of the land.

John had recommended a parcel not far from the acreage he'd acquired. Frederick was struck by the rolling hills and sweet water that flowed over the rocky bottom of Dutch Buffalo Creek.

One day he would own the rich soil by the creek. As if to lay claim to it, he buried his bayonet. The War for American Independence went on with one less weapon aimed at the rebellion. He wasn't searching for fame or glory or gold; he just wanted to farm. The blade slipped beneath the mud of the water-starved flow.

This was no ordinary bayonet. It was a unique German/Dutch-made knife-blade design. Considered too horrific a weapon, it was outlawed by all nations except Germany. It was banned by the commander-in-chief of the colonial army.

Washington warned the enemy that no quarter would be given to any soldier captured with this bayonet. Frederick was thankful that he had never used that blade in battle. 2.

Frederick planned to retrieve the bayonet but the water had risen by the time he returned. It hid that reminder of his military past. He never again saw the blade. It took months for a letter and reply to link destiny and destination. Over time he lost touch with Joseph and Sarah. Frederick put the bayonet and the gold ring into the treasury of his memories.

Jackson paused to reflect on the section of the preface they'd just read. They returned to the restaurant and sat in a booth next to the same two men whom they had encountered the previous week. They were still talking about Frederick.

The patron was sure that his ancestor Frederick should have been able to find gold on the farm that was handed down through the family. Some day he planned to retire his cane fishing pole and set up a sluice box.

Jackson encouraged James to thank the men for helping her to construct a comprehensive preface. He approached them with a friendly greeting:

"Y'all have a great story; didn't mean to listen in, but glad I did."

It was an awkward moment. He realized that he had just met the owner of the adjacent corn field. He knew his neighbors to the north, south, and west of the house nestled on the edge of the development; he never thought to consider that the owner of the farmland on the eastern side of the creek was also a neighbor.

The arbitrary property line between suburban lot and country meadow was confirmed by some surveyor along the way. It was positioned at the halfway point in the water, twenty feet to the east of the western bank.

Defined by the location of the find, the bayonet belonged in the den overlooking Dutch Buffalo Creek. Yet this direct descendant of Frederick might have some ancestral claim to the weapon. He might also make some very incidental claim to the gold ring that found a way back to Mont Amoena. He could have no remote ownership of small nuggets that were discovered within a foot of the western bank. Maybe they contained gold.

Information about the bayonet, the ring, and the rocks would be withheld at this initial encounter. There would be time enough to share when more was known about this accidental acquaintance. James would be more than willing to ransom a few stones for the ring and the blade.

In the meantime, Jackson could develop the chapters that were beyond the reach of the patrons in the restaurant. She had seen what they had only heard through generational word of mouth.

Her chapters would reveal the emotional conflict that Frederick faced when he first wore the uniform. They recalled the drill when he carried his musket with bayonet.

They expanded on his life in the county, his marriage, and the birth of his children. Subsequent chapters traced the contributions of their offspring down to the seventh generation.

Other chapters tracked the lives of Joseph, Sarah, and their progeny.

Another week passed and they resumed reading. Jackson now encouraged James to affix a yellow sticky label to each chapter in the book during the course of his reading.

CHAPTER I

Around A Georgia Campfire

The hot ashes refused to be extinguished. Frederick paused for a moment and then decided to rekindle the flame. He placed some dry branches upon the glowing embers and waved his scarf to fan the fire. A flicker caught the first twig, then a second. His friend Joseph arrived with some heavier logs.

Soon thereafter Johannes arrived. He carried a newly-slain hog to the campfire. They prepared a feast and began to recall the times that drew them close to each other. Three fireflies circled in the evening air.

Johannes, Joseph, and Frederick were more than best of friends: they grew up in the same small village just down the road from Frankfurt, Germany. Their childhood was full of fun and mischief. As they approached adulthood, fun was harder to come by, and the mischief of other men had led to war.

They entered service within weeks of each other. They were told that they would be fighting Indians. Proud of the new uniforms, they were not thrilled about the endless drill, marching, and more drill that were a part and parcel of military life.

On a trip that seemed to last forever, they continued to practice for conflict. They paced the wooden deck of a cramped and crowded war vessel bound for the British colonies in America. Joseph watched with some envy when sailors hoisted new canvas from the main mast. He was sure that their view was preferable.

Shortly after their arrival, they made their way south from Long Island to join comrades assigned to duty in South Carolina and Georgia. A flood of memories filled the early evening hours and held their attention throughout the night.

Frederick kept ample fuel on the fire that warmed their hands and roasted their meal. Johannes provided a steady stream of beverage to warm their spirits. Joseph longed to warm their hearts. They sensed that he was bursting with some new revelation. Good friends could always tell.

He sipped from his cup and whispered, "Sarah—her name is Sarah."

Frederick poked him with the tip of his bayonet. "You mean the Indian girl? Has her family threatened you? They are patriot sympathizers and would love to destroy us."

Joseph pushed aside the blade. "They mean us no harm. I am quite sure that I will spend the rest of my life with her. Lord permitting, that life will unfold in Germany. My tour is almost over and I can return home within the year. Sarah already told me that she had no real home on this side of the ocean. We would make a new home together."

Johannes and Frederick tried to absorb the information. She was a beautiful young woman and educated well beyond her station. They paused for a moment and then each in turn slapped the back of their comrade-in-arms.

"Congratulations, my friend; remember us when you arrive back in the land of castles, counts, and dukes."

Frederick tugged at his pinky finger. With a gentle twist he was able to remove a ring of yellow gold. It had been given to him by his mother on his seventeenth birthday. "Consider this a wedding gift, my friend," he said. "Embrace your bride."

Johannes stoked the flame and surveyed the surroundings. He too had something to share and was careful to lower his voice.

"I have no war bride. You two are the only friends on this side of the Atlantic. I won't be there to bid farewell next year. Within the week I plan to shed this uniform, change my name to John, and head north. Rich farmland is waiting for a strong body like mine to till the soil. I have been offered fifty acres.

"Frederick, you are more than welcome to accompany me. Joseph can bear witness to our departure. Create a convincing story for our superiors. They must not suspect that we would desert service to King George."

Frederick was intrigued by the offer. He tried to come to grips with the opportunity and the inherent danger. He had seen first-hand the consequences of capture following desertion.

Many of the local citizens were former German countrymen. However, they would be the first to turn them in if their treachery was discovered. They were ardent loyalists to the British Crown.

He couldn't comprehend their loyalty. They weren't Englishmen and yet they seemed to prosper from British law and structure. Hadn't they considered that this empire had also brought a measure of sorrow to this new continent?

Frederick could still hear the furtive groans of some and the anguished pleas of other African males bound in chains. Their wives and children cried and screamed in despair when they were pulled away from their husbands and fathers to be sold into slavery.

Patriots, even those with real English roots, fared no better. They were hunted down and dispatched without compassion. Native Americans were forced to decide their allegiance in the struggle that had assumed global proportions. If they were on the wrong side, they were parted from their scalps—a very bloody affair.

At this point, Jackson encouraged James to suspend reading from the book about Frederick.

Subsequent chapters would document his encounter with Native Americans, displaced loyalists, and enslaved African Americans. They would also trace his journey to Mecklenburg and the formation of his family to the fourth generation.

Meanwhile, Jackson's companion James thought that perhaps she wanted to return to *The Book of The Neverborn*. James had barely begun to read her story. A gust of wind had deflected the opportunity to read about the other Neverborn authors. It was arranged by their first name in alphabetic sequence. Maybe his viewing had missed something about these Neverborn ghost writers.

She suggested that he begin to read instead from the books they helped to write. Other chapters in *The Book of The Neverborn* contained dark elements that would distract from his search for the meaning of the bayonet and the hunt for hidden treasure.

"Focus for now on the other lives washed by the Hidden Treasure of Dutch Buffalo Creek," said Jackson. "You can still follow an alphabetic path through those high water marker works."

He followed her instruction and began to read. The first book was written by Anna.

[Book 4]

The High Water Markers of Anna's Observee

Copyright © 2015 by Jackson Badgenoone

About the Author

The complete dossier of Anna, aka Abadgenoone, is available in the first section of *The Book of The Neverborn*. Anna completed this work under the tutelage of JBadgenoone, aka Jackson.

Anna was commissioned to observe the life of a man that she would come to identify as the Knowledge Navigator, Nav, or simply KN. In his earlier years, KN had earned the nickname of Traveler, shortened to Trav.

She believed that KN would more accurately capture the natural progression of his life. A traveler will wander from point to place. Sometimes in a fictionalized rendition, he/she would travel from time to time.

A Knowledge Navigator could sift for truth through time and distance without ever leaving the desk in her or his den.

[At that moment, James realized that Anna was observing him. It was a surreal moment. The reading and the narcotics eased the physical pain that continued to pierce his consciousness. He watched his name evaporate into the nicknames that partially defined his personalities. The story continued to unfold.]

ABadgenoone had recently read a compelling novel titled *Traveler*, written by Elaine Fox. In that story, a Civil War Union soldier was transported in time from an 1862 Fredericksburg, Virginia battlefield to that same site in 1996.

In that latter year of reflection and exuberance, the battle site was grounded in a distant suburb of Washington, DC. In Elaine's novel, the appearance of the Northern Lights during the earlier year of reflection and incursion set the stage for an encounter between a nineteenth-century man and a twentieth-century woman.

Anna loved to consider time travel, especially when it flowered around a human relationship. Another story united a father and son with the occurrence of the Aurora Borealis. She watched that late twentieth-century movie *Frequency* in a DVD rendition on the small screen in KN's den. KN looked to the northern sky from time to time. He longed for another way to understand his dad.

Jackson and Anna conceded that time travel was possible. The catalyst may have been a fire in the sky, a reversal of the rotation of the earth, a solar eclipse, a bump on the head, or the appearance of a NEAT Comet. A whole body of science fiction sub-genre and alternate historical fiction literature was constructed around a galaxy of possibilities.

They agreed that time travel was possible for people. On a one-way journey into the future it was certain for the objects that they possessed.

Jackson did her best not to interfere with Anna's interpretation of the story. She was concerned about Abadgenoone's tendency to infuse her own recollections of people and places into the storyline of her observee. The reading continued.

Preface to the High Water Markers
of Anna's Observee

Anna's book swirled around several personalities. The least among them was a man named Traveler, Trav for short. He was also known as Knowledge Navigator (KN, alternately Nav), Point Man and the Wannabe Cisco Kid.

At times the four became one, on occasion conversing with each other. His (their) journey was set against a backdrop of tumultuous times.

In time, KN managed to hear the voices of distant relatives and ghostwriters who were never born. The Neverborn provided a portage between waters of contentment and struggle. They revealed submerged truths with spiritual sonar pings that bounced from mind to heart to soul.

They rescued two hundred golden thought flakes that were suspended in the living water of ten ordinary human vessels.

The Neverborn linked the voices of those who wrote history to those who lived through history. They would help Trav to appreciate the places he had seen and the people he met along the way. They would encourage KN to discover the deeper meaning of life. They would challenge Point Man to take risks. They would remind the Wannabe Cisco Kid that sometimes reality emerges from fiction.

Anna wrote the book for the prevailing bridge generation. She was well aware that every generation provided a bridge between the past and the present. One journalist referred to the contemporaries of Trav's parents as "the Greatest Generation."

They had bridged the unfinished business of the Great War to the beginning of space exploration. In a sense they laid the foundation for a transition between two millennia.

A previous generation was just as sure that it had changed the world. It referred to the Greatest Generation in different terms. These children of theirs were the Flappers and the Roaring Twenties crowd. When they came of age, they did indeed tackle the challenges of a global depression, followed by a second world war. Their parents and their children were proud of their accomplishments.

The Greatest Generation decided that their children would be called Baby Boomers. The Boomers were shaped by a fecundity differential between the winning and losing sides of another great war. Trav was on the winning side.

Human population on the third planet from the Sun would double within a few decades. American, Belgian, Canadian, Chinese, Dutch, English, French, Indian, Irish, Russian and other Allied Nations Boomer babies contributed large numbers.

Each generation assumes the task of applying a label to their parents. They usually wait until only a handful of their number still draw breath. Generation X or Y will apply an appropriate tag to the post-World War II collection of souls as Boomers approach the end of their course.

They couldn't be called the Revolutionary Generation. That identity had already been assigned to the founding fathers of the United States and their counterparts in France. They overthrew kings on both sides of the Atlantic. One in France paid with his severed head; the other in England lost his treasured American colonies.

Despite the perceptions of their parents, most Boomers weren't about revolution. They could be defined as the Challenger Generation. They were sufficient in number to challenge the unfinished business of the Greatest Generation.

Improved race relations, containment of war, and space exploration are part of their legacy. The Challengers pass a torch of unfinished business to Generation X and the Millennials. They will face global warming, increased pollution, untamed disease, resource inequality and worldwide hunger. Love and hate will be defined anew. They will determine their relationship with God and each other.

Boys and girls born to attain adulthood in the first quarter of the twenty-first century stand on the shoulders of all those who occupied center stage before they arrived. Hopefully their children will provide a more fitting label than X or Y.

These newer generations drew first breath at the dawn of the Internet Age. They expect to document progress and communicate in new and exciting ways.

The text of this narrative could be understood by the souls of the Greatest Generation and their predecessors. In keeping with convention established by her Neverborn colleagues, Anna employs an industry standard vehicle to transport more than words to a technology receptive audience.

Other data elements accessible through blue underlined hyperlinks are introduced in an eBook version. In one rendition, multimedia anchors secure into a common seabed beneath the water of life. A collection of images and sounds reflective of ordinary people punctuate the treasure of their memory.

When juxtaposed to similar collections, they might serve to connect people of all nationalities, languages, races, and religions. Anna couldn't talk back to the dead. She hoped to reach a few more of the living and those not yet born of flesh with the cloud-enriched eNovel.

The novel and the eNovel share identical objectives. Anna hopes to uncover the multiple personalities of KN's adopted alter ego. She attempts to shed some light on previously undiscovered treasures hidden in souls within his circle of influence.

Several treasures are like small flakes of gold that generate a smile. Larger nuggets elicit laughter and song. The largest evoke the currency of spiritual development.

Trav would have recognized Fredericksburg. There in 1994, a year of reflection and reservation, his youngest daughter had attended a college named after the mother of the father of the nation.

He had travelled with his daughter and her sisters to countless campuses a few years earlier. They were on a search for the perfect environment suited to the academic calling, taste, and temperament of each young lady.

Her older sister attended the second-oldest college in the country. It was named after a king and a queen regnant. The college was just a few Amtrak train stops southeast of the home of Mary Ball Washington.

Trav never missed the chance to stop and shop with his daughters at the local malls. He would dine with them at any one of the several restaurants that catered to the college students and their parents.

Nav (KN), on the other hand, seized every opportunity to visit the historical campus in Williamsburg, the alma mater of several presidents. The restored town also provided a glimpse into a colonial past.

In Fredericksburg, he slowly paced the battlefield described by Elaine. He could appreciate the image of a fallen soldier at the foot of the ridge.

The vignette captured in this preface represents a microcosm of KN's life. It unveils the tension between Nav and Trav, the two most dominant of his alternate personalities. It attempts to reveal a more comprehensive portrait of the man.

It identifies the high water markers that he left behind during his need to observe, chronicle, and participate in events. Along the way, he pursued a relentless quest to discover the meaning of life. Trav thought that good works would accompany the journey. Perhaps they could mitigate the carnage strewn along the way. Nav believed that lasting peace emanated from a deeper source.

In his golden years, he made a promise to his grandchildren: He would attempt to preserve precious moments that had a direct bearing on their lives. Many people influenced the life of Trav and Nav. Some were contemporaries. Others walked the Earth long before his birth. He grew up in the shadow of the Roman Empire, and was a product of modern-day Western Civilization.

Trav witnessed the influence of that society on other people. He observed the displacement and control of indigenous populations. KN considered the consequences of war, exemplified by the bayonet, rendered futile by atomic bomb.

Trav participated in the life of a career military officer father and followed him beyond army service into a civilian world. Anna's colleagues chronicled dad's journey and that of his very young war bride, one of millions to assume that mantle through the ages. Anna also kept a keen eye on a number of other souls who touched KN's life.

KN was thankful for a lifestyle that permitted him to participate in numerous circles of influence. He was intrigued by the Venn diagram view of humanity that those circles represented. At times he confessed a jealousy of the stay-put people.

Trav wrote his first short story in year one of his second decade and presented it as a gift to his grandfather. He continued to observe events throughout his lifelong work. Armed with a degree in Political Science, he never entered the world of formal politics. He fashioned a career in educational publishing and technology.

At the beginning of the sixth year of his sixth decade, KN began to pen his novel. A year later it would incorporate a lifetime of experiences. They forged station to vocation, linked place to time, and spiritual development to physical deterioration.

That book was originally intended as a gift to his grandchildren. He realized that it really belonged to an extended audience of family, friends, neighbors, colleagues, co-workers, classmates, and possibly at least a handful of heretofore strangers.

In a translucent version of the story, a ghostwriter named Jackson would devise an engaging title that spoke of hidden treasure. JBadgenoone would also assign other Neverborn observers to document supporting stories.

In a closed loop environment, Jackson would assign the story of Trav to a ghostwriter by the name of Anna. Jackson Badgenoone didn't have the positional authority to formulate a proper dedication to Trav's original work.

Trav, Nav, Point Man, and the Wannabe Cisco Kid would joyfully embrace that opportunity in a purely autobiographical version that he someday hoped to publish under a different title. It would declare,

> This story is dedicated to my (our) LORD and Savior, Jesus Christ, the source of living waters. It is meet indeed and just, right and helpful onto salvation, always and every- where to give thanks to Thee, holy Lord, Father almighty, eternal God, who with Thine only-begotten Son and the Holy Ghost art one God, one Lord; not in the unity of a single person, but in the trinity of a single nature. Thank you LORD for the gift of life, the gift of salvation, the gift of all the lives that you have shared, brothers, sisters in Christ and those soon to be so.

Jackson was eager to absorb the story as interpreted by her Neverborn compatriot, Anna Badgenoone. This adopted sister chal- lenged Jackson's management skills.

CHAPTER I
Born For The Journey

He grabbed the plastic wheel and pressed hard on the play horn. Pretending to drive his fathers' brand-new 1953 Chevy along the Will Rogers Highway, he believed he had complete command of the road.

Decades later, a boy his age would not have been permitted to sit in the front seat of a motor vehicle. He would have been required to wear a seat belt, would have missed the opportunity to co-pilot a dream car down an endless two-lane road.

The year before, the boy was mesmerized by the strain of metal wheels on train tracks that radiated from their temporary home in Chicago. He thrilled at the sound of the boat whistle and horn that announced the lifting of an anchor in San Francisco Bay a year later. Propeller airplane engines buzzed in his ear with every flight to every new base.

Fast forward four years to 1957, a year of reflection and adjustment. It was the year he left Yuma. The peaceful western town had withstood the vagaries of time. A post office, pharmacy, library, museums, several houses of worship, two banks, and a number of restaurants provided meeting places for local residents.

Every year, the rodeo came to town. It was announced by the formation of a parade down the main street. The local high school marching band, a bevy of beauty queens, and an occasional princess provided additional flair to the entertainment.

Fire engines and police car sirens announced the beginning and the end of each event. Young children tossed candy from horse-drawn floats to the younger children lining the parade route. The American flag waved from every home.

Local men and women were festooned with appropriate dress and or uniform from several periods in American History. Equestrians displayed their skills during the parade and at the rodeo on the following day.

The town had deep roots that hearkened back to native populations. For a time, the region was governed by Mexico. Ten years after the end of the American Civil War a territorial prison was constructed. He tried to imagine life within its walls.

Trav joined his dad and family on the 1957 trip back east to Fort Hamilton. It was a base situated in the shadow of New York City. During the twentieth century it was named after the first secretary of the US Treasury.

The military significance of the site was first realized in 1776, a year of reflection and revolution. In 1841, a year of reflection and acquisition, Robert E. Lee served as the post engineer. Also serving at the fort in the pre-Civil War era was one Lieutenant Thomas Jackson.

One day, this fort would represent his father's final duty station. Dad would return to civilian life not far from where he started his uniformed journey two decades earlier, but not this time. Within a year he would be deployed to Korea.

He made a concerted effort to provide a suitable base of operations for his wife and children, a safe and comfortable setting. They would be surrounded by friends and family, stateside. Years earlier he had returned to his father's house. Now he returned again.

The boy in the Buick Special listened to his dad bragging about how everything back east seemed so much grander. Route 66, where they began this eastbound journey, was alternately two-lanes and four-lane highways. Dad announced with some pride as they entered the Pennsylvania Turnpike, "No more two-lanes from here on in." It was a model for the emerging Interstate Highway system.

On the approach to the New York City skyline, the one-year-old 1956 Buick climbed up an elevated road, the Pulaski Skyway, an engineering marvel. The metal structure could have formed ten million "steels."

Somewhere between the Ohio border and Valley Forge, Pennsylvania, his dad realized how much his son loved to travel. It wasn't just about the sound of wheels and engines—he absorbed every landmark along the way.

His dad gave him a nickname that would stay with him for years: Traveler—no relation to the character in Elaine's book. Sometimes he just called him Trav.

This trip back east would be a bittersweet journey for Trav. He knew that he would probably never again pass through the gates of a military installation, at least not to live, and certainly not as a boy.

He would leave the neatly-ordered military base life and enter into an uncertain civilian world. The guard soldier's parting salute represented a high water marker that he hoped to savor in his memory bank.

Trav relished meeting new family and friends but he left behind in the Yuma desert five formative years of his life. There he could venture out toward the mountains, the very image of Gary Cooper, humming the theme song from *High Noon*.

On other days he could fashion himself as The Cisco Kid, Gene Autrey, Roy Rogers, Hopalong Cassidy, Zorro, Davy Crockett, or Daniel Boone. Any number of western action figures leapt from the screen. A few were pure invention, some reinvented. They all helped to fashion the worldview of a pre-teen boy.

He'd once met Romanian-born American Duncan Renaldo, the actor who portrayed Cisco. He also met his horse Diablo. The boy cherished an autographed photo that reminded him of the meeting. He also treasured a wooden coat rack plaque painstakingly crafted by his dad. Dad painted *Cisco* across the top of the hanger.

For an all-too-brief period, he was the wannabe Cisco Kid. Wannabe remembered his dad every time he went to hang a jacket or a coat.

Many of Cisco's Hollywood colleagues made it to the Yuma Rodeo. Autographs from some of the other actors were lost along the way. He found other ways to store their memories.

Of course, the world beyond his boyhood fantasies was very different.

Just before he started his journey back to the east coast, the Soviet Union launched Sputnik, the first artificial satellite to orbit the earth. It served as a high water marker that challenged the United States to rethink the ground game.

President Eisenhower signed the Federal-Aid Highway Act a year earlier. Initially inspired by the German Autobahn as an efficient way to move troops, it would lead to the creation of the Interstate Highway System.

That affected the growth patterns of the civilian population for the next half-century. It sealed the fate of a high water marker for passenger rail ground transportation in the United States.

The automobile would define the next half-century. Two-lane roads would follow the wagon trails into a nostalgic bypass. Postcards and books like *Where the Old Roads Go* kept alive their memory.

During those years in the desert, above the ground, the Americans and Soviets tested nuclear weapons. Later tests were conducted beneath the surface, less damaging to the atmosphere.

Intercontinental Ballistic Missiles (ICBMs) would be able to carry the ever-perfected weapons over land and sea. Mutually-assured destruction (MAD) was the prevailing goal. Like many in his generation, Cisco learned the art of duck and cover. His worldview began to expand.

Submarines went nuclear; aircraft carriers were the new battleships. Jet engines replaced propellers on planes. Trains were relegated to cargo, oil, and coal-carrying assignments. Automobiles from Detroit grew larger and more powerful with each new model year. Eventually they grew fins symbolic of the speed of a rocket age.

Mankind made progress on other fronts. Cisco was among the first to receive a vaccine against polio. His house had one of the first television sets, albeit with just one channel. It went off the air at midnight following a rendition of the national anthem.

The shows were wholesome enough—plenty of cowboy westerns punctuated by the Texaco Star Theater featuring the humor of Uncle Milte. The Dinah Shore Show, sponsored by the Chevrolet division of General Motors and the Mickey Mouse Club, rounded out the entertainment. Kate Smith belted out "God Bless America."

The following year, the King of Rock and Roll would wear a US Army uniform and would be stationed in Germany. The ruins there were almost fully restored in the years since Trav left Bad Nauheim in that country of his birth. By 1957, Disneyland was drawing thousands to a fantasy world ruled by a mouse and a princess.

Other changes carried more weight. The civil rights movement gained momentum, especially in the southern states. A century earlier, Americans on both sides of the Mason-Dixon line were still talking about compromise over slavery.

A civil war later, an aborted attempt at reconstruction, decades of Jim Crow laws, and the resurgence of the Ku Klux Klan swelled a wave of discontent that approached the shore of racial justice and equality.

In the following decades, it gained volume and strength as it moved across the land and around the world. In 1954, a year of reflection and reversal, the Supreme Court decision in Brown vs. Board of Education created a new high water marker for race relations in the United States. Sadly, it wasn't able to create a new nation of the United People.

He figured that out during a road trip the following year. He recalled a moment when he sought a sip of water from a colored drinking fountain. The white one was dry. A local teen encouraged him to quench his thirst elsewhere.

In 1955, a year of reflection and upheaval, the stage was being set for the eventual destruction of apartheid in South Africa. Foment brewed in a thousand hotspots around the globe.

Rewinding to that same year, two years before the family headed east, the boy played out his cowboy role. A Stetson hat covered his head and a red scarf bandana was fastened around his neck. His official Boy Scout canteen was strapped from his left shoulder and lodged near his right hip. Leather cowboy boots protected the soles of his feet.

The boy who would later be called Trav left his home and headed toward the distant hills. He felt that some destiny awaited him on the eastern face of those peaks that framed the sunrise.

A mile away from his concrete house, he entered a dried-out gully. Shallow at first, it expanded to a height of twenty feet and width of thirty more within a half mile of the entry point.

The sandstone cliff wall provided some measure of protective shade from the rising sun. He paused from time to time along the gully floor to inspect rocks and minerals that peaked above the barren dry bed. He had amassed a modest collection of stones and was eager to add more. Mica quartz, pegmatite, and pyrite were among his favorites. He was always on the lookout for gold but didn't expect to find any in this trench.

He emerged from the topographical depression, climbed brittle rocky cliffs, and marched through desert sands. Along the way, he chanced upon a host of fascinating creatures—lizard, Gila monster, scorpion, tarantula, rattlesnake, and roadrunner. Coyotes made their presence known to his ear, but eluded his eyes. Vultures circled overhead.

Tumbleweed bounced off the tall Saguaro and lodged in driftwood. Dust devils carried a million particles of sand skyward into the bone-thirsty air. They swirled on the advance edge of a dark cloud that released a flood of life-sustaining water.

Within a few hours, the sweet scent of cactus flowers filled his nostrils. They reminded him of how much he loved this place.

When he reached the summit of the westernmost peak, he paused to quench his thirst and refill the canteen from a spring nourished by the recent rain. For the first time, he was able to discern a voice that had spoken to him long before that moment. He'd heard her voice in the ruins of buildings destroyed by war.

She met his ear with the sound of waves and ship anchor chains. She found him perched between two rail cars traveling with clank and clatter on ribbons of steel. She whispered to him in the back seat of an automobile that glided down a country road.

The voice carried a gentle warning: *Don't tempt the LORD and don't return through the gully. Pyrite and gold alike will be swept away.*

Soon the sky cleared, and the rain ceased to fall.

He descended from the hill but he didn't enter the ravine. Instead he made his way home along the southern ridge.

Within thirty minutes, a wall of water rushed by his feet; along the ridge, creatures emerged and scampered up to the crest; below the surface, rocks were washed clean. He recalled her words: *Don't fear the water. Respect it.*

Back at the main section of the base, he crossed the road, entered the stucco-covered house, and paused to reflect on this recent adventure. He began to feel a sense of purpose. His daily journeys into the wilderness had evolved.

They were no longer a stage for fantasy western episodes. He was more aware of the miracles of life that were hidden in the gully and dunes. The transformation of the boy from Trav to Nav had also begun to take shape in that desert sand, even before he assumed either nickname.

Later that week he attended Mass at the base chapel. There was only one house of worship on the post. The religious denomination was determined by the day of the week and time of day. Ten on Sunday morning was reserved for Roman Catholic military and families.

The boy who would one day be nicknamed Trav wore the black cassock robe of an altar boy and assisted the priest who performed the liturgy in Latin. The altar boy memorized the words and knew the responses by heart, but he didn't understand their meaning. Fortunately, he could refer to *My Sunday Missal—Explained by Rt. Rev. Msgr. Joseph F. Stedman.*

On page forty-seven, he read, *"Vere dignum et justum est, aequum et salutare, nos tibi semper, et ubique gratias agere: Domine sancte, Pater omnipotens, aeterne Deus:"*

Rendered in English translation: "It is meet indeed and just, right and helpful onto salvation, always and everywhere to give thanks to Thee, holy Lord, Father almighty, eternal God."

The voice he heard in the desert followed him into the building. Anna added a sweet soprano strain to the chorus as they sang the recessional hymn following the Concluding Rite.

> *Holy God, we praise Thy Name;*
> *LORD of all, we bow before Thee!*
> *All on earth Thy scepter claim,*
> *All in Heaven above adore Thee; Infinite Thy vast domain,*
> *Everlasting is Thy reign.*

His father had first embraced that as his favorite hymn while stationed in Germany during the Second World War. From the last pew in the chapel, Dad sang it with particular gusto that day.

The colonel's baritone voice rose above the congregation. It joined the voice from the desert and reached the ears of the altar boy with incredible force.

CHAPTER II
Fifty-six Steps

The boy carried those memories and a thousand more on the road trip in 1957. The family explored abandoned gold mines, old forts, deserted towns and a cave where outlaws created their own law. They travelled some of the most scenic vistas on the continent. The Mother Road traversed paths forged by migrations of tens of thousands over the course of several millennia.

Those migrants included early Native Americans who followed game; other later tribes were led on a Trail of Tears. Spaniards searched for gold and the fountain of youth. Paths were formed by Eastern shopkeepers headed west in covered wagons.

Prospectors searched for precious metals. Settlers looked for new land to farm. Farmers displaced by a land turned to dust rode the road less than a century later.

They left the highway on occasion to visit a battlefield or historic site. They paid homage to Will Rogers in Oklahoma. In Springfield, Illinois they made a pilgrimage to the resting place of the sixteenth US president, Abraham Lincoln.

In Hodgenville, Kentucky they visited a log cabin representative of the one where he was born just a few miles away. This new cabin was protected from the elements in a stone memorial building. They climbed up fifty-six stairs to reach the entrance; each step represented one year of Lincoln's short time on earth.

Farther down the road, the family paused to gas up the car and grab a bite to eat. While his dad talked with the station attendant, his mother, sister, and brother sat down for lunch at a restaurant, large sign post outside that spelled out eat.

For a short time, Dad had been attached to the 101st Airborne Division and was stationed at the stateside base of the Screaming Eagles. It was not far down the road from the eatery. Trav did remember watching the blue sky fluttered with puffs of white silk as paratroopers made practice drops over the rolling countryside.

His dad recalled a time when the division withstood a German army advance in the dead of winter in a little-known town in eastern Belgium. When asked to surrender, the commanding general responded with one word: "Nuts."

Dad was part of a relief column in the Ardennes forest that December. Later in his life he would often utter that one word in response to any challenging situation.

They wouldn't have the opportunity to revisit the base during this trip. A second visit to Fort Knox was also ruled out. Dad promised that on the next trip the family would be sure to return to the site that contained the wealth of the nation.

During the Second World War, it also provided a secure home for precious stones and irreplaceable original documents. Several were inked on parchment. Among them were the Magna Carter, the US Constitution and the Declaration of Independence. The vaults also contained a sizable number of gold bars, although no one outside of the fortress knew just how many. They were protected by modern-day weapons of war. There were no bayonets within immediate sight.

They finished their meal, topped off the gas tank, and continued to travel to the Northeast. Kentucky unfolded before them, a beautiful tapestry of blue grass, thoroughbred horses, rolling hills and considerate people. Trav affixed another state decal on the driver side rear window of the Buick.

The family continued the journey.

CHAPTER III

A Golden Cross And Silver Streams

In the years following his arrival at Fort Hamilton, he made the transition from army brat to just another kid in the neighborhood. His first exposure to civilian life came in the small town of Mount Holly, New Jersey.

His first memories centered on a parade that featured the local high school marching band. A bevy of beauty queens and an occasional princess added flair to the event. Local men and women were festooned with appropriate dress or uniform from several periods in American History. Equestrians displayed their skills to the delight of the roadside audience.

Fire engines and police car sirens announced the beginning and the end of the parade. Young children tossed candy from horse-drawn floats to the younger children lining the parade route. The American flag waved from every home.

While Dad was completing an assignment at nearby Fort Dix in preparation for his duty in Korea, Trav was completing fifth grade. The next month Trav hugged his dad one more time before he moved to his next tour. Dad remained on that Korean peninsula for almost four years. In the meantime, his family returned to Hudson County.

The parades there assumed county-wide proportions. Troops marched and tanks rolled up the Hudson Boulevard to celebrate the

Memorial Day weekend. A thousand different flags flew from the homes that lined the county streets.

A month later, Trav enrolled as the sixty-first member of the sixth grade class of Saint Joseph's Grammar School. Sixty participated in the commencement exercise three years later. His classmates were somewhat deflated when they learned that sixty-one in 1961 was not going to happen. One of their classmates had fallen.

The following year, the parish celebrated its 75th Diamond Jubilee as the school marked another high water marker year. It was located on the north side of 14th Street and had hosted a landmark performance of Veronica's Veil in the first-floor auditorium.

His fifth-floor class window provided an excellent view of the church and steeple bell tower on the south side of the block. On the top of the tower was a golden cross that held his attention between lessons about the crusades and exercises in mathematics multiplication. During the winter, snow melted from the base of the cross and formed silver streams that froze solid when they reached the roof of the church. The cross could be seen by tourists in a New York City skyscraper to the east and by farmers in the town of Secaucus to the west.

From the Dominican Nuns he learned how to diagram a sentence and recite the Baltimore Catechism. He also promised to explore the real meaning behind the pat answers to the questions posed in that book: "Who is God? Why did He make you?"

(He also made a personal vow to interject at least a few compound, complex sentences into any story he might someday come to author.)

At Saint Joseph's, Trav discovered that eating meat on Friday was a mortal sin, punishable by eternal damnation. Yet with a dispensation available on the military base, just two years before, he could enjoy a hamburger on that day without suffering any consequence other than indigestion.

He continued to serve Mass, sometimes in a cassock of red. He and his very best friend would venture to the Blue Chapel just a few blocks from the cross on Saint Joe's. Cloistered nuns lived behind a thick brick wall and spent their entire lives singing praises to the Lord. Anna would have added her voice to the choir had she been born in 1936, a year of reflection and recovery.

Other than the priest, they were the only males permitted to enter the building behind the blue stone wall. Inside, the altar was always alive with the color and scent of fresh-cut flowers.

Sister Gemma provided to each of them two bright red apples and two large oranges as a reward following the six am serving. They posed for a photo with another altar boy a few hours after they returned to street clothes.

His friend encouraged him to join the Columbian Squires and the Third Order of Saint Francis. He was becoming more Catholic with each day. It wasn't until after they had both graduated from the same public high school that Trav questioned the entire position.

Following high school, his friend went on to college in New Mexico, then service in the Peace Corps. His experience there and in subsequent job assignments led him to serve his country and mankind. He shared his experiences with Trav in a stream of letters and postcards that spanned several decades. Eventually he transitioned the discourse to email.

By 2014, he shared from his vantage point as an instructor in China. He confided to Trav that the West had impressed a stamp on the culture. They enjoyed Bach and Beethoven. They wore blue jeans and sipped Coca Cola. Some contemplated Buddha, while a few studied the teachings of Confucius. Others venerated saints, and more than a few embraced Jesus the Christ. Maintaining their Asian culture, they amassed many Occidental artifacts. They assumed a portion of the mantle of western civilization.

The professor remained resolutely Catholic but acknowledged a very personal relationship with Jesus. Peace signs appeared everywhere in his presence. A lifelong friend validates a life in a treasured sort of way.

The meat-on-Friday edict was the first in a string of rules that made no sense to the future Knowledge Navigator. One day during a visit to the confessional he questioned the authority of the church. The priest provided an easy answer, stay on the very large ship or face the perils of the sea of life in a very small life boat. All he could hear was Titanic.

It wasn't an indictment of Catholicism. It was more about a search for spiritual awakening unavailable within the constructs of any brick and mortar environment or religious denomination. He couldn't accept deism; he had seen too many proofs of the evidence of Christ.

CHAPTER IV
The Altruist

Geographically, the public high school was really not too far removed from the parochial elementary school. Stylistically it was a world apart. There were no uniforms, no nuns, and no cross. In substance they had much in common, such as dedicated teachers and students who were eager to learn.

Trav would attend and graduate from Emerson High School, EHS, the alma mater of his father. Dad shared the pages of his 1928 yearbook and pointed out classmates who now held teaching or administrative responsibilities at the school. Trav was amazed by the predictions made by the class of that year. He was entertained by the descriptions under the name of each graduating senior and took special note of the lines under the photo of his dad:

> "Jimmy"
> *Emerson Grammar Business*
> Gym exhibitions 1926; class baseball and basketball,
> 1926; A. A. 1927; typing awards; bank awards; football
> squad 1926 – 27; civics debate; stage manager, senior
> play, 1927; One-act play, 1927.
> *"Curly locks, wilt thou be mine?"*

Trav's yearbook was printed in 1965, a year of reflection and provocation. It would provide similar descriptions and predictions, all of them bearing some element of truth. Labels like *class clown, most athletic, best dressed, most likely to succeed,* and *class sweethearts* all contributed to the casual high water markers of each life.

The classmates were almost always identified by some fitting nickname. His best friend was Gaz. His other best friends, Eddy and Bob, were among the few to dodge the nickname frenzy. Joe was sometimes called Slim.

Slim literally ran circles around Trav on the track. His stamina on the basketball court led EHS to a number of victories. Trav kept in touch through the years and was able to share a cup of coffee with him at the LAX Los Angeles Airport decades later.

An older version of the vibrant athlete met Trav at the baggage claim area that day. They approached one another, each with the aid of a cane. By then Trav was in considerable arthritic pain. Joe was dealing with a potentially life-threatening medical condition. It took all of his stamina to defeat that struggle.

In typical Hudson County style, he won the battle and added that conquest to his many high water markers. Trav eventually went under the surgeon's knife and emerged with a new plastic hip and a Titanium rod in his thigh bone. Three years later he repeated that exercise on the other hip. These two old boys weren't going to run the quarter mile anytime soon except in their memories.

Eddy and Trav found a peaceful meadow in Englishtown. The local farmer had given them permission to target shoot on his property. Discharging a weapon in the city would have placed them behind bars. In the country, they took careful aim at little black dots at the center of four concentric circles on a piece of paper. Trav couldn't resist the temptation to obliterate one of the targets with a blast from a twelve-gauge shotgun. Ed was a more deliberate marksman.

With precision, he perfectly placed 30-30 and twenty-two caliber rounds. They pierced the paper and lodged into the supporting straw and wooden platform. Following graduation, Eddy would brandish a different kind of weapon in the countryside of Viet Nam.

He returned home with a Bronze Star and a number of high water markers. Years later, Nav would be thankful that he spared the future in-laws of his daughter. During the conflict, Ed kept Trav informed of the highs and lows. He shared information about a chance encounter with two former high school buddies.

The classmates forged a special bond in the crucible of war. All three recalled memories created on the eastern shore of another ocean. They roasted a hog and for a brief moment reminisced about stateside days. Ed murmured something like, "This is my weapon; this is my gun." [It reminded Jackson of a moment in Georgia shared by Frederick, John and Joseph.]

Bob had been a classmate at SJS and continued his education in Catholic institutions. His high school was named in honor of the first pope. Jesuit priests also provided undergraduate instruction in Bean Town.

His graduate work began with preparation for a career in medicine. Midway through the program, he decided to change course and pursue an advanced degree in law. After he passed the bar, he went on to commendable public service. Now he had a nickname: Esquire.

Decades after high school graduation, Trav shared a cup of coffee with Esquire at a Jersey diner, not far from his office in the state capital. They were able to relive the old days and consider the numerous high water markers in their lives. Neither could comprehend the passage of time.

Eddy, Bob, and Gaz would be ushers (modern-day groomsmen) at Trav's wedding. Joe's sister-in-law and Trav's sister would serve as bridesmaids. Trav's brother would serve as best man. Trav's sister-in-law would be the maid of honor.

Another Bob was nicknamed Moose, a daunting tackle on the football field. Moose left Emerson in junior year and moved to a new home in suburban Bergen County. He stayed in touch through the next decade, returning to the city for a brief visit during a rest and recuperation (R&R) visit from Air Force duties in Okinawa and Southeast Asia.

Gaz captured Moose, Bob, and Trav in a photo taken in the house on the Transfer Station. Later that day, Trav planted two maple trees. They were from Moose's Mahwah backyard. Someday they would provide shade in the eastern corner of the city lot. At the time of planting, they measured less than an inch at the base of the trunk. Six decades later, the diameter of each tree was measured in feet.

Jackson made a promise to Anna Badgenoone: Jackson would assign more Badgenoone compatriots to document the high water markers of all of Trav's family and friends. The stories would include the friends he had made in grade school, high school, college and graduate school.

She promised to include the friends he made as an army brat, the neighborhood friends, and the workplace friends. It would require her to requisition a second storage trunk and additional space in the cloud. She welcomed the task.

Teachers at Emerson High School were usually referred to by the first letter of their last name. On a few occasions a letter would be shared by two teachers. Students would find a way around that; Mr. T taught Social Studies, Coach T was there for the sports teams.

Mr. T set up a challenging debate for Trav and Gaz during their senior year. They would each take a pro and con position on the merits of the atomic bombing of two Japanese cities in the final days of WWII. They grilled each other for an hour, each certain in their supporting arguments. Then Mr. T, without warning, required them to change positions. For him, it became a teachable moment. For the students, it unleashed an epiphany.

Trav participated in the full measure of high school life. Encouraged by Mr. R, his ninth-grade English teacher, Trav joined the staff of the school newspaper. It shared a masthead of the same name as was assigned to the yearbook: the *Altruist*. That was fitting since it reflected the better nature of the namesake of the school.

Mr. R guided his young charge. There was so much to learn. The mechanics of creating the page of a newspaper was just a piece of the puzzle. A page layout marked the beginning of the process and provided a template for arranging the articles. The actual placement of a story was determined by newsworthiness. Content, style, and relevance to surrounding stories were also factored into the equation.

In senior year, he was named editor-in-chief of the paper and assistant editor of the yearbook. Those high water markers were reflected in his book. He was humbled by the talent that surrounded him, inspired by classmates and teachers. JBadgenoone promised to add them to her list. By now it exceeded five hundred.

As an undergraduate student, Trav would join the staff of his college newspaper, the *Bulletin*. It captured events both local and global. He continued to follow the dictum of Mr. R, supposing that someday he might embrace a career in journalism. Instead, Trav chose a somewhat-related career in book publishing. His cousin would carry the mantle of newspaper reporter, editor, and eventually publisher of a large metropolitan newspaper chain.

He also included a stint at the *Altruist* among his high water markers. Trav first met him, his sister, and parents during one of the several sojourns at the Transfer Station between the army base assignments. Jackson added them to the list.

Mr. R provided an opportunity for Trav to intern at the New York Herald Tribune. Tribune offices were just across the river from the high school upon the summit that towers over the Hudson still.

Trav was pleased to see that the building was still standing when he returned in 2012, a year of reflection and commiseration. He was somewhat taken back when he realized that it had been converted into a middle school. Across the Hudson, the doors of the *Tribune* were closed altogether. The *Tribune* represented a high water marker in journalism. It brought to life the lessons taught under the tutelage of Mr. R. Trav wasn't there to learn about page layout and design. He was there to improve his journalist writing style.

Two years later, in the year of reflection and reconciliation, Nav wondered if the time at the *Tribune* had also influenced his political leanings. He considered the possibility that his writing or politics might have followed a different stream had he interned at the New York Times.

EHS and its rival, Union Hill High School, had been merged into a city-wide building constructed on the site of the venerable Roosevelt Stadium. That stadium was a focal point in Trav's life much as it had been in the life of his dad.

It was constructed by the Works Progress Administration as part of FDR's New Deal. A replacement sports field was actually built on top of the academic building. Something was lost in the process. The Thanksgiving Turkey Game football rivalry on a chilly morning was the focal point for thousands of families for the better part of the twentieth century.

The Emerson High School Bulldogs and the Union Hill Hillers memories would be preserved behind glass shelves and in fading newspapers and yearbooks. The new consolidated high school football team would be known as the Soaring Eagles.

Trav was pretty sure that Mr. R would have had no comment on the merger. He was the faculty advisor to the yearbook and the school newspaper back in 1965, a year of reflection and provocation. He made sure that extra reporters were at the stadium to cover every game.

Mr. R reminded the young reporters and editors that every newsworthy article is defined by facts and story. It was their responsibility to provide the proper blend of both before the type was set.

His standing order to them was simple and easy to remember: "Answer the questions to the following words; Who, What, Where, When, Why, and How. Bring common sense and your experience to the article. Save your opinion for the editorial column." He also suggested that they follow the example of Ralph Waldo Emerson: "Keep a journal." Trav began his lifelong log that same year.

Trav took time to reflect on his good fortune at EHS. Miss C helped him to appreciate the form and function in every work of art. At her urging, he picked up a paint brush and experimented with acrylics at first, then with oil. He looked forward to expressing his thoughts on every new canvas. She always reminded her students to apply a solid white gesso foundation layer before adding colors to their creation.

At her urging, they pored through books that reflected the contributions of the masters. Like many of his classmates, he started his collection with the fifth printing of *History of Art* by HW Janson. Years later, with urging from Anna Badgenoone, he was compelled to add a work titled *Roman Art, Romulus to Constantine*. ABadgenoone also recommended that he add two additional works to help him discover the hidden treasure. He didn't know at the time that it was by her direction that he acquired *Leonardo, Artist, Inventor and Scientist*.

Soon thereafter, *Native Grace, Prints of the New World 1590 – 1876* joined twenty-two other art books in his library. Most of them would survive on shelves in the den overlooking Dutch Buffalo Creek decades later.

Mr. P created harmony from a seemingly inharmonious collection of vocal chords. Mr. C awakened his interest in all things Latin. Trav wished that he could have embraced the dead language years earlier. His understanding of the words might have brought the Roman Rite to life for the little altar boy in the desert:

> *Munda cor meum, ac labia mea, omnipotens Deus, qui labia Isaiae Prophetae calculo mundasti ignito: ita me tua grata miseratione dignare mundare, ut sanctum Evangelium tuum digne valeam nuntiare. Per Christum Dominum nostrum. Amen.*

Rendered in English, it would summon a plea to God:

> Cleanse my heart and my lips, O almighty God, who didst cleanse the lips of the prophet Isaiah with a burning coal: design of Thy gracious mercy, so to purify me that I may worthily proclaim Thy holy Gospel. Through Christ our Lord. Amen.

Italian and French language instruction was also available at EHS. Trav didn't want to favor the language of one parent over the language of the other. Miss H did make it possible for him to transition his father's native Italian *per favore* into her Spanish *por favor*. His mother encouraged him to learn every language.

The early and mid-sixties was a heady time to be in high school. Kids gathered at the Dairy Queen across the street. A recent graduate, Marty Spin (vowel guy) would cruise New York Avenue in a brand-new, highly-polished red Chevy Corvette. School dances, football games, basketball games, track and field events were usually capped off with a Coke and a slice of heavily-coated mozzarella pie at Christina's Pizzeria.

At their fortieth reunion, an adopted classmate tried to capture it all in a sequence of paintings. They found a home in a New York art gallery and were recorded on a video. She filtered through the times to create a third-party perspective of the class of 1965. Laurie managed to capture a few precious memories.

No such recollection was captured for Jimmy's class of 1928, another heady time in a year of reflection and without limits.

The world beyond the halls of EHS continued to ebb and flow. In the late roaring twenties, the world was on the brink of a financial calamity, a perfect prelude to a second world war. They dared a prediction for the year 1950, a year of reflection and sober expectations.

In the mid-sixties, a third world war was averted with US support for another domino in Southeast Asia. The Beatles led a British invasion on the music front.

An Irish Catholic became the youngest elected US president. By junior year he was gone. Everyone would recall where they were on that fateful day.

Kids from high schools in fifty states and several territories came to grips with life after graduation in those challenging times. Many like Slim, Moose, and Ed entered military service. A sizable number joined the civilian labor force. Others like Trav, Bob, and Gaz continued their education in colleges and universities.

The baby boom provided an endless stream of bodies to fill all of the requirements of the times.

As the year of reflection and reconciliation unfolded, Trav continued to provide information to Anna Badgenoone. He was by then well aware of her presence and wanted to help her with the task of writing about his life. She took careful note of his train of thought.

In 2014, he thought to himself that his life had progressed on a somewhat prescribed path beyond EHS: college, graduate school, work, marriage, children, and grandchildren. His job assignments provided a travel redux of his days as an army brat.

At that moment, Trav thought that he heard laughter. He realized that he wasn't alone in the den. JBadgenoone and Abadgenoone were at his side. He was reasonably certain that Jackson and Anna had no capacity for humor. They promptly disabused him of that notion.

You make us laugh, they said. *Do you really think that you have any control over the events in your life? You might make a decision or two along the way, but the river of life runs its own course. Not everyone has an opportunity to graduate from high school or attend college or graduate school. Not everyone finds meaningful employment. Not everyone gets married. Not everyone who gets married stays married. Not everyone has children or grandchildren. Yet every one of them can lead a rich and meaningful life. Look no further than to your own circle of family and friends for confirmation. Then consider why we chuckle at the arrogance of your statement. Anywhere along the way your life could have been inexorably altered.*

He reflected and apologized. It was ignorance, not arrogance.

They continued to mine his thoughts.

There would be no military service on his resume. He carried a 1A card until the day he drew draft lottery number 319. Had he been called, he most likely would have volunteered for service in the Navy. He hoped to be considered for duty on a ship. It would be a great opportunity to serve his nation and return to the sea. Years later, he resurrected that dream on the deck of a battleship anchored in North Carolina. It was nicknamed *Showboat*.

His father didn't discourage him from joining the service, nor did he offer encouragement. It wasn't about a separate branch of service; he had a deep respect for the Navy. They watched the nightly news images of classmates and friends returning in body bags. Both questioned the proposition of expanded hostilities.

The news reporters of that day must have taken a lesson or two from Mr. R. The way they combined story and fact eventually helped lead the nation away from the entanglement.

Boomers who served on land, air, and sea performed admirably. They deserved a much better thank you from their country. Jackson made a promise to Anna: JBadgenoone would find a way to thank

Ed, Slim, Moose, and all who served, especially the 58,209 who never returned.

She added that thanks were also appropriate and long overdue for a generation that served quietly in remote corners of the world, representatives of America in the service of the Peace Corps. She projected thanks to Gaz and his compatriots.

Other boomers stayed home and pursued civilian careers. They populated the ranks in law, medicine, education, and business. Some launched new enterprises. They created new ways to print a page. Then they found ways to obviate print.

They discovered different ways to transmit data and new ways to store the information. JBadgenoone had thanks in mind for Bob, Joe, Mimi, Bill, John, Steve, and Steve, and millions of others who contributed to the journey.

CHAPTER V

What's In A Color?

College years evaporated with the times. Trav's future wife, Mimi, kept a diary that captured the highlights. They began to establish a place in the workforce before exchanging marriage vows on a snowy Easter Sunday. More about that day is recorded in subsequent chapters of this book. *The High Water Markers of FBadgenoone's Observee* also documented the event.

Mimi embarked on a career as an elementary school teacher. Her first class inspired twenty-five energetic second grade students. He landed a job at a New York City-based trade book publishing company. His first assignment was in the catalog division that dealt with remainder titles.

Her spring vacation seemed like an appropriate opportunity to finally exchange vows in public. Easter Sunday arrived early that year. Siblings, along with best friends from high school and college, formed the wedding party on March 29, 1970, a year of reflection and maturation. Ed was back from the war; Bob was about to enter graduate school; Gaz was heading for the Peace Corps; young brother John was old enough to be best man.

A cold and biting wind laden with silver dollar-size snowflakes blew in from the north that day. By the time of the service, several feet of the white stuff covered the ground. Only a handful of local relatives made it to the church. More guests arrived in time for the reception later that evening. Trav and Mimi were thankful that everyone made it there and home again without incident.

The next day, they packed the little red car and headed for a small cabin in the Poconos. It was one of a dozen nestled around a main lodge centered in a valley covered with snow. They had planned for a spring wedding and honeymoon but absorbed the cold and quiet moments that came to them in that place.

Those cabins were just a few hours and a world away from the hustle of the big city. On a map they still appeared within the boundaries of the megalopolis. Horses that pulled the sleigh were unaware of the Metropolitan Statistical Area. Trav and Mimi didn't consider the map.

They enjoyed the horse-drawn events, the candle making, and arts and crafts offered at the main lodge. The facility provided an indoor swimming pool, recreation room, country dining and a roaring fire place to take the chill out of the mountain air.

After a week, the snowpack melted away. She returned to her students, and he returned to his desk. He shared a commute into the Big Apple with thousands of others. They packed trains in underground tubes. Buses and cars travelled below the Hudson through the Lincoln and Holland tunnels or over that river on the George Washington Bridge. A relative handful of commuters arrived by ferry.

The trip into the city was just the first leg of his daily adventure. During the spring and summer months, he took special note of a large willow-like tree on 32nd street, not far from the main post office building. The leaves reminded him of leaves of grass shimmering in the morning sunlight.

Each leaf was suspended from a singular stem. The arrangement permitted them to twist independently in the wind. They were like a poem that was forever changing. Every new breeze infused a new interpretation of the stanzas. When the rays settled on them they were transformed into so many golden-green sequins.

Trav usually closed his eyes with that image in his mind before the bus veered onto the Lincoln Tunnel approach ramp. During the winter months, his eyes were shut before he reached the barren tree.

On the other side of the tunnel, the first and last stop in Manhattan was the Port Authority Bus Terminal. Passengers formed a single line in the exhaust fumes that filled the upper platform. He joined them in the daily procession down the stairs to the main building. A quick walk down a long underground corridor led to the Cross-town Shuttle. He exhaled traces of carbon monoxide and inhaled a huge volume of carbon dioxide during that part of the commute.

At Grand Central Station, he packed into an IRT subway that carried him to within walking distance of his office at 29th street and Park Avenue South. He emerged from the platform without fail every working day. There were no trees, no leaves, just an elevator ride to the 18th floor.

He paused to consider the pros and cons of this routine. He loved the excitement of the publishing world. His coworkers and supervisors were sharp, articulate people. They genuinely enjoyed showing up for the job each day. Much of their day involved finding new ways to move titles from the backlist.

Trav started to think of it as more than just a job. He tried to construct a path to a genuine career. With a better understanding of the mechanics of print, he might be able to appreciate the science of publishing.

He enrolled in a course on Offset Lithography and sought additional knowledge from local print shops operators. He hadn't considered that there were different printing methods available at that time. They filled in the blanks and raised the bar.

Later in life, he realized that publishing could survive without print and print could survive without publishing. Learning about publishing by knowing print was like knowing the bible by learning about Gutenberg.

Within the year, a printing company opportunity knocked on his door. It was on the Jersey side of the Hudson River. This was a step removed from the publishing world. The company printed boxes, not books.

It didn't seem to matter. Print was print, and the huge four-color presses consumed an enormous volume of ink. At this stage of the

Jackson Badgenoone

journey, he was more interested in the mechanics of this industry, less on the science. The move also had a positive impact on his daily commute. Two pointless hours were recovered each day, time he could spend with Mimi.

On the downside, there was no way to observe the trees on Tonnele Avenue. And it was all he could do to avoid a collision with the truck traffic that dominated the old Route 1 and 9 Highway.

Most of the cardboard boxes ended up on supermarket shelves. The company had carved out a niche in the pasta trade. Pasta boxes came in an assortment of shapes and colors. Blue was a most recognizable brand color of the company's largest client.

The president of the company that made that pasta insisted on a special hue of blue. Any departure from that shade would spell immediate cancellation of a print job, and that meant a serious loss of revenue.

Trav was able to spot any deviation from the standard. His boss recognized the keen eye and special talent. He assigned Trav to the duty of quality control spotter. He would often get the call in the middle of the night. The presses had to roll. Trav had the power to stop them for a simple color correction. He wondered if customers glancing through the supermarket shelves could tell the difference.

Within a year, the printing concern became a target for acquisition. A Charlotte, North Carolina firm was interested. That company printed cartons for another niche market, ice cream. The combined output made sense at some level.

The reconfigured company would produce ice cream cartons for the summer months and pasta cartons for the winter. It seemed like a logical match.

Trav assumed that he and his new bride would be heading south, but his immediate supervisor dispelled that notion. The acquiring company planned to shut down the New Jersey operation and move the business to an upstate New York plant.

The blue macaroni boxes would be manufactured in Newark, New York. The white ice cream cartons would be produced at a Charlotte, North Carolina facility.

What's in a color? He might have guessed when pure white snow fell at their wedding that he and Mimi wouldn't continue their journey in the Sunbelt—at least not for now. They packed the car and headed north.

Along the way, they made time to visit reminders of a distant past. In Newburgh, New York, they visited the headquarters of General Washington. They stood in the room where he delivered a defining moment speech to his officer corps.

The tour guide relived the moment when he removed spectacles from his vest and began to read from a scrap of paper. The original delivery left no eye dry in that room. It kept the Republic alive.

They spent a short time at Fort Ticonderoga where, at the general's urging, heavy cannons were removed to challenge the British in Boston Harbor a few years earlier. Trav and Mimi considered the scale of the stone fortress and couldn't imagine the man and mammal toil required to dislodge and transport the mammoth guns.

Farther up the road they stopped at Fort Stanwick. They learned about the impact that site had on the movement of British troops determined to split the northern colonies. Trav considered his growing-up years. He wondered if there were any army brats housed behind the timber walls.

Trav shared with Mimi recollections from the auto trips he made as a boy. These trips strengthened his resolve to never pass by a battlefield, fort, or museum without stopping; it solidified his conviction that one should take in all the roadside commemorative plaques; it taught him to consider the people that travelled these paths. He promised her, "If the good LORD blesses us with children, they'll have the same opportunities."

On the third day, they arrived in Newark, New York. His immediate supervisor welcomed him to the plant. He was anxious to learn more about the customer requirements of the new line of business that would be manufactured at his facility.

The new company provided temporary housing. That gave them time to find a more permanent dwelling place. They took out the map and drew a circle with Newark at the center. He had done the commuting thing downstate and was in no hurry to relive that hassle. Locals informed him that this was Western New York.

There was some consideration given to the immediate surroundings, and they enjoyed a brief visit to the Newark Rose Garden. In 1908, the Dorothy Perkins Rose received special recognition from the National Rose Society of Great Britain. These many years later, they took the time to smell the roses. They didn't know it at the time, but Bernadette Badgenoone, Frederick Badgenoone and Anna were there that day to help savor the moment.

Later that day, they sipped a cup of coffee at Scofield's Diner and reflected upon an acceptable commuting range. They agreed upon a diameter of twenty miles with the plant at center point. The northern fringe was bound by Lake Ontario. The New York Thruway was a comparable distance to the south. The eastern commute would bring them closer to Syracuse.

Mimi and Trav decided to start the search for a house on the western side of the circle. That ten-mile radius would put them closer to relatives in Rochester. A voice seemed to whisper to them as they approached a drumlin on the westernmost point of their third exploratory trip.

They followed the tree-covered hill. It tapered off within a few yards of the New York State Barge Canal. A bridge across that still-active shipping waterway brought them up a slight incline and into the heart of a small town. They made a left-hand turn at the Four Churches and drove east along the main street.

Another cup of coffee, this time at the Blue Ribbon Dairy, gave them time to consider this place. It fit the criteria that they had agreed upon. It offered a Post Office, a pharmacy, a library, museums, several houses of worship, two banks, and a number of restaurants. The local volunteer fire department kept a proud fleet of firefighting equipment. Thinking ahead to a possible family, they considered the local schools, parks, and recreation.

Within three weeks, they found a perfect starter home in this little northern village identified by locals as Canal Town. It was within convenient walking distance of the Wayne County Fair Grounds, far enough away from the noise of carnival barkers and the demolition derby.

The district middle school was across the street. The high school was just around the corner. One of two district elementary schools was just a few blocks away.

CHAPTER VI

A New Family Emerges

Mimi and Trav settled into the new environment. His commute meandered along country roads through farmland and gentle rolling hills. She was able to continue her career as a teacher in the local school within walking distance from the house.

He had learned just about everything there was to know about the construction of a box. Cartons would be printed, scored, glued, and folded to exact specifications. Trav enjoyed the smell of ink and the sound of enormous presses on task.

Coworkers in Newark and townspeople in Canal Town helped to reshape his quick downstate speech patterns. It didn't take too long. Those patterns had been acquired in a relatively short span of time. They served him well during his tenure in the Megalopolis and resurfaced on occasion when needed during his career.

The new pace of speech was reflective of country life. The word *pajama* was pronounced with an emphasis on jam. *Soda* was referred to as *pop*. *Insurance* sounded a lot like *Inn*-surance. *Italian* was *Eyetalian*. Everything was *fannntastic*.

He relearned how to step back and appreciate a slightly slower rhythm of life. He genuinely enjoyed this new circle of friends. From his days as an army brat, he learned how to connect with people very quickly. He got to do it all over again.

His colleagues at the publishing company let him know that life in the Big Apple moved at the same hurried pace. High school and college buddies still kept in touch. Gaz sent pictures of young children under his care at a Peace Corps camp in Africa. Eddy, Moose, and Slim sent regards from military bases located around the globe. Some came from the war zone in Viet Nam.

In conservative western New York, time seemed to have taken pause. Their lives had apparently escaped the events that swirled around them. Then he received not totally unexpected news at the office: The Carolina firm was going to spin off the Newark plant. Colors that bled from a press proof littered the concrete floor.

He had lived through the acquisition and relocated. Now he felt the sting of a divestiture. The newly-formed company would continue to service the client base but he was unsure of the long-term implications. His eye for blue was replaceable.

Trav thought about a return to publishing. Rochester was home to at least one firm. If he could find work there, his morning commute would take him away from the rising sun. He searched want ads in the largest circulation regional newspaper, the *Rochester Democrat and Chronicle*.

It seemed as though a voice spoke to him on his third visit to the newspaper classified ads. Five lines in the second column leapt from the page. An educational publisher was looking for a candidate.

He/she would be responsible for representing a line of textbooks and supplementary materials to educators in western New York. Base salary, commission, benefits, and a company car would be provided. The book line included titles in social studies, history, and government. Candidate had to possess a bachelor's degree and have experience in publishing or printing industries. Resumes were to be submitted in confidence.

Trav had floated into another stream in his career. He would be saddened to leave his coworkers and boss. They had become an extended family. He wasn't sure about driving the roads from Syracuse to Buffalo. The previous winter provided a reminder of central and western New York seasonal weather perils.

Mimi completed her contract as a Title I Reading teacher and had recently accepted a full-time position back in the classroom. Trav would have a company vehicle; she could drive the Corvair to work. He interviewed and within the span of a few weeks received the news. The job was his if he was still interested.

He secured county maps from every courthouse in his territory. They provided school building locations. His manager supplied log books that contained account history and contact names. He also provided an initial inventory of sample texts.

Trav filtered their content through the lens of his undergraduate study and his own life experiences. He then formulated a presentation for each title that would capture the attention of his prospective customers. He cross-referenced the log books of his predecessor with the county maps and began this new chapter in his career. This wasn't a dream job, but it was close enough.

He entered another sphere of influence and made more friends along the way. Many of them were nominal competitors. At a time before large corporations devoured educational publishing, travelers would often exchange leads.

They made an effort to ensure that educators selected the titles best suited to their curriculum needs. The behavior reminded him of the Macy and Gimble exchange in the movie *Miracle on 34th Street*.

[JBadgenoone approached Anna and politely inquired about this seemingly incongruous reference.

ABadgenoone paused, and replied, "Ms. Jackson, you asked me to produce chapters that would reflect the life of this man. You instructed me to make available only those chapters that could be read by the grandchildren. Is this inquiry part of my performance review? At the time of this rendering, his identity was clearly linked to Trav. My objective was to reveal hidden treasures that Trav found in his new job. The *Miracle on 34th Street* seemed a readymade analogy for the younger crowd. Even his five-year-old granddaughter could understand."

And so she continued with the story.]

Trav would load his company sedan with sample books, two wire book racks and sufficient literature for the weekly tour. It had replaced the daily commute. His nickname acquired new meaning.

On a brisk autumn day, Mimi broke the news. They were going to have a baby. He was about to become the sole breadwinner. Within the year, she held their little brown eyed girl. A view of Lake Ontario was framed by the hospital window.

Sixteen months later, twin daughters arrived at the same hospital. Trav was now the sole breadwinner for a family of five. Their arrival brought a tremendous amount of joy into his world. It also focused his attention on the responsibilities of parenting. On occasion, the focus was lost, but the loss heightened his quest for the deeper meaning of life.

CHAPTER VII

A Chance Encounter

He loaded the brown sedan and prepared to head west. There were reports of white-out blizzard like conditions between Rochester and Batavia.

[Jackson interrupted Anna again. She reminded her that this chapter and several to follow were off-topic and inappropriate for younger readers. Hadn't ABadgenoone agreed a few moments earlier that only chapters suitable for viewing by the grandchildren would be accepted into *The Hidden Treasure of Dutch Buffalo Creek*?

Anna seemed to smile. "Just keeping you on your toes," she said. "In these selected chapters, I had hoped to provide *stasis* and *trigger* points in a modified eight-point story arc. In the comprehensive version, I would attempt to demonstrate points of *quest* and *surprise*, *critical choice*, *climax* and *reversal*. The larger story will culminate with a point of *resolution*. My Badgenoone counterparts struggled with similar limitations when they developed their 'child-friendly' observations.

"I know that I am difficult to manage. I honor your editorial advice and will do my best to develop the story in an engaging manner. Please pardon me if I slip in a double entendre every so often. I hope to interject some entertainment into the story of my observee. He is a complicated character who embraces a sense of humor even in the most difficult circumstance. He deserves a laugh or two."

Jackson made a note for the weekly meeting. Anna skipped to Chapter 10.]

CHAPTER X

A Warm Fuzzy

It was his fifth year on the job. During those years, he made every effort to better understand his clientele. Years before, he had gone to work for a printing company to better understand publishers. Now he pursued an education degree to better understand educators. Abadgenoone smiled at his thought.

Practice teaching was the final requirement in his graduate program. It would require a two-month leave of absence from his company. He had been led to believe that would not present a problem. Turned out it did. In January, 1977, a year of reflection and illumination, his immediate supervisor greeted him at the door. Joseph was there to pick up the keys to the company car.

He was about to drive away when word came over the radio that a storm had just closed the New York Thruway. Joe was going to have to spend the night at the house. Trav, Mimi, and the three girls met him for breakfast the following morning. After breakfast, they bid goodbye to Joe. Sometimes seemingly bad news arrives in successive waves. They had recently learned that Governor Carey had closed all public schools because of a natural gas shortage, and the Corvair had just given up the ghost. Trav scratched his head in disbelief. He thought he had done the honorable thing.

He could have taken a pass on the degree. He might have worked out an arrangement for covering the territory. A colleague advised him to fudge the log books and formulate some disingenuous explanation for his boss. Trav dismissed that out of hand as he thought, *Tell the truth and shame the devil.* Now he faced the aftermath of a biting cold blizzard and a student teaching experience put on hold.

There was no car and barely a week's supply of food in the pantry. The bank account was one Hamilton shy of four-hundred Jacksons. With five mouths to feed, for a brief moment he longed for the sands of Yuma.

The sun returned, the schools reopened, and Trav walked across the street to the middle school where he began his practicum. Many of the sixth-graders in his class had fond memories of the time when Mimi was their third-grade teacher. Three weeks after the blizzard, life seemed to recover some sense of purpose.

He wasn't sure about how to instruct his young charges. Until that moment, his learning was in the hands of college professors. Now he would observe and work with a practitioner in the field, thankfully one of the best around. Trav tried to recall his time as a sixth-grader in the shadow of the cross.

It was a lifetime and a world away from the experience of these children. Trav wanted desperately to bring the subject matter to life. He drew from every bone in the corpus of his knowledge. He considered the military bases, travel, job experiences, education, a library of books, and the perspective of his friends.

They would all find a way into his lesson plans. The knowledge would wash over adolescent minds and pubescent bodies. It was the toughest two-month assignment in his life up to that time. It was also a very fulfilling experience. He never knew what wisdom would surface from their young minds.

One bright student named Joel had all but given up on any sort of academic involvement. He saw no point to the history lessons, no need to study grammar, and had little use for mathematics. The young boy's father was a well-respected local electrician. Perhaps a science lesson could provide a key to unlock the youngster's talent.

Trav set up a lesson on electricity. He instructed the students to construct an electrical maze arranged with circuits—some in parallel, others in series. They set up light bulbs to test the current strength and circuit breakers to manage the flow.

Construction materials consisted of cardboard strips, brass fasteners, paper clips, copper wire, and dry cells. Many of the materials were purchased at the local supermarket. Joel set up the most elaborate project in the class. He went on to explain how he had constructed a battery from three dry cells as his power source. Then he demonstrated how bulbs remained uniformly lit when arranged in one circuit. The other circuit produced diminished light with each successive bulb added along the copper string.

Trav took note of Joel's command of the language, his grasp of mathematical concepts, his understanding of the science, and his ability to communicate his understanding to his peers. Joel addressed the class. "We don't purchase batteries in the store. We buy dry cells. When we combine two or more, then we have a battery. The brand name doesn't make much of a difference in performance, but shelf-life matters."

Another student seemed to challenge every historical event. Brad had his own ideas and was only too willing to share them with his classmates. Trav appreciated Brad's rhetorical capacity and suggested that he pose the next question to the class. He obliged and framed one that had been gnawing at him for quite some time.

"Why do you suppose that Jesus Christ chose that particular place in history 1977 years ago to make his appearance on planet Earth? Why did he wait so long? Why didn't he wait a little bit longer?" Brad acknowledged that the question really wasn't that simple and actually amounted to several questions in sequence.

In typical Brad fashion, he answered his own question when no one else ventured a guess. "Simple: The Romans had a unifying system of law, language, and roads. If Jesus wanted to get the word out to the greatest number of people in the shortest amount of time, that was as good a time as any in recorded history."

Trav took a page from Mr.T's playbook. He challenged Brad and another classmate to develop alternate possibilities. Three weeks later, they defended the merits or lack of merit for the arrival of the Christ at different points in time.

In pendulum fashion, they moved from the Bronze Age to the Middle Ages, and from the Iron Age to the Renaissance. Brad finally blurted out that the entire question was without merit.

"If Jesus is the Christ and Christ is God, then His Word could be delivered at anytime and anywhere."

He concluded that the Word would be written on the human heart. It wasn't dependent on roads of stone overcome by weeds. It didn't rely on a dead language or an empire that decayed into dust.

Trav was humbled by the insight. It added fuel to the spiritual search that raged in his soul.

On the following day, Trav's supervising teacher approached him about the discourse. It might have been challenged by parents who held alternate spiritual views. He was reasonably sure that there was at least one atheist in town.

There were a number of people who didn't believe in the deity of Jesus. He encouraged Trav to stick with the curriculum and avoid potential controversy.

Trav thought back to his own education. He remembered opening bell, the pledge of allegiance, the Lord's Prayer, roll-call, and announcements over the public speaker—not necessarily in that order.

The daily ritual was repeated at the base school, the public schools off base, and the parochial institutions. No one seemed too concerned when a student or a teacher mentioned the name of Jesus. Times had changed.

The village was at one time in the heart of spiritual revival. Worshipers gathered to praise around campfires and left behind what would be referred to as the Burned-over District. A hill just to the south of town on Route 21 was the birthplace of an American religion, The Church of Jesus Christ of Latter Day Saints, the Mormons.

Trav recalled spending long hours in the Sacred Grove just down the road. It was a focal point for the founder of the new religion. JBadgenoone joined him there from time to time but he was unaware of her presence. Her mother had contemplated the Universe in the very same strand of forest.

On a Monday following a weekend visit to the Sacred Grove, Trav returned to the classroom with a new sense of appreciation. His charges would find their own interpretation of God. If the revelation came inside the walls of a public institution, it would come from a higher source. It would be impossible to silence Him.

The sixth-grade curriculum provided ample opportunities to spotlight the talent and treasure of every student. Trav employed a presentation of the play *Our Town* as a vehicle for showcasing young actors, providing backstage opportunities for future set designers.

He was reasonably sure that no objections would surface from that assignment. At the final performance, all the people from this town applauded their youngsters who poured so much of themselves into the production.

For an art project, he asked the students to imagine and then construct representations of a warm fuzzy and a cold prickly. One girl brought in a swath of fantasy fur (not real fur) that she had purchased at a local arts and crafts store.

She believed that she could fashion a really cool warm fuzzy from that material. The rest of the class soon adopted the blue fantasy fur as the warm fuzzy standard. They invented renditions in various sizes then added button eyes and noses.

Cold pricklies were fashioned from an assortment of thorny or jagged edge objects. One girl brought in multipoint jacks. A boy introduced recently-recovered prickly tree spurs. Another brought in pine needles. No cold prickly standard emerged from the exercise. The children were asked to consider their feelings when they received one or the other—cold prickly or warm fuzzy.

Every one of them decided that a warm fuzzy was preferable. The art lesson took on attributes from his undergrad courses in

Psychology and Sociology. Trav asked them to attach a magnet to the back of each hunk of fur and keep it as a souvenir.

He assumed that they would bring them home and place them on a refrigerator door. His master teacher told him that might not be a great idea but he didn't interfere with Trav's decision.

The next day, the principal called Trav into his office. The custodian had lodged a complaint. He was obliged to spend the better part of three hours dislodging blue furry creatures from the metal roof that ran the entire length of the hallway. Trav had been reminded that these were, after all, just sixth-graders.

At the end of that semester in 1977, he stood on the platform to accept his master's degree in education. He considered a change in career. The recent months had provided another high water marker in his life and awakened in him a passion to teach. He had just heard about an open position in the school across the street from his house.

The first day of school would be in September. There were still enough Jacksons in the bank account to fund the summer months. Mimi might be able to return to the classroom. Their combined salaries could provide an adequate if somewhat humble lifestyle. They discussed the ramifications of creating three latch-key kids.

Before they could dwell on that decision, the phone rang. The call was from another educational publisher. DC Heath and Company, DCH, had heard that Trav might be available and wanted to schedule an interview.

The company carried a comprehensive line of books including several targeted to the elementary and middle school market. They preferred to hire someone with book experience and a graduate degree in education. His career continued to evolve that June, and the stream seemed to widen just a bit.

[Jackson encouraged Anna to remain focused on the search, avoid age inappropriate content, and bypass the remaining pages in chapter ten. She complied and continued the reading at chapter eleven.]

CHAPTER XI
What's In An Imprint?

World events sometimes change the behavior of citizens. Tourists' visits to a paradise of flowers are curtailed when red-hot napalm scorches the earth. When airfares skyrocket, people drive more cars. Gasoline prices escalate, and people cut back on driving.

Corporate citizens are no less sensitive to an evolving environment. People fly less, and airlines merge. They drive less, and automakers resize vehicles. Wars wind down, and defense contractors look for new ways to balance their asset portfolio. Just like the military, they perform a reduction in force (also known as RIF).

[Jackson and Anna were intrigued by naming conventions that seemed to overlap their stories.]

Mohawk Airlines and Allegany Airlines combined forces at about the same time that Trav first carried the book bag for Allyn and Bacon Publishing.

That company was formed three years after the end of the American Civil War. USAir emerged from Mohawk and Allegany in 1979, a year of reflection and possibilities. Two years prior to that event, Trav began to carry an expanded book bag for DCH.

Daniel Collamore Heath founded that company in 1885. Heath survived an identity transformation before Trav arrived. Prior to his arrival, the corporate parent name overwhelmed the publishing imprint.

Educators didn't recognize the new entity. Sales recovered when the venerable publishing company regained its former luster and original name. By 1981, a year of reflection and deliverance, DCH acquired the American Book Company, ABC, assets from International Thompson Organization. They celebrated the event with a company picnic.

Years earlier, Thompson had acquired ABC from Litton Educational Publishing, Inc. a creation of Litton Industries. ABC built a niche dynasty upon book spines of the McGuffey Readers. It continued to mine the niche until days before the divesture.

[This time it was Jackson's turn to smile. Anna wasn't around to see a generation of young students weaned on the Sixth Eclectic Reader.]

Chapter XXXVI of that book describes the speech of Paul on Mars Hill. Students back in the good old days (late 1800s) actually learned how to read by reading. The bible wasn't off limits. Reading companies weren't concerned with readability formula. Content was king.

Oh, there were plenty of examples from secular works, including classic literature. Children were introduced to short works of poetry. They read a speech before the Virginia Convention and learned about the character of Napoleon Bonaparte.

[The Acts of the Apostles that engaged the learner, Acts 17:23, was still Jackson's all-time favorite story: "For as I passed by, and beheld your devotions, I found an altar with this inscription: to the unknown god. Whom therefore ye ignorantly worship, Him declare I unto you." Jackson was driven by the message.]

Most of the old-line publishers were long gone by the time Trav retired. Textbooks and reading series would be constructed by committee and influenced by state adoptions. Eventually the web provided a reasonable alternative.

Long gone by then was any pretext of friendly competition. To be understood in pre-technology parlance, acquisitions, mergers, spinoffs, and divestitures required acetate overlay presentation. [Anna, for the benefit of the grandchildren, recalled the anatomy illustrations of the human body presented in Trav's biology text. Bones, blood vessels, nerves, skin, were all perfectly aligned to create a complete anatomical portrait.]

The additional DCH books presented some logistical challenges. The company sedan was replaced by a station wagon. The larger vehicle was not large enough. There wasn't sufficient room to accommodate all the titles. Trav opened the new log books and the old maps to construct a different way to approach his territory.

1978 was a year of reflection and rebirth. On the third day of the first month in this second calendar year with DCH, Trav packed the brown Ford LTD wagon and headed toward the morning sun. He made an impromptu visit to his former employer in Newark.

They continued to produce cartons for all manner of pasta: bucatini, cannelloni, and capellini.

Trav loved to listen to the ice cream crowd pronounce the labels in slow and deliberate manner. They hadn't forgotten the Italian pronunciation he had coached them through a few years earlier. Sherman's favorite was the *occhi di lupo*, the eyes of the fox.

Norm's biggest pronunciation challenge came from the gnocchi. *Najokee* rolled off his tongue, close enough to satisfy the downstate customers. These friends and former co-workers recalled what seemed to be an easier time. He just needed to know the difference between hyperlink blue and Ronzoni blue.

After a cup of coffee, he continued on his prearranged route. The first stop was a school in the nearby town of Seneca Falls. He had been there before with his wife and daughters to learn more about the Women's Rights Movement.

During that visit, they learned about the canal construction that linked the village with their Canal Town. They heard more about the Underground Railroad. Local citizens also shared with some pride that their little hamlet served as the inspiration for Bedford Falls. That village was portrayed in a classic movie replayed on the small screen every year during the Christmas holiday season.

[Jackson concealed the violent clash that took the lives of Sarah's uncles in the surrounding countryside. They perished in the aftermath of the Sullivan Expedition years before Sarah's mother surrendered her spirit within sight of the Mississippi.]

Trav put it all aside and focused on the task at hand. His first presentation was to an elementary mathematics committee. Two hours later, he would meet with several high school department chairs to address their respective curriculum needs.

He continued to follow his appointments calendar, south to Cincinnatus, then north to Cicero. By the time he arrived in Rome, New York, the sun had disappeared on the horizon over Wayne County. This Rome was a world removed from the center of the empire he'd visited during his first European adventure.

His wife and children were sound asleep by the time he arrived at his hotel room. The first presentation on the next day was scheduled in the early afternoon. He allowed the morning hours for travel. It was often interrupted by the central New York weather, but not on that day. The sky was overcast and there was a chill in the air but no new snow in sight.

Trav ventured from the motel to a nearby church. This was the second time in as many months that he entered that building. On his first visit there, he observed the motion of a priest after the morning Mass.

Following the Mass, the priest produced a wicker flame and began to light several candles contained in red and gray colored glass jars. It reminded Trav of his days at Saint Joseph's and the Blue Chapel.

At this second visit, he sat still for the eight o'clock service. Sometime between the reading from the Old Testament and the reading of the Gospel according to John he challenged God. His wife and children were hours away. His career seemed hostage to an endless round of acquisitions, mergers, spinoffs, and divestitures.

He feared he had lost his capacity to love anyone. His challenge to God was straightforward: *Please Lord, talk to me. I am ready to listen to your story.* He suspected that he had heard the voice of God before this moment.

This church building was connected to the Vatican by one of the most enduring political organizations ever constructed by man. The prevailing line was that it was formed upon the rock that was Peter. That church of Peter rose as the empire fell.

Trav took some solace from the stained-glass windows much as he had in the cathedrals of the eternal city. Some presented images of saints, martyrs, and popes. He was drawn to the representations of Christ, the Father, and the Holy Spirit.

In the depth of his soul, he was sure that no colored glass could represent the Creator of the Universe. Transfiguration accepted, he was certain that the Creator made His appearance known in a number of ways.

He could also accept the doctrine of transubstantiation but was of the mind that biblical injunction was straightforward. "And He took bread, and gave thanks, and brake it, and gave unto them, saying, This is my body which is given for you: this do in remembrance of me." (Luke 22:19, KJV)

Trav could find no reference to placing the bread in a house of gold hidden behind a silk or satin curtain. Surely Jesus couldn't be contained by a lock and key. The imperative was clear and immediate: Participate in the life of Christ. Remember the price He paid for your sins. Remember Him.

Following the Concluding Rite, the priest and one altar boy exited to the right. The scent of incense lingered in the aisle. Moments later, another priest appeared. He produced a pewter candle snuffer and extinguished the flames from three flickering wicks in front of a white marble statue.

He walked down the center of the church and approached Trav. Head bowed in prayer, he knelt in the last pew. It was similar to the one most frequented by his dad at his favorite house of worship. Trav was determined not to leave that spot until he heard from God.

The priest tapped him on the shoulder.

When Trav lifted his head, the priest spoke with a firm but tender voice.

"Wipe away your tears. The LORD told me that you wanted to hear from Him. Meet me in the Sacristy at 11:00 am and we'll continue the conversation."

Trav had no planned calls to make and he wasn't in the mood for another cup of coffee. He asked for permission to wait in the room on the other side of the Sanctuary. Permission was granted.

The room was sparsely decorated. It received some light from a lamp overhead. Gray daylight filtered through two frost covered windows. Unlike the windows in the church building, these did not contain stained glass. There was a plain cross on the wall, no image of Christ affixed to the wood. It was reminiscent of the cross that hung in the base chapel in Yuma.

There was an end table next to his sofa. A single book placed there invited his reading. Within a few chapters, he learned that anything of worth usually required patience and time. It described the forty years that Moses wandered in the desert. It recalled the forty days when Jesus was tempted in the flesh. Surely forty minutes in this room would yield some kernel of hope.

[Jackson interrupted Anna. She reminded her that this part of the story was best rendered as a prelude to Mimi's salvation experience. The imprint of nails on the hands and feet of Christ would define the rest of their lives as husband and wife. This moment in 1978 was the highest water marker in a long string of events and messages leading up to that day. In the interest of efficiency relative to the master book they skipped ten chapters and began to read again.]

[Book 4]

CHAPTER XXI

Super Bowl Reducere

Super Bowl XLVIII, played on February 2, 2014 at the Meadowlands Sports Complex in East Rutherford, New Jersey, was hyped as a classic match, worthy of any gladiatorial arena. It would pit the best offense against the best defense in the league. Both teams had reached a high water mark.

Trav watched the game from a color television in his father's house. The game unfolded just up the hill from the meadowland where his dad played as a young boy shortly after the turn of the century. Trav sat in the same recliner chair that belonged to his hero. The moment released a flood of memories.

It seemed like yesterday when, from that very chair, his father cheered on the AFC Los Angeles Raiders in Super Bowl XVIII on January 22, 1984. That was a year of reflection and awakening.

That game at Tampa Bay Stadium unfolded on a black and white set in same room—same home, same room, same chair; it was as if time had stopped dead away.

On that day, from across the room, Trav rooted for the NFC Washington Redskins. At the time, neither man was much concerned about the conference implication. Neither stopped to think about the name attached to either team.

Against his inner voice, Trav took a bet with his dad at the beginning of the game, so sure that his team would prevail. Trav paid off his bet with a brand new ten-dollar bill. These years later, his dad was there now only in spirit.

On this new day in 2014, kickoff was just moments away. Trav settled back into his father's recliner chair. With memories of other teams he supported during a travel-filled career, this game was purely about the contest, with no favorite, no foe. He cheered on the Carolina Panthers for over a decade.

His adopted team had seen their high water marker earlier in the playoff season. Maybe they would fare better in the following year.

Trav's mother entered the living room and handed over a still-crisp image of Hamilton. Trav thought he would never again see that bill. Along with the money was a note of a different kind, this one addressed "to my first-born son."

It read, "The figure on this bill has more significance in your life than the earned interest it might have brought to me in mine. This is in your hands now because I have no further need of it. Put it to better use than as a wager for a game that could go either way on any given Sunday. Be kind to your mother, sister, and brother."

His mind drifted back through four decades of Super Bowl odysseys. The contest in 1984 changed the direction of his life. It was not so much the contest as a Super Bowl Ad sponsored by a personal computer company. The tagline was simple but brilliant: *Why 1984 won't be like 1984*. It culminated with a young woman shattering a giant telescreen, setting free row upon row of seemingly brainwashed figures.

The ad prompted him to read again a novel that he first digested as an undergraduate student almost two decades earlier. That book was penned two decades earlier still. Some elements of the world of George Orwell survived.

After viewing the ad and rereading the book, Trav was drawn ever closer to the adventure. At the time of the 1984 Super Bowl, he was still an educational publisher's representative.

The rep was sometimes referred to as a traveler and the traveler carried books, usually in a leather case. How appropriate to match a job description with defining elements of his life—another high water marker.

He was thankful for this occupation. It allowed him to share his love of literature, music, art, mathematics, science, geography, and history with dedicated and thoughtful educators.

His was a jewel of a territory. It encompassed the whole of the Hudson Valley, the Leather Stocking District, and the length of the Erie Canal. It included the Finger Lakes, The Niagara Frontier and the ancestral home to six nations of the Iroquois Confederation.

When he first started to carry the book bag, Buffalo was partially defined by steel mills. At kickoff time for the Super Bowl in 2014, the mills had long since ceased to spew ash into the air. Just south of Buffalo, they had been replaced by wind farms built on a former slag heap.

Rochester was the proud home to the Eastman Kodak Company in 1984. Eastman Kodak missed the digital photography revolution. By 2014, the city had to reinvent itself in high tech following the aftermath of the plants closings.

On another wintery day, months before the 1984-scheduled rendezvous between Washington and Los Angeles, Trav pounded through a winter white-out just north of the Finger Lakes in western New York. On the other side of the snow-laden cloud, a textbook adoption committee was eager to learn more about the content in his book bag. For a brief moment he considered the world of Orwell and thought to himself that perhaps it didn't really matter.

Twelve months after he viewed the 1984 Super Bowl ad, Trav covered the same geography. This time as a senior account executive for a personal computer company, Trav was to deliver a technology story. The audience wondered if he would talk about the Apple II or the Macintosh.

When asked what he would share he immediately blurted out, "FAMPS!" It was an acronym that he coined to keep his presentation on track. The audience of educators was somewhat taken aback. There was no line item funding for FAMPS. It wasn't listed in the technology budget. It didn't sound like anything provided by textbook money that they could shift to make the purchase.

He was there to help them do just a little bit more efficiently what they had been doing all along. They nodded enthusiastically when he described the acronym for *find, analyze, manage, present* and *share* information.

What they held in their minds was infinitely more valuable than the intellectual property contained in any one title. Technology could unlock the meaning behind every word. It demanded a complete revision to the Orwellian construct of an ever-diminishing vocabulary. Words matter, images matter, thoughts matter.

Had he been invented in this era, Winston—the lead character in the novel *1984*—wouldn't have to sneak into some out of the way shop to find an unadulterated passage from the past. He wouldn't need to rely on fragmented and disassociated commentary from aging patrons at a local pub.

They couldn't help him to discover any meaningful counterpoint to the historical view proffered by the Ministry of Truth. They couldn't ameliorate the negative consequence of thought control. In the actual year of 1984, information would be digitized. People could consider the philosophical, mathematic, and psychological multiplicity of source documents to validate their beliefs.

Information hidden in a million shops, library dens, and home collections would become available for inspection. These educators were about to embark upon a brave new world.

FAMPS assumed the magnitude of a mission statement for Trav. It would redefine his nickname and alter his sense of purpose in the workplace. He had already discovered the spiritual treasure that gave meaning to all life. Trav paused to consider that somehow the two were connected.

Several times since his return from Rome, New York, he reflected on a passage from the Old Testament. He considered two interpretations:

But thou, O Daniel, shut up the words, and seal the book, even to the time of the end: many shall run to and fro, and knowledge shall be increased. (Daniel:12:4, KJV)

But you, Daniel, keep these words secret, and seal the book, until the end times. Many will travel everywhere, and knowledge will grow. (Daniel 12:4, GW)

Was it possible that all the travel and turmoil in the workplace brought him to a place where prophesy might be fulfilled? He thought about all the people who passed by him in airports, ship docks, train stations, bus terminals, and highway rest stops. He placed a checkmark next to the requirement about travel.

The increase in knowledge was problematic. He held out the thought of a man challenging God. One man, even the most knowledgeable person ever created, would be humbled in the presence of the Creator of the Universe.

This new technology might provide mankind with a second path to rebellion. It was ludicrous to think that one man or one woman could out-think God—after all, Adam and Eve had tried and failed.

The knowledge of all those who had returned to dust was added to the collective wisdom and experience of seven billion living souls. With cumulative acumen, mankind might be foolish enough to issue the challenge. He placed a checkmark next to the second line in the passage. Trav didn't comprehend the full meaning.

There was a tangent reference concerning two men on opposite banks of a river. Maybe the importance of that would be revealed at a later time. In the meantime, he carried this passage into and beyond the workplace.

Three years later, the company released a vision of the future. Released in 1987, a year of reflection and prediction(s), the concept video was still alive and well on the web in 2014. [Anna made a point of sharing it with JBadgenoone.]

The video carried a title that had little to do with driving through snow drifts in central New York. Dubbed *The Knowledge Navigator,* it portrayed an exchange of ideas and information between two university colleagues.

They were exploring the possible connection between the expansion of the African sub-Saharan desert and the defoliation of the tropical rain forest in South America. Comparing and contrasting information, they collaborated in a knowledge construction enabled by two devices. They bore a striking resemblance to a 2014 iPad. It anticipated a delivery system akin to the Internet.

It was one of several concept videos that helped Trav expand upon his mission statement just as the 1984 Super Bowl ad changed the course in the river of his life. [At that time, Anna grabbed the KN label and applied it to Trav. She knew that he was ready for new epistemology and identity. He could find a new theme song. "I'm driving my life away" and "The Wanderer" were no longer fitting. Anna chuckled again.]

Following the Super Bowl XLVIII game in 2014, his mother brought to him a book titled *So Far: The First Ten Years of A Vision*. He had given the book to her in 1987, the same year that KN (Nav) was formally recognized by the Neverborn. The book was printed and bound by the personal computer company.

It was a memento for employees who served during the first ten years of the journey. The cover featured a picture of ripples in a pond, representative of the ripples emanating from the idea that was the company. An audio rendition of ripples modified contemporary music to motivate the team. [Jackson made the MP3 file available upon request to her email, jbadgenoone@yahoo.com.]

His mother opened *So Far* and found his name. It was imbedded alongside so many others who had contributed to the journey. Trav was humbled by the presence of these bright and talented colleagues.

The book was printed just three years after his arrival at the emerging high-tech powerhouse. Years later, the company would surpass rivals. It would claim another enviable high water marker. In the meantime, his adventure continued.

Over time, his journey had also become a family affair. His daughters embraced the technology from the moment Trav brought home his first Apple IIe. He inserted the appropriate boards and connected the disk drives. The daughters immediately saw the value proposition of this device. A robust library of educational software enriched their learning experience.

It also provided a compelling story to counter the FUD (Fear, Uncertainty and Doubt) stories circulated by his competitors in the education market space. The most formidable was headquartered just down the highway. It boasted a single-color logo, a slightly different hue of blue than the one on the spaghetti carton.

Within a year, he was connecting a Mac to a LaserWriter. That combination launched a desktop publishing industry. He recalled how type had to be set for the Altruist in 1965 and the PCB and OBC catalogs published in 1970.

At the Park Avenue South office in New York City that year, he cut pages with an X-acto knife and pasted galley proof copy with rubber cement glue. He recalled a conversation with his then-supervisor, predicting a time twenty years into the future when all that would be done electronically. He was off by five years.

In 1988, a year of reflection and reiteration, Trav helped to arrange a joint project developed by the personal computer company, a media corporation, and a neighboring high school. Some very talented young students and a dedicated newspaper advisor launched the premier issue of *GHS Today*. Nav imagined how much fun his staff could have had with this kind of technology back in the production room of the *Altruist*.

That *GHS* issue would incorporate many of the elements found in a national newspaper. The lead story featured a comparison of national candidates in the US presidential election held that year.

Back in Cupertino, there was a lot of discussion about which platform would dominate the company balance sheet. At this stage of development, KN was convinced that there was ample room for both into the foreseeable future, at least in the education market that he served.

He was thankful to work at a company that encouraged field representatives to initiate such projects, as long as they helped contribute to the bottom line. The projects redefined the mission. Expanding technology implementation in schools assumed almost scriptural significance.

His colleague and higher education counterpart gave him another nickname: Point Man. It was reflective of KN's penchant for pushing the sales and marketing envelope.

The colleague went on to establish an enviable career of his own. He also leveraged the lessons learned at the personal computer company. He became an accomplished speaker and author. One title focused on ways to deliver a message through remarkable presentations.

Trav, Nav, and Point Man reflected on the wisdom that surfaced from that book. It placed a punctuation mark on FAMPS.

Another co-worker sometimes stood point with Nav during his PC journey. On one occasion, he helped to construct a project designed to enlist the talent of students with special needs. It provided opportunities for students to repair and refurbish computers and printers. A number of the youngsters went on to find rewarding employment in the electronics field.

He was on a mission to help everyone to secure meaningful employment. Years later, he too would leverage the lessons learned and publish a book. It provided real-world advice for college graduates preparing to enter into the job market. The book also offered suggestions for returning military veterans and others seeking job guidance in a perilous and ever changing economy.

[Jackson made a promise to Anna: Additional Badgenoone colleagues would be assigned to both authors.]

With measured steps, Point Man's daughters moved into the Macintosh platform along with many in their generation. The Mac 512K fit neatly into a canvas carrying case that became somewhat of a status symbol on many a campus.

They also acquired his desire to travel. Two years after he had presented the book to his mother, his daughters and wife joined him on another trip back to Europe.

That trip in 1989, a year of reflection and refinement, started with a British Airways jet flight from Kennedy (Idlewild) to Gatwick. With a week in London they took in all the sights. Trav agreed to visit Harrods Department Store and the Hard Rock Café.

At the British Museum, KN and his family pondered at length in front of a painting that depicted the execution of Lady Jane Grey. Her hand was outstretched, searching for the executioner's block. The next day, they visited the tower where the hatchet severed her head. Her final words: "Lord, into thy hands I commend my spirit!"

The continent was just a ferry ride away from the white cliffs of Dover. Trav perched on the bow and rode the waves to the Belgian port. He recalled how he had followed the whales on the USS Mitchell.

KN predicted that the long-anticipated Chunnel would create a new high water marker for cross-channel navigation. He encouraged his daughters to save their British pound and pence, as well as the Belgian franc and centime.

They would represent high water markers of a different kind when a European Union might replace them with a universal currency in the not-too-distant future. His uncle had predicted that transition years ago.

Once on the mainland, a short train ride brought them to their next destination: Brussels. Who could imagine that someday it would become the seat of power for continental affairs? Queen Victoria or King Leopold II might have made that prediction.

They returned to the house of his uncle, since departed. It was now occupied by his first cousin. His uncle left four treasures to his son: a golden rose, a Meerschaum pipe, a violin, and a rusty bayonet.

His cousin gave the bayonet to Trav. It was a relic from the battle of Waterloo. Trav was relieved to learn that it was not employed by some German practicing how to use it on Belgian babies during WWI.

[Anna wasn't laughing this time.]

Originally one of thousands that glistened in the sunlight on a hill, this bayonet never left the gentle ridge. A bullet struck his ancestor silent before he could employ the metal to enemy flesh. His dying body lingered on the field of battle.

A note from his younger brother who carried the blade home invoked the final wish of his sibling. "If you are reading this, I am passed. Remember how I loved. I will most likely be buried in my uniform. Find some other use for the bayonet, this sliver of iron. The new Caesar Napoleon will have need for it no more."

His memory and the bayonet traveled through distance and time. It would eventually find a place in the den overlooking Dutch Buffalo Creek. Trav would mount it above the door on the north wall. KN treasured the memory and the bayonet that was never christened with blood. Eventually it would be mounted in cross-sword fashion with a bayonet employed by a former enemy.

The next day, KN, along with his wife and daughters, climbed the stairs leading to the monument at Waterloo. From the top of the hill, they could survey the entire battlefield. In the visitors center rotunda, they could interject themselves at different vantage points of the conflict as depicted in a 360-degree diorama. The hill where his ancestor had fallen was clearly marked in the painting.

On the way back to the city, they rested at a small campsite and reflected on the sacrifice made by so many young men so long ago. Their collective actions altered the course of history.

Their individual struggles were lost to the history books but kept alive in the letters that they wrote to loved ones at home. The next week they trained to Paris. After a few days in the city they motored to Versailles.

At this point, Jackson intervened. She asked Anna and KN to suspend reading in the book of his life for now. There would be time enough in subsequent chapters and other books to learn about KN's life after his journey at the Infinite Loop.

They would also reveal the moment he met Jesus. They would describe Nav's transition into the role of grandfather, author, and sage. Jackson asked Anna to dog-ear the page and move onto the next book.

Jackson Badgenoone

Anna couldn't restrain herself. This was the fourth time that Jackson had interrupted her story. She wasn't sure, but she suspected that she felt an emotion, dynamic tension, more likely confusion. Hadn't Jackson entrusted to her the rendering of this story?

Jackson apologized and reassured Anna that she had done a commendable job. She had captured the salient highlights of a complicated life. She had provided appropriate hyperlinks for one of the eBook versions, although Jackson suspected that several more were as yet undiscovered.

Anna hadn't dwelled on every job assignment. She highlighted the printing plant because it provided a link to a shifting national and international manufacturing landscape. The publishing companies reflected a philosophical transition. Guardians of intellectual property morphed into content brokers.

The technology corporations were a logical work extension of men like the Wizard of Menlo Park and his inventive contemporaries. They brought light and sound to the stage of life. Jackson had tracked their entrance onto and exit from the stage.

She was witness to the moment when Louis Daguerre seized the light. Photos could support a story from that moment and into the future. Jackson was also in the basement chamber when Samuel Morse signaled his famous words from the US Capitol building: "What hath God wrought?"

Jackson was there when Alexander Graham Bell was awarded the Mohawk Indian title of honorary chief. She was in the room when Bell spoke the famous sentence, "Mr. Watson—come here—I want to see you."

Anna and her colleagues tracked the contribution of their observees. They found purpose in the organizations spawned by Thomas, Louis, Samuel, and Alexander. Anna was the first to appreciate the links.

JBadgenoone felt a measure of disappointment. It must have been her fault as author's guide. She enjoyed the give-and-take dialog but hadn't adequately conveyed the mission to her favorite Neverborn colleague. She thought that she had provided plausible explanation for the interruptions at the time they were required.

Jackson seized the moment and convened the first weekly meeting of the Badgenoone cohort. Even though they comported themselves in the finest circular tradition of the ancient Greeks, she summoned them to a makeshift oval Roman amphitheater in the woods. She began the meeting with a roll call and a call to order. Anna, Bernadette, Christopher, Daniel, Elizabeth, Frederick, George, Henry, and Israel all responded *here* or *present*. She began to review the mission.

Their books were never meant to be totally absorbed into *The Hidden Treasure of Dutch Buffalo Creek*. Anna should reflect solely on chapters that cast a lighthouse beacon on the primary work or the other books in the High Water Marker series.

Jackson took this opportunity to expand her initial commentary. "As I said, we can return to the 'High Water Markers of Anna's Observee' at any time during the rendering of this reading in *The Hidden Treasures of Dutch Buffalo Creek*."

Trav's salvation was a deeply personal moment in his life. Anna had described it in some detail in the comprehensive version of her work. She had brought to life the struggles and the endless soul-searching leading up to that moment.

The first interruption was occasioned by a point of clarification. The second was presaged by age-inappropriate content in the original work.

The third halt in the reading came because it affected another work. Trav's salvation was dynamically linked to Mimi's. Jackson quoted a verse from the New Testament to make her point:

"For when two or three are gathered together in My name, I am there among them." Matthew 18:20

Jackson believed that Anna had superbly described the experience in her hidden chapters. But Frederick Badgenoone had also captured the moment. He was able to bring to it a different focus when it was coupled with his rendering of Mimi's experience. Trav and Mimi would be gathered in His name for the remainder of their lives.

Obviously, Anna hadn't read the book compiled by Frederick.

Jackson went on to compliment Anna for additional hidden chapters she developed following Trav's salvation moment. In chapter twelve, she captured the immediate rush to witness following his salvation experience.

She also bore witness to the struggles faced by a new Christian. Nuance carried her character through revisited relationships with family, friends, neighbors, coworkers, colleagues, and acquaintances.

Subsequent recondite chapters explored his interactions with other cultures and societies. One relived his visit to Frankfurt when he participated in the annual book fair. The city was totally modern by then but still held the seeds of his birthplace. It also formed a connection that dated back 500 years to Johannes Gutenberg.

Other chapters were set against backdrops in Egypt, Algeria, Libya, Kenya, the Democratic Republic of Congo, and Zimbabwe. Trav made a point of looking up some of the former students Gaz had taught during his Peace Corps days.

There were two chapters about his journey to Central and South America. His brother-in-law had worked for the airlines. He provided an awesome array of out-of-the-way spots to visit and provided introductions to some extraordinary people.

Anna dedicated a chapter to a very special Christmas celebration at Trav's New England home in 1989, a year of reflection and refinement. The observees of each Badgenoone observer were at Merryall that evening. Trav watched as they peeled back the wrapping paper that covered a special gift that he had purchased for each member of his family.

His three daughters joined their mother Mimi, Grandpa Jimmy, Grandma Charlene, Grandpa Fred, and Grandma Mary as they gathered by the fireplace. The gift was a book titled *Apples of Gold*, a compilation of encouraging quotes. He hoped that they would provide inspiration when life presented challenge in the future.

In the final chapters of Anna's work, Trav experienced physical limitations accentuated by two major surgical procedures. He had already gone through a crisis of faith. At the time of the second surgery in 2014, he withstood a crisis of confidence. On the way to the operating room, he was bolstered by a quote from the very book that he had gifted in 1989: "All I see teaches me to trust the Creator for all I do not see." (*Apples of Gold*, p. 67)

Anna understood all that but genuinely believed that the fourth intrusion seemed more a disruption that an interruption. She had so much more to share, so why stop at this point? She voiced her opinion for the benefit of her colleagues.

JBadgenoone responded with advice to all the Neverborn ghostwriters. She asked them to read the complete works that each had helped to create. After they had accomplished that task, they would be more than welcome to question any further interruption by the author's guide.

To underscore her point, she also encouraged them to read all four of the New Testament Gospels. They provide an excellent example of how a story became more powerful when told from alternate vantage points.

Matthew, Mark, Luke, and John brought the story of Jesus to a world hungry to hear His word. (And hungry it still is.)

Each evangelist approaches identical events through different passages. The primary Author knows that the message would be carried around the world throughout the ages. He knows that an intended disciple might miss the message put forward in a first, second, third, or even fourth reading.

Ultimately, the message of the gospel required no printed word at all. It was to be written on the heart of the recipient. It was, and is, a gift.

GBadgenoone interrupted. "You are a wonderful editor, but I wonder about your statement."

Jackson reminded him that she was not an editor; she was a guide.

George acknowledged her role and continued to challenge Jackson's comment. "If the printed word doesn't matter, then why are we taking the time to record the lives of this handful of souls?"

Jackson responded with a question. "Have you stopped to consider why you now experience human emotions? The Neverborn are all aware of the existence of the Creator. Yet we will never know Him. He reserved that privilege to souls granted a time in the flesh. That flesh awakens the passions that lead women and men to seek their spiritual roots.

"We are granted a handful of those emotions to hone our documentary skills. Neverborn know that God exists, but we will never know Him in the same way. Humans have the capacity to know Him without knowing about Him.

"A person born with no ears or eyes would not be denied a place in Paradise simply because she was born deaf and blind. Written scripture was designed to enlighten. It was not crafted as an obstacle to salvation. The Creator's love could bypass transcribed physical barriers and imprint directly on the heart of a receptive soul."

This time Anna interjected a question. "Why did Jesus assume flesh? Didn't He already know the full range of human emotions?"

Jackson responded with several questions. "Did He do it for His benefit? Was it done to establish an umbilical connection between Creator and creation? Didn't the gospel suggest that He offered His body as a propitiation for sin?"

Jackson hoped that her suggestions would enrich each story. The intentionally hidden chapters revealed conflict and resolution common to the species. Interested readers could explore the complete works at an appropriate time. She concluded the meeting. Israel Badgenoone seconded the motion for closure.

They thanked Jackson for the guidance. Each Badgenoone agreed to revisit their observation. Bernadette was responsible for the next story. Her relationship with Jackson rested on stronger foundations, in part due to her senior tenure in the group. She paid close attention to Jackson's critique of Anna's rendition.

James swallowed another pill. He began to sympathize with the Badgenoone observers. Jackson could display tyrannical tendencies. He tried to walk a mile in her moccasins. He understood Jackson's instruction about chapter selection. He was disappointed because so many of the comprehensive chapters were omitted.

He didn't fault Anna. She was following directions. Still, James felt that the selected chapters represented an overly pasteurized version of his life. He also questioned Jackson about her selection of the next eight observees. There were other souls that impacted his story.

Jackson knew that she now had more than one management challenge. She patiently explained her selection.

"You have extended families with roots in Africa and Asia," she explained. "Their worlds are sometimes filtered through different religions and philosophy. I have revealed your connection to the First People of Canada and to Native Americans south of the border. Your immediate family—Dad, Mom, mother-in-law, father-in-law, spouse and children—have a more proximate influence on your worldview. I also took into account genetics and their personal salvation experience.

"The lives in this immediate circle would validate the influence of western civilization on the character of James. At defining moments in their lives they were likely to quote from the same bible. They shared the same traditions and entertained a similar worldview. By the way, I am not a tyrant.

"I gave the other Badgenoone observers permission to insert your name on occasion. Anna also has my permission to insert your name in the yet-to-be published chapters of her book."

The reading continued.

[Book 5]

The High Water Markers of Bernadette's Observee

By Bernadette Badgenoone,

Preface to The High Water Markers
of Bernadette's Observee

BBadgenoone was only too eager to help uncover the meaning of the artifacts attached to the life of the colonel. She would refer to him by his nickname, Jimmy.

He left a treasure trove of books, magazines, maps, photos, record albums and music song sheets. A reader mining the pages of *The Hidden Treasure of Dutch Buffalo Creek* would have discovered reference to some of them in that book.

In the den overlooking Dutch Buffalo Creek, a photo of Jimmy at the piano hung above the fourth shelf. It was lined with copies of *The Armed Forces Song Folio* from April 1952 – April 1957. They were issued monthly by the departments of the Army, Navy and Air Force of the United States. The folios provided a snapshot of music that was popular at the time.

His son remembered how they came to life when Dad moved his time-worn fingers across the black and ivory keys. Trav's grandfather taught his son to embrace every note in every song. He provided a piano and lessons. Music would fill the modest home of this immigrant from Italy.

There were resources sufficient to feed the family, provide piano lessons for one son, violin lessons for a second, cello for a third, and saxophone for a fourth. Long before he held rank, Colonel Jim's sister Connie received voice lessons. She helped bring life to the lyrics of the instrumental renditions provided by her older siblings.

Even after her brothers had passed, in the choir of Saint Anthony, Connie's voice continued to praise the Lord. In the period between two world wars, her music provided a high water marker that couldn't be heard or appreciated until years after they faded from sight and sound. Memories from Connie were recorded and saved to VHS at a family reunion convened long after the colonel had retired.

At that reunion she shared that her father delighted in the classical music that permeated his home. He was chagrined when Jimmy transitioned from Chopin to ragtime within the span of less than a dozen keys.

No recordings were ever made of those happy transitions. Their memory was kept alive only by the recounting of his sister and imagination of his children. The colonel did leave a wonderful collection of long playing record albums that influenced his music.

They too found a home in the den overlooking Dutch Buffalo Creek. On the sixth shelf, they included contemporary orchestral and instrumental recordings: Beethoven Complete Nine Symphonies, Berwald Symphony in C Major, Brahms—the complete cello sonatas, and the colonel's favorite, Chopin—Piano concerto No. 2 in F Minor, Opus 21.

Also on the shelf, "Voice-O-Graphs", audio messages recorded and mailed to him from his wife. The voices of his children sang Christmas carols. Before zip codes, the mailing label was addressed to Jimmy at the Rycom Motor Command, 8109th Army Unit, A.P.O. 719, c/o PM, San Francisco, California.

One record contained a very personal message, spoken from her heart with sentences that took form in English, French, and Italian. Her loving refrain was simple: "I love you, *mi amore*." His children rendered childhood songs that tugged at his heartstrings.

A stereo-to-PC recording kit brought the LPs and voice letters into the digital world. They joined an ever-expanding body of artifacts that lived on in digital format in a cloud unseen by human eyes. The cloud had no form, hid no sun, chilled no air, shed no rain or snow, and produced no lightning or thunder.

This cloud wasn't formed by evaporation. It gained strength from artifacts that measured the high water markers of an entire species. The den overlooking Dutch Buffalo Creek fed to it a steady stream of memories.

Bernadette reserved presentation of Chapter 1 in the book about Jim. That chapter assumed two signature proportions. It began by tracing the journey of Jim's father through the period of Italian unification. A backdrop of world events set the stage for his journey. Geopolitical struggle had a direct impact on his family and ultimately presaged his departure for America at the turn of the twentieth century.

Bbadgenoone was certain that an entire book could be written about the diminutive man named Umberto. All of five feet in stature, his presence dominated the pages of the first chapter in the book by Bernadette Badgenoone.

Victoria Badgenoone spoke from the back of the room. She had already written the story and was waiting in line to have it published. Her brother, Victor Badgenoonev, subtitled it *One Immigrant, One Dream*. The book would also reach into the life of Umberto's wife, the former Anna Coppola and her Fedele and Romognola family roots. In the meantime, readers could observe more about Umberto and Anna in the comprehensive version of Bernadette's book.

CHAPTER II
The Tracks From Transfer Station

Just a few months and one state line removed from the birth time and place of another Jimmy, this Jimmy was born in a lower section of Manhattan in New York City. The other Jimmy was born in a small Pennsylvania town and went on to a dual career that linked the world of entertainment and the military.

This Jimmy would weave a career defined by business enterprise and the US Army. His journey started on Mulberry Street in the Little Italy section, an ocean removed from the back streets of Naples.

At the time of his birth in 1908, the world was lunging headlong into a new century. In his lifetime, that world would survive two world wars, countless conflicts, a worldwide pandemic, and an economic depression.

The US would grow from forty-six states to fifty. Dirt roads would be paved, many then paved again into an Interstate Highway system. Civil War veterans still marched in the parades of his youth. Native Americans who had survived the Indian Wars toured in the Wild West Show.

Soon after his birth, Jimmy's father decided it was time to move the family, now two boys and his wife, to a comparatively uncluttered environment. He had left his Napolitano homeland in search for a better place to raise children.

The excrement-ridden cobblestone alleys of the lower east side were not what he had in mind. [Bernadette was well aware of the physical and human squalor in the two neighborhoods on opposite shores. She didn't plan to document any of it for the purpose of this book. Anyone interested in knowing more about that blight could read any number of non-fiction or fictional works about the time leading up to that period. Her favorite was *The King of Mulberry Street.*]

Across the Hudson River, in what was then West Hoboken, Umberto purchased a modest two-family home in the Transfer Station Section. Passengers would transfer from one trolley line to another in their daily journey from home to work. Lines ran north, south, east and west from the Fifth Street terminus.

Jimmy thrived in the new environment. He was within reach of the movie studios that produced an endless stream of cliffhanger westerns. Many of those silent movies were filmed against the backdrop of the nearby Palisades.

A curious blend of fact and fiction emerged during his formative years. Actors portrayed real-life action figures. They were still very much alive. It was nearly impossible for the young boy to distinguish between actor Tom Mix and lawman Wyatt Earp. Jimmy was sure that he wanted to be the marshal.

Years later, Mix would join fellow actor William S. Hart as a pallbearer at Earp's funeral. It was the year following Jimmy's graduation from high school. Movie production had shifted to Hollywood. High water markers were set up on both sides of the continent.

A crash of gun shots and the sound of galloping horse hoofs enlivened the westerns in the new age of talkies. Later that year, a different kind of crash would impact an entire generation of wannabe marshals.

Jackson Badgenoone

CHAPTER III
A New Order Emerges

The town prospered and grew in that first decade of the new century and in the decades that followed. By 1925, a year of reflection and sobriety, the town merged with Union Hill and assumed a new name. Jimmy enrolled in the high school that was nearest to his home, Emerson.

It was named for Ralph Waldo Emerson, a literary giant who amassed a sixteen-volume journal. He believed in the "still, small voice," and that voice is Christ within us.

He was one of the most influential writers of nineteenth-century America. Some pundits held the belief that Walt Whitman, Henry David Thoreau, and William James were Emersonians. His influence was not diminished by time.

Emerson was quoted one hundred and thirty years after a new flag was hoisted at Fort Sumter in 1861, a year of reflection and division. Emerson's comment about the destruction of the south supported a narrative on the use of force to unite two populations at the point of a bayonet.

Herman Melville, Nathaniel Hawthorne, and Henry James often took different positions from the Concord Sage but respected him nonetheless. Mark Twain commented on Emerson's grammar: "It isn't wrong, just awkward: it all at once arrests the flow of your serenity for a moment, like gravel in the bread."

In his early years, the Sage would dream about freeing the slaves. He became an ardent abolitionist. He referred to America as a smelting pot, a culturally and racially mixed society.

At the time when Jimmy entered the school, most of his classmates were vowel people (meaning that their last name ended in a vowel), a euphemism for Italians. Special emphasis was placed on the first letter, *I*. The smelting pot had become a melting pot.

Union Hill High School, located in the north section of the newly-named city, drew a German-American student population from that part of town. Over the years, the schools developed a long-standing rivalry. The annual Thanksgiving football game between the two schools marked a high water marker for both teams every year.

As the city grew, so did Jimmy's family. Two more brothers and then a sister brought a vibrant life to the second floor of the two-story home. They preserved memories of those days in an oral tradition and with numerous notes and letters that survived the years.

The roaring twenties brought a bevy of entertainers to the city. By the thirties, burlesque and comedy found expression in a theater on 48th Street. So too did the longest running passion play in the United States. To those who had moved there, the new city was no longer in the shadow of the metropolis to the east.

From her window at EHS, Jimmy's sister could see the Empire State Building reaching for the clouds, one story at a time. It was opened for business just as business was failing during the Great Depression. She delayed her entry into the job market and enrolled as an undergraduate student at New York University.

She was the first of her siblings to earn a baccalaureate degree, impressive for a young woman at that time. She still displayed her youthful smile at her high school reunion twenty-five years later.

After completing his studies, Jimmy graduated and entered the labor force. He felt the sting of that depression as he lost one job after another in the banking industry. Following the election of 1932, a year of reflection and restored confidence, things began to turn around for that segment of the economy. President Franklin D.

Roosevelt declared a bank holiday. A few months later, Jim found a job that would bring a measure of stability.

Happy days were here again. By 1939, things seemed to be returning to normal. In July, Jim joined his friends at the World's Fair in Flushing Meadow. They spent most of the time in the Communications and Business Systems Zone. Jim was particularly impressed by what he saw at the International Business Machines pavilion.

IBM displayed an electronic calculator that used punched cards. His friends were amazed when they entered the AT&T pavilion. It featured the Voder, a synthetic voice that spoke to the audience.

They compared notes on the way back to the Embroidery Capital of the United States. Jim was the only one who could offer a comparison to an earlier fair. He had accompanied his father and older brother on a trip to visit relatives in San Diego more than two decades earlier.

Anna and newborn Connie remained at the Transfer Station. Father and sons took in the continent with a sense of wonderment.

[Bernadette recorded every moment of the adventure in the expanded version of her book. Victoria Badgenoone provided a deeper view of the journey in her unpublished manuscript. She also revealed the struggle that visited Anna during the absence of her husband and the boys.]

Jim was all of seven years old when they visited the Panama California Exhibition in July of 1915, a year of reflection and prelude. He had vivid memories and kept a copy of the official guide book as a reminder. The highlight of his visit came when he had the opportunity to listen to the former president of the United States.

Teddy Roosevelt, often referred to by his initials, TR, wanted everyone to consider the utility of the canal that was constructed under his watch. San Diego was the first northbound stop for ships steaming west through the canal. Jim appreciated the significance of the undertaking during his future service in the military.

A chance meeting with his childhood hero helped to form his view of America and the world. TR was born in a brownstone building on East 20th street in Manhattan, exactly a half-century before Jimmy entered the arena of life. Teddy had a frail physical beginning but was larger than life by the time he grabbed the attention of the little boy from the lower east side.

The visit to the earlier fair was twenty-four years earlier, almost to the day. So much had taken place since that time. This new fair was truly a World's Fair, much larger and more expansive in purpose and presentation.

The Fifth Street boys, now young men, discussed their impressions of different national pavilions. Their favorite was the Italian pavilion. It brought a measure of ethnic pride. However, they were miffed by the absence of a German pavilion. A few months later they understood. The world seemed peaceful enough for now.

In the following months, the lights went out in pavilions maintained by countries that were overrun by the Nazi Juggernaut. The Polish doors were among the first to close. The United States seemed immune to the turmoil.

Then the Japanese attacked Pearl Harbor.

Everyone could remember where they were on that day. Jimmy and his family were gathered around the dining room table when the radio announcer interrupted his regular broadcast.

The Transfer Station continued to evolve. At the advent of WWII it was a busy hub. During the war, uniformed servicemen hurried through the area on their way to their duty bases. After the war, the trolley lines were torn up and the cobblestone streets paved. The Fifth Street neighborhood withstood all the change.

CHAPTER V

The Last Supper

His friends respected his athletic prowess on the football grid-iron and on the tennis court. They were entertained by his unique piano style and occasional foray into alternative music via ukulele or harmonica.

Jimmy also harbored a lifelong interest in painting. Most of the canvas was lost to time. However, one did survive. It was a replica of the Last Supper that he painted during his time between the wars.

He was inspired to render it after having attended *Veronica's Veil*, another passion play performed by locals in the first floor auditorium of Saint Joseph's School. Jim was moved by the passion of the Christ and by the events that led up to that moment. He always seemed to bring the Old and New Testaments into alignment. His favorite psalm was 23. His favorite New Testament quote was John 3:16.

For him, the Last Supper was really the first supper. The oil on his palette brought to the canvas an expression of peace in the portrait of Jesus. Jim conjured up images of the many dinners he had shared with his family. He somehow managed to bring those emotion-filled events to this work.

Bernadette took note of Jackson's gaze. Just as she had skipped chapter four in the interest of efficiency, she now moved beyond the rest of this chapter and the following six to focus again on the mission of the **Hidden Treasure of Dutch Buffalo Creek.**

CHAPTER XII

Rails To And From A Windy City

The New Year brought yet another measure of change into his life. He had received his orders to report to a new duty station in Korea. His wife, Charlene, and three children had returned with him to the Transfer Station, fresh with memories of Fort Dix and the little eastern town of Mount Holly, New Jersey.

They considered their housing options in the wake of this new assignment. Lodging for dependents might be available in Japan. He never considered exposing them to shelter on the Korean peninsula in 1958.

Charlene came up with a reasonable suggestion: She would stay in the city with the children. It would become their base of operations. She didn't plan to spend the entire four years of his next tour strictly within the confines of Hudson County.

Brussels was selected as the site for the World's Fair that year. She could craft a visit to her homeland with extended trips during the summer months. There would be time enough before the start of school. The first month would provide ample time to visit the Fair and meet with her parents, brothers, sisters, nieces and nephews.

She would set aside the second month to train to Rome. Then she would motor from there to Naples. Jimmy's siblings had a long list of relatives that she could look up when they arrived in Italy.

They could spend the following summer visiting with friends back in Kentucky and with family in Rochester, New York. The autumn, winter, and spring of each year would pass quickly enough under the tumult of the school calendar. Jim agreed. It was a reasonable plan for starters.

Jim kissed them goodbye and headed for the Penn Station. That venerable New York City landmark was at a high water marker. A few short years later, the terminal would be demolished in the name of progress.

The train was comfortable enough. He watched the platform fade from view as it pulled out of the station. The first significant stop for him would be in Rochester, New York.

Locals referred to it as the Flower City. It was home to the Lilac Festival each year, an event that supercharged his sense of smell and sight. The first organized event was hosted at Highland Park in the same year that he was born.

His older brother met him at the train station. The festival had taken place two months earlier. Gennaro extended an open invitation to return to the city when Jim returned from this new overseas assignment.

They spent precious hours recalling the good old days on the Transfer Station. The following day, both considered the expanded size of Gerry's vegetable garden. He had just added a greenhouse, which enabled him to cultivate his plants from seed.

That evening, they sipped a glass of wine from Gerry's homemade stock. Umberto would have been pleased to see his two oldest sons embrace the nectar of life. The following morning, Jim boarded the westbound train.

It rolled on ribbons of steel to Buffalo, cities in Ohio and Indiana, finally into the Union Station in Chicago, Illinois. In a few years, that building would also reach a high water marker. Automobiles and airlines were exacting a toll.

He sojourned in the Windy City for a few days, catching up with old buddies who rode the rails with him during his years as a bank representative. The city had gone through quite a transformation in the years following the war. A place where the skyscraper was born had given rise to a forest of steel and glass buildings.

A whistle blew and the train lurched forward. He was on the next leg of his journey to the west coast. He pressed his hand on the window and then waved farewell to his friends. Within the space of an hour, the sound of turning iron wheels lulled him into a deep sleep.

His mind raced back to his boyhood days. Brothers and friends would venture to the edge of the meadowlands. Automobiles were scarce and the air was still breathable. An odiferous reminder of nearby pig farms was the only despoiler to an otherwise perfect summer day.

Back up the hill, trolley cars clanked down the center of cobblestone streets. An Italian church was erected just blocks south of the German spires to the north. The dream continued racing through the years.

Memories of the first job, second, and third caused his body to stir. The newspapers of that day carried the bad news, depression, unemployment, dustbowl, and drought. The bank failures were beyond his control. He could only hope to carve out some meaningful career through the chaos of the times.

He heard the countless clicks of counting machines in his undergraduate business classes. Maybe numbers had meaning beyond the world of banking. Numbers without banks, banks without numbers, and the thoughts raced through his mind.

Pearl Harbor brought into focus different calculations. He remembered the day when he first got the news. His family was gathered around the table, and the radio announcer interrupted the broadcast.

Within a year, he was drafted into the military and earmarked for officer candidate school. Memories of his training base in Mississippi entered his slumber. When the dream continued, he found himself in the winter snow just outside of the Belgian town of Bastogne.

Moments later, his mind reflected on a blurred image of his future wife as they strolled down a street in Brussels. He called her

Mon chéri. Within a moment, another image of her with his children flashed before his mind. They were on a visit in Mexico. It was a comfortable car ride from his duty base in Yuma.

The years seemed to race along with every mile of track. The seconds were measured by a thousand wooden railroad ties. The train was approaching Saint Louis when he awoke. For a brief moment, he thought that he saw the family again, this time in Belgium. The image faded and he realized that he wasn't part of that picture. His wife and three children were boarding an eastbound flight from Idewild at that very moment.

His journey led him ever farther west. By the time he arrived in Korea, his family was already lodged in Brussels, half a world away. The strain of this assignment weighed heavily on his spirit. He longed for a time when they could be reunited.

Jackson intervened. She complimented Bernadette for her thoughtful selection of chapters and her willingness to skip over those that were best left for a more comprehensive read.

Jimmy had so many high water markers in his life: son, brother, husband, father, grandfather, uncle, businessman, soldier, gardener, pianist, painter, and wannabe marshal. The chapters in this book would barely scratch the surface of the contributions he made to society or the joy he brought into the lives of those he touched.

[Jackson knew that Bernadette had amassed an incredible treasure of information about her observee. JBadgenoone reassured her that the comprehensive version of the life of the colonel would be published in short order. She directed Bernadette to skip ahead to the last chapter in Jimmy's book.

There was no push-back. Anna delivered an acknowledging gaze toward Bernadette. Abadgenoone had even learned a bit more about her own identity from the reading. She too would now trust Jackson to help publish her complete work in the appropriate season. Bernadette skipped the chapters and began to read again.]

CHAPTER XXVII

Rings of Smoke

Jimmy enjoyed a good meal, a fine glass of wine from his father's homemade stock, and a King Edward cigar. His brother's oldest son was entertained for hours by the smoke rings that Uncle Jim would puff into the air.

At a family reunion years later, it was one of the recollections that he shared, captured for the family in a VHS format video. They took this time to pay tribute to the memory of Jim.

He recalled a time when he would visit his uncle Jim on the army base in Yuma. It was just a car ride away from his San Diego base. He also had fond memories of the times when Jim and family would visit the naval base. They were sure to visit the world-famous zoo and the grounds of the former Panama California Exposition.

The one-time sailor shared stories about his time at sea and the respite provided during Rest and Recuperation, R&R, at Uncle Jim's house in the desert. He didn't talk about service branch, his rank, or his uncle's rank. He just recalled how wonderful it was to sleep in a real bed instead of a navy destroyer hammock.

Years earlier, Uncle Jim would take his R&R in Rochester at the young sailor's house, home to Jim's older brother. Jim and Gennaro were more than brothers; they were the best of friends.

One by one, Jimmy's siblings, nephews, nieces, children, and grandchildren pieced together fragments of the memories they had shared with him. His oldest son was the second to step up to the lectern that evening. Trav began to speak in a somewhat subdued voice.

He recalled the times they (he, his sister, and dad) fished in the Gila River. They managed to land some catfish and carp. On many a day they returned home with just an empty pail. It didn't matter. It gave Dad the time he needed to share all the stories that sprang from this water.

Dad told of Spanish explorers in the mid-sixteenth century. Then he recounted the 1846 movement of a detachment of US cavalrymen led by Kit Carson. The Wannabe Cisco Kid added him to his western action hero list. Cisco still remained Trav's lifelong favorite.

Trav attributed his passion for technology and all things mechanical to his dad. He recalled how Dad helped him to assemble his first crystal radio set, graduating to transistors over time. Along the way, he also learned how to construct and fly a gas-powered model plane and launch a plastic missile with baking soda and vinegar.

Trav's brother, younger by seven years, was too young to participate in those early morning adventures. He took his place at the lectern and relived his memories of Dad. Jimmy nicknamed him Honest John. John recalled posing for a picture with his siblings and dad in front of a missile that engendered his new handle.

His stories were grounded in a mainly civilian experience. The picture in front of the mounted projectile was one of the last taken on a military base. John's memories were formed around the Fifth Street neighborhood and stories his dad shared about that place, then and in times long gone.

He recalled the time when Dad spoke of a meadowland that harbored wildlife, fish and fowl. Concrete buildings and parking lots would eventually displace the snakes, bullfrogs, turtles, songbirds, and other animals that found shelter in the reeds.

Some of the uncles in the room nodded in agreement. They were there to explore those marshes with Jimmy.

[BBadgenoone wished that someone had remembered to bring a Brownie camera. It was a teachable moment for Bernadette. She had ignored an injunction provided in 1908 during the year of Jimmy's birth. It urged ordinary people to employ this people's camera to capture moments in time. Bernadette Badgenoone shared the realization with Jackson and the other Neverborn observers. They realized that they should encourage their collaborating authors to document written stories with supporting images.

Jackson Badgenoone seconded her motion. Photo-enhanced moments had slipped through the events on her watch. She bore some responsibility for the lack of photos associated with the name-sakes of Bbadgenoone. The technology was available during the lifespan of Bernadette Soubirous, and it was pervasive by the time Jimmy's cousin Bernadette drew breath.]

Jim was equally at home in a small town or a large city. He never lost touch with nature, managing to cultivate a modest garden no matter where he lived at the time. John's dad taught him about the fine art of raising tomatoes in one's own backyard. [This time, Bernadette made sure that her collaborator had a lens available.]

John learned to appreciate the culture and entertainment provided by the city across the Hudson. Dad opened John's eyes to Broadway Theater, the New York Philharmonic, museums and art galleries.

In the final hours, Dad made an effort to comfort his second son. Dad had secured copies of a book that he had received from older brother Trav a few years earlier. Dad gave a copy of *Apples of Gold* to John. Several quotes were underlined. John was drawn to one as he opened the book for the first time. "Death is not extinguishing the light; it is putting out the lamp because dawn has come." (p. 68) John recalled the moment for the benefit of his family gathered at the reunion.

He wiped away a tear and handed the microphone to his sister.

Sister recalled that to her, father was Daddy. He lavished all the love a father brings to a daughter. She talked about the times he would accompany her on Father-Daughter Day during their time on the Test Station.

It was a wonderful time in her life. On the weekends, Dad would break out a cane fishing pole and head with her and Trav to the Gila River. They never caught much of anything except some incredible stories about that place.

She felt a little sad that her younger brother was too young to scale down the cliffs to the river basin. She was sure that he would have enjoyed those special times.

The trips from base to base were of some interest. While Trav seemed happy enough to visit forts and battlefields, his sister was entertained more by the museums and shops along the way. The stops made the countless hours in the car more bearable.

Dad was always there to render some word of wisdom. It would usually elaborate on a factoid delivered by a tour guide. He also provided a fatherly assurance that all was well in the face of danger.

He was there to catch her when she slipped during a visit to an underground passage in the Carlsbad Caverns. When they continued deeper into the cave, he explained the story behind every underground stalagmite and stalactite.

The side trip delivered a measure of relief on the southern leg of their journey. The white Buick wasn't air-conditioned. A dashboard fan was no match for the increasing heat of the day. She had all she could do to fend off barbs from her brothers in the back seat of the car. They made up games to while away the time, taking note of every state border crossing, every different license plate that passed.

She recalled a more recent time in the city. Every year before the leaves would turn her dad would escort her to the Feast of Saint Gennaro. It was celebrated each September in the Little Italy neighborhood where Jimmy was born.

The feast also provided an opportunity to catch up with her Rochester relatives. Her uncle made a point of visiting his roots at the feast of his patron saint without fail every year.

She also followed her dad and her older brother to Emerson High School. She began to describe the times when Dad would ignore the chaos in a house filled with their teenage friends and the young buddies of her brother John.

The weekends were always a challenge. Dad loved to watch his sports shows on the little screen. He had a particular liking for football, baseball and boxing. His favorite pugilist was James Braddock, The Bulldog of Bergen. He earned the title with a unanimous decision at Madison Square Garden in June of 1935, a year of reflection and plebiscite. Her dad caught the action from a ring side seat.

There was no television at that contest. The scene came to life in subsequent years. She watched the movie *Cinderella Man* in 2007. Even though he was no longer in the land of the living, her dad's voice seemed to reverberate throughout the house with the ring of every bell emanating from the small screen that recounted the match.

While he still had breath, he had cheered on Jersey Joe Walcott, Rocky Marciano, and Floyd Paterson. When she was still in high school, she remembered that he rooted for Cassius Clay. A few years later, he favored Joe Frazier.

In Dad's world, The New York Giants trumped the Jets. The Yankees towered over the Mets. Dad shared memories from games at Ebbets Field, The Polo Grounds and the House that Ruth built. TV wasn't even a close contender to the stadium atmosphere. It was a lot more convenient, more so with each passing year.

Dad didn't seem to notice when Gaz, Slim, Bob, and Moose took over the kitchen and the living room areas. He even invited them to watch along from time to time.

Her friends tended to hang out in the other rooms. Janet, Linda, Claudia, and Kathy were respectful of the colonel's space. They tried to stay clear of the cigar tobacco cloud that wafted in every direction from his recliner.

She was with her siblings and Dad at the hospital during his final weeks. He reassured her that he was moving on to a better life. He also gave to her a copy of *Apples of Gold*. She was drawn to a quote on page 23: "God does not deduct from man's allotted time those hours spent in fishing." She shared the memory of the moment with her family at the reunion. At that point she really couldn't carry on much longer and handed the microphone to her aunt.

Jackson Badgenoone

Aunt Connie proceeded to awaken memories from an earlier time. She went on to share that Jimmy wore a kind heart on his sleeve but displayed a firmness of purpose when it came to protecting his family and friends. No one messed with the brothers and their buddies on Fifth Street.

If a picture could capture a thousand words, she would direct anyone in the restaurant that day to a photo of the boys in front of a Model T. They posed with their friends Anthony, aka Tony, and his brother Salvatore, aka Sal.

Her brother Jim brought laughter and song into the home on the Transfer Station. He carried his songbooks through the good times and those times that were challenging. Jimmy always managed to find a well-tuned piano.

He played on through the Roaring Twenties, the Great Depression, World War II, The Korean Conflict, and the Viet Nam War. She recalled how he thought that a well-rendered song would help to calm Thomas and Andrew Jackson in difficult times. Ditto for Harry S. Truman.

Oftentimes his brothers would join in to create an impromptu band. Of course, his sister would add her voice to many of the renditions.

Jimmy had his somber moments. When he returned from Okinawa, he brought home a golden pocket watch. Connie recognized it before he flipped open the gold thin-plated lid. It contained an endearing sentiment that she had inscribed for her fiancé just seven months prior to December 7, 1941, a year of reflection and retribution. The inscription read, *Love overcomes time.*

No words needed to be spoken. He just provided a much-needed Jimmy hug. She recalled the event for the benefit of family gathered at the reunion. Connie could share no more at that moment in time. She handed the microphone to Gennaro.

Her older brother captivated the family with stories from the very early days on Mulberry Street and the neighborhood in West Hoboken. Gennaro and Jimmy were inseparable. Another picture of the two before the other three arrived reinforced the story when it flashed up on the screen behind the head table.

Gennaro was the only sibling who could speak with some authority on the old country. He did and it was all captured on a video tape. It was a family treasure that might someday join the artifacts in the cloud. For now, only family members with access to a VCR or DVD player had access to those private reflections.

Charlene couldn't bring herself to address children and in-laws. She had given up everything and everyone she knew to follow Jimmy around the world. The people in this room were now her family. They expected that she would be the next to speak. The Transfer Station was now her home.

She was sure that her bittersweet thoughts were best left unspoken that evening. Her granddaughters sensed the pain, so they surrounded her with gentle hugs and took their turn at the front of the room. The second-born twin spoke first, then her twin sister, then the first-born daughter.

Their first recollections of Grandpa were formed in the little starter house in Canal Town. A screened-in porch was a perfect place to play and he loved to play. They never knew about his military service.

To them he was always Grandpa. Each girl took time to reflect on a special moment that he shared with just that one granddaughter. There were memories from the second house on Maple Avenue. In the pool behind that home, he taught them how to float on the water.

Other memories were formed when they lived in the Nutmeg State. He would spend hours with them on the Village Green of this eastern town. He shared stories about his visits to this town when the train still made a stop at the local station. Then the stories bubbled up about the really old days before he was even born.

Didn't they know that this place had a role to play in the Revolutionary War? Why, George Washington himself held camp just down the road under a still standing Oak Tree in the neighboring town of Sherman.

Jackson Badgenoone

When they entered high school years, his conversation became less informative and more instructive. "Don't accept a glass of wine on a date. The boy isn't thinking of Napa Valley or the Finger Lakes wine growing countryside. Humor your dad when he tells you stories about the past; most of his life is there. Hug your mother once in a while; you represent a large part of her life."

They left the stage and put their arms around Mimi. Then they planted a gentle kiss on their dad as he headed back toward the podium.

Trav approached the lectern and tried to wrap up this part of the evening. He went on to describe Jim's final days.

Sixty-two of his eighty-two years were spent in civilian life. Yet it was his twenty years in the army that placed punctuation marks on his time here on the planet.

In a Catholic hospital in Hoboken, Jimmy's bed was surrounded by flowers and cards wishing a speedy recovery. He knew that none was available after this most recent heart attack. He confided to his oldest son that he would welcome prayers to Saints Anna, Bernadette, and Christopher.

Nav reminded him of a story that Dad shared with him years ago. It was soon after the time when the banker received his draft notice. It was within a year following the attack on Pearl Harbor. At thirty-two years of age, he was pretty sure that he was too old to render any meaningful service in uniform.

He considered writing a letter to his Commander-in-Chief, Franklin Delano Roosevelt. It would warn FDR that drafting a guy that old might hurt the allied cause. He would also remind the president that a number of banks failed while he was their employee. Why risk losing the war?

Jimmy never sent the letter, but he told his son that if he had, it would have to be addressed to the head guy. Sending it anywhere else invited a miscommunication in the chain of command.

Just weeks before his final day, Nav reminded him of the letter. "Dad, there is no reason to go through the ranks. Talk with the head guy, His name is Jesus."

His dad already knew that; he just wanted to hear it from his son.

In the final week, Jimmy was sure that he heard the voice of two women. They were there to welcome him home. Bernadette and Jackson assured him that he was destined for a better place. Bbadgenoone directed him to page 9 in *Apples of Gold*. She listened to him read for the last time, "Where love is, there God is."

On his final day, Jimmy—son, brother, husband, father, grandfather, uncle, businessman, soldier, gardener, pianist, painter and wannabe marshal—folded his arms. With the most peaceful smile on his face, he went to meet his LORD and Father. Nav wanted his family to embrace the memory of his countenance.

There was no camera in the intensive care room. Trav pressed the slide projector button and an image of Jimmy taken just days before his passing appeared on the large screen behind the podium. He knew that he was Heaven bound.

He was laid to rest at a cemetery that was within view of his birthplace. His coffin was lowered into the ground, placed between the graves of two army privates. One had sacrificed his life in World War II, the other in the Korean Conflict.

They were not yet twenty years of age when they perished. The colonel chose his plot beforehand. It was his way of saying *thank you* to them for their sacrifice, and *thank you* to his God for the extra years granted to him.

His daughter continued to decorate Daddy's tombstone with flowers on the anniversary of his birthday every November and on Father's Day every June. She would also place a floral bouquet on the headstones to the left and right of his.

Jackson convened a second weekly meeting. She began the meeting with a roll call and a call to order. Anna, Bernadette, Christopher, Daniel, Elizabeth, Frederick, George, Henry, and Israel all responded here or present. Victoria and Victor joined them at the makeshift oval Roman amphitheater in the woods and signaled their attendance.

They put a strain on Jackson's span of control. She welcomed their presence nonetheless. At the appropriate time they would provide links to the early days of Jackson's observee.

Anna sought to be recognized. She wanted to formally applaud the chapter selections submitted by Bernadette. They seemed to have a tighter chronological flow than those rendered by Anna in the previous book.

Jackson interrupted her again. "Don't be too hard on yourself. Your observee shared many of his stories while he was under the influence of oxycodone prior to and following his surgery. We're thankful that you captured the relevant memories.

"We laughed when we read some of the chapters in your comprehensive work. His wish to have titanium bones mounted in cross swords manner over the den door after his demise was classic Trav. It even brought laughter to the nurses and staff at the rehabilitation center during the year of reflection and reconciliation."

Jackson Badgenoone then sought feedback from her colleagues. They agreed with Anna. Bernadette had presented a tighter verbal narration. They believed, moreover, that the selections drew interesting parallels between father and son when they were framed on the same canvas.

So much had happened on the world stage in the 106 years between 1908 and 2014. Through it all, Dad was always his hero. He taught the wannabe Cisco Kid to appreciate the characters in his life, real and imagined.

He encouraged Trav to chronicle his journey. Both men held various staff and line assignments, dad in the military and son in the corporate world. Dad assured Point Man that taking risk steepened the learning curve. He provided navigational tools that enabled KN to link the dates, years and events that set the stage of his life.

George Badgenoone ventured a comment. It seemed that Anna and Bernadette had bounced from one year to another and then back again. Jackson acknowledged his concern. "Years are artificial markers. The observers used them to anchor timeless events that ultimately radiate from 33 A.D. They exist for the benefit of the reader, not the observee."

Jackson acknowledged their critique and challenged each of them to step up their game. She reminded them that her role was that of general guide and mentor. A formal editor would be enlisted to help them to further craft their message. She kept the meeting in session so they could critique the next story in real time. She asked Christopher, aka Cbadgenoone, to share the story of Jimmy's wife.

[Book 6]

The High Water Markers of Christopher's Observee

By Christopher Badgenoone,
Copyright © 2015 by Jackson Badgenoone

Preface to The High Water Markers
of Christopher's Observee

Her first great-grandson was four years old in 2007. The little boy needed to find a way to differentiate between his two great-grandmothers. During some conversation, he had heard her referred to as NuNu. From then on, to him she was Grandma NuNu. The concept of Great-Grandma was too esoteric.

NuNu embraced the identity. It signaled a high water marker in her life. Not many of her siblings survived to see the generation beyond the next. She would actually live to see four more great-grandchildren.

Her three granddaughters had provided the next generation of two boys and three girls. Each one of them would follow the lead of the first-born great-grandson and call her NuNu. She was surrounded by them on the covered entrance to a house during a family reunion in 2014.

The first-born twin granddaughter managed to bring her branch of the next generation back to Hudson County. An aroma of brewed coffee and fresh-baked bread drifted from the kitchen and out onto the porch of her new home.

Her grandmother enjoyed the view, the progeny, and the memories. Sweet fragrance transported her back to a childhood when she was alternately referred to as Georgette and Charlene. Georgette recalled the day she left the school kitchen and entered her class at Chambery School in Brussels, Belgium.

These seven decades and six years later she would still have vivid recollections of cleaning the chalkboard with her friend, Marcel. After their task was complete, the nuns would reward them with hot coffee and fresh-baked bread. On rare occasions they would produce an orange or polished red apple.

Charlene would treasure the images with her eyes closed and her mind wide open. A photo collage of memories formed in her subconscious world.

It contained an image of the girls from Chambery in a religious procession, her mother, a walk with her husband on a Brussels street, her first-born son in front of the house on Transfer Station.

Seven years before the 2014 reunion, she had returned to Brussels with her oldest son. During that visit, she invited herself back into Chambery. The school was still standing but it was no longer a school just for girls. By 2007, it served a multinational coeducational clientele, many from Pacific Rim nations.

The journey in 2007 provided a wonderful opportunity to share the high water markers of her life. Her son had her undivided attention, and she had his. He was able to gain a different perspective on the same cities, villages, sites, and dwellings that he had visited with his wife and daughters two decades earlier.

This time NuNu, aka Georgette, aka Charlene, aka Mother, allowed him to see the tapestry through her eyes. She was fourteen years old when Germany invaded Poland in 1939. She began to frame the view through the lens of that year of reflection and reckoning. Her young eyes saw no discernible change in the streets of Brussels. School continued. People were still out and about.

Christopher added a color from his palette. In that same year in the United States, the Coca Cola Company printed an ad for their flagship product. It featured a picture of the World's Fair in New York City and another of the Golden Gate International Exposition. The tagline read "Drink Coca-Cola, Delicious and Refreshing, the drink everybody knows . . . from New York to San Francisco."

During the 2007 visit, Charlene shared a view from the vantage point provided by the highest window of the Atomium. She gazed down upon a platform of stairs where her sister, mother, and grandmother had posed for a photo taken at a time between the two world wars. The picture conveyed a sense of survival and determination. Those women were not going to let conflict dictate their lives.

Charlene's mother would nurture thirteen children to adulthood. The family would survive the depression and the war. They never lost touch with the little sister who moved an ocean away soon after she entered her third decade.

Jackson complimented Christopher for the thorough preface and promised to place his book in the publishing queue. The first six chapters contained a lot of happy moments. There were also way too many examples of society gone awry. Christopher Badgenoone appreciated the guidance, acknowledged his peers, and skipped to Chapter Seven.

CHAPTER VII
Print Shop Prelude

In post-war Belgium during the fall of 1945, Charlene found a way to earn a living as a typesetter in a local print shop. She recalled the moment less than a year later when a US Army captain came into the establishment to examine a printing job requisitioned by his unit.

She won his attention and his heart. Despite warnings about fraternization, they started to see each other on a regular basis. She introduced him to her mother and family. They enjoyed the sites and life that was reemerging from the years of conflict and rationing.

Within a year, they were married in a modest ceremony in Brussels. His friend stood in for best man Dominic, and her sister served as maid of honor. Soon after the wedding, duty called again, and they moved to Frankfurt, Germany. Their first son was born within a year of their arrival in the land of castles, counts, and dukes. Charlene sent the joyful news to her family in Belgium and to her husband's family on the other side of the pond.

A year later, at the time George Orwell was penning his iconic novel, Charlene was with child again. Her daughter joined the family soon after they made the trans-Atlantic voyage to the captain's new stateside assignment. She had a new home and family.

Her father-in-law and his family embraced the bride from northern Europe as one of their own. She added a unique French twist to the Italian dinners served every Sunday afternoon. Charlene had several high water markers by then: wife, mother, daughter-in-law, sister, chef.

Decades later, she thought about writing a book. Instead she tucked away the memories and photos. Then she read about others who experienced a similar journey. She began with *War Brides of WWII* and *Bittersweet Decision: The War Brides 40 years later*. Her library continued to expand well into 2014.

The most recent acquisition was a book with the title, *GI Brides: The Wartime Girls Who Crossed the Atlantic for Love*. She placed the books next to the instruction manual that the army gave to her when she made her first transatlantic voyage.

Jackson thought about her sister Sarah. No one had ever written a book about her journey. She was also multi-lingual and ready to adapt to a new continent. Maybe it was because her journey was carried on the sails of an eastern wind. Perhaps it had something to do with the fact that her husband was considered a mercenary.

Christopher Badgenoone gazed at Anna and Bernadette. He needed no urging from Jackson. He moved through the pages and picked up the story several chapters later. He skimmed through a number of them before relinquishing his role to writing confederate DBadgenoone later that day. For the moment, Christopher continued to read.

CHAPTER VIII

The World is a Big Round Sphere

The USS Mitchell had sounded her horn on that misty day in 1952. Charlene knew that they had to get to the ship soon in order to join her husband on the other side of the Pacific Ocean. Her oldest son was visibly shaken. He was sure that they were lost and wouldn't find the assigned pier. The young boy feared that he might never see his dad again.

She took a deep breath. Charlene recalled her previous Atlantic journey and the countless number of journeys across the continents. Mother held her hands together in a gesture suggesting a circle. Pointer finger met pointer finger, left thumb met right thumb.

You see, the world is like this—a very big circle, her gesture conveyed. *You can't really get lost. You may just take a while to get to where you need to be. We will get to the ship on time.*

James cherished that treasure. The memory came back to him on several occasions and proved instructive later in life, especially when he read *The World Is Flat* by Thomas L. Friedman.

He looked up at the Golden Gate Bridge, and then looked back at the city skyline. It would be just a while longer before he could see his dad again. In the meantime, Mother continued to provide a stream of wisdom with each passing day. She made sure that he knew the moment when the gulls no longer shadowed the ship.

She made him aware of the signal bells and then shared stories about her past. All this instruction and information was provided in broken English that was improving with every new jewel of wisdom. Without benefit of continued formal higher education, Charlene had mastered five languages.

Charlene and her husband communicated at first in Italian, the language of his parents. Charlene relied on her French at times. She interjected phrases from her knowledge of German, Flemish, and Spanish.

Little Belgium had been sometimes referred to as the Battlefield of Europe. Overrun and ruled by a number of nation states and empires, it emerged in the mid-nineteenth century as a constitutional monarchy. It was a country defined by language, religion, and tradition. Her language acquisition reflected the powers that overran her homeland.

By the end of that century, her king would gain control of the Congo Free State. He exacted treasure from the African nation at the point of a bayonet. His excess and the image of dead black Congolese babies caused an international uproar that forced a divesture. Samuel Langhorne Clemens added his voice to the crescendo.

The Belgian Congo was created in the same year that her future husband Jimmy was born. His son recalled the regalia of Belgian-Congolese troops marching through Brussels as a tribute to the mother country during a celebration for the 1958 World's Fair. A few years later they would march under their own flag.

Charlene was actually of Dutch decent. Her native language would have been Flemish. She grew up with the language of France because that was the prevailing tongue spoken in the capital city. She suspected that German blood also ran through her veins. A Conquistador might have contributed Spanish genes. Eventually convergent languages morphed into a Mediterranean Lingua Franca.

She had shared an ocean full of stories with her children by the time they arrived in Okinawa. Her husband greeted them with wide-open arms when they climbed down the gangplank. On assignment

Jackson Badgenoone

with her husband on that island, she managed to pick up survival Japanese. The children were exposed to a different culture.

Her husband sometimes affectionately referred to her as his *Chéri*. Regardless of the language spoken by the native people, Chéri was sure that they all shared common wants and needs. She brought home a postcard as a remembrance. It depicted ordinary people going about the work of the day.

They laughed and cried and loved. Sometimes they were taught to hate. Too many times their collective hate led to war. Like her husband, she hated war and the exploitation it harbored. It was all so senseless and counterproductive. She found a way to convey that disdain to her children in terms they could understand, delivered at a teachable moment.

One such moment was presented when her son spat at his sister during a sibling argument. Charlene didn't spank or scold. She reminded the young boy of a time when Jesus was brought before the elders.

Before they crucified Him, she told him, before they beat Him, they spat upon Him. Violence starts with a thought, then a gesture. It ultimately leads to death and way too often ends in war. Her son would likely have forgotten a swat. James never forgot the way she connected the dots. She continued to share pearls of wisdom.

Some of her friends had selective amnesia when it came to the abuses perpetrated in search for treasures hidden in Congolese minerals, trees, and elephant tusks. Chéri wasn't born when Leopold II sought wealth from rubber tree plants. She wanted to learn more and opened the pages of *King Leopold's Ghost*.

A decade after the formation of the Belgian Congo, little Belgium was on the receiving end of atrocities administered at the point of a Boche bayonet. Dead white Belgian babies produced an outcry from the civilized world that cascaded into powerful Allied propaganda.

She did consider the many contributions made by this little kingdom. She shared stories of the accomplishments and alliances that framed the story. Christopher penned chapters in the book dedicated to the Trade Guilds, famous painters, Belgian lace, Belgian chocolate, Belgian beer, and all things Belgian that influenced or were influenced by her family.

Charlene's favorite story was captured in a chapter that traced her family involvement with Father Damien. His mission was to care for poor souls warehoused at a leper colony in Hawaii. On her first trans-Pacific journey, she had made it a point to visit the tiny island of Molokai.

Jackson seized the opportunity to query her Badgenoone colleagues. Did they comprehend the influence that Charlene had on her son? Did they appreciate the impact of the lifestyle on the family?

Anna Badgenoone volunteered the first comment. "The whole world seemed to be in motion. Charlene exhibited some interesting parenting skills."

Bernadette commented that Chéri provided Jimmy with a soul mate who displayed wisdom and grace beyond her years and station.

Christopher inserted a side note and then picked up the story at chapter nine:

Decades after following her husband around the globe, she attended her granddaughter's college graduation ceremony in the Pacific Northwest. She sipped a morning Mimosa at a restaurant overlooking the Oregon coast and reflected that perhaps Jules Verne selected a suitable site for a utopian experience.

[Book 6]

CHAPTER IX

Champion for a Cause

In 1954, they settled into a new duty base in the desert sands of Yuma, Arizona. Barely a hint of her Belgian-French accent remained. She was the colonel's wife. She supported him with an English language presentation that could have been cultivated at any stateside institution of higher learning.

Charlene also learned how to master games of Bridge and Canasta. She hosted afternoon tea and attended the prescribed social functions.

During the third year of his assignment, the colonel had an opportunity to serve as military technical advisor to a Hollywood movie filmed in part at the base. He had a lifelong interest in filmmaking that began on the banks of the Hudson.

In her role as social hostess, Charlene helped to provide a welcoming environment to stars and cast alike. Her son's favorite movie hero assumed the lead role of that film. It satirized the life of a Hollywood version soldier. Charlene was rewarded with an autographed photo for her son James, the Traveler, aka Trav.

That treasure was framed and eventually added to another that found a place in the den overlooking Dutch Buffalo Creek. Years later, Trav admired the actor-comedian's sense of social purpose. He went on to host an annual telethon designed to help stricken children.

The entertainer would become a hero to a new generation. His signature comedic gestures could not conceal the fact that now he was a champion for their cause. There were so many high water markers for this kid from Newark, New Jersey.

These experiences were wonderful reflections of her husband's high water markers. She sought to define her own and signed up as a volunteer for the Red Cross. Within the year, she had organized relief efforts, streamlined operations, and established a mobile unit. She would become a lesser-known champion for others.

Her favorite picture of herself was one taken that same year. She was behind the wheel of a Red Cross station wagon en route to another mission. This was a high water marker uniquely her own. A picture of her in uniform with her Red Cross team also found a way into the den and then to Jackson's cloud.

Jackson spoke up. She had just completed reading Christopher's unabridged version of the story. There was remarkable similarity between the life of Charlene and Sarah, the sister of JBadgenoone. Both brides had followed a husband in uniform across the same ocean, albeit in a different direction. Jackson encouraged Christopher to resume reading at chapter eleven.

CHAPTER XI
Cascade, The War Bride Returns Home

She tried to absorb the consequence of his announcement in 1958. Her husband had just confided his recent orders: He was headed for Korea. Even though a truce was still in effect, she knew that the peninsula was not a safe place for her family.

They could anticipate a four-year separation, the longest in their marriage. It would come at a time when she and the children needed him at home more than ever. She knew that military families faced stress points unimagined by many of their civilian counterparts, but Charlene was going to figure out a way to make this work.

The summer months were going to present the greatest challenge to her sanity. School provided some structure for her children from September through June. She had to come up with a plan for July and August of the first two years.

Her Belgian family invited her to return to Brussels. The World's Fair of 1958 would be hosted on ground not far removed from her childhood home. The first summer was all but signed, sealed, and delivered.

Eleven years earlier, she had crossed the Atlantic in a single-stack troop transport ship. The voyage took days at sea. Now they would cross in an airliner that would measure the trip in hours. She mapped out the itinerary. The first month would be a Belgian holiday. There would be time to visit the Fair. Most of the first few weeks would be shared with relatives in Brussels.

Beyond Brussels was a country rich with history, art, literature, and tradition. At least one or two castles were on the schedule. Visits to the countryside provided a glimpse into a bucolic past with scenery unchanged by time.

Only in her mid-thirties, she was now tour guide and sole protectress to three young children. The first significant challenge came during a visit to a local stream. Her nephew had invited her children to raft the waterway.

Against her better judgment, she agreed to allow Trav and his sister to join Mark and his friend. There was no way that she would allow John to enter into one of those rubber rafts. He was just too young.

Mark assured Tante Charlene that her children would be safe with him and his friend. Charles was a direct descendant of one of the Mohawk Indians who managed the headwaters of the Nile for the British during the last century.

She watched two of her children descend the cliff face to the water. It seemed tranquil enough at the spot where they climbed into the flimsy rafts. She watched as Charles and Trav moved toward the center of the stream. His sister and Mark were close behind.

Charlene and John walked along the ridge and followed their downstream progress. Within the space of a few meters, rapids marked a pickup in the speed of their adventure. She stopped at a clearing and began to scream to her nephew. *Cascade! Waterfall!*

Mark couldn't hear her voice. The rapids had grown too swift and the sound of the rushing water all but drowned out any other sound. Charlene held John tight to her chest and cried when she saw both rafts slip out of sight.

She made her way down to the water's edge and followed a path to the lee side of the falls. Her children were sitting on the bank. Mark and Charles were securing the rafts.

Charlene couldn't believe her eyes. Maybe God had crushed the rocks that would have torn apart the little rubber boats.

Jackson Badgenoone

Charles could sense her concern. He pointed to a spillway on the side of the waterfall. He knew that it was there and had navigated the rafts over the smooth concrete bypass. She thanked Charles for his skill and then turned to scold her nephew for putting her through this ordeal.

By nightfall it was all behind them. They were back in the city and preparing for a different kind of adventure on the following day.

The air was cool. Their bags were packed. They were going to leave the little kingdom and head south. Her children had other genetic roots in Italy. She had promised her husband's family that they would find a way to spend time with them before returning to the States.

They boarded the train at the Midi Station and waved goodbye to their Belgian family. They were headed to Rome and from there to Naples, Italy. After the children went down for a nap she closed her eyes.

Moments later, her mind reflected on a photo collage from her childhood years. It contained images of her family at the beach, her mother, siblings, and friends. Another collage captured reminders from the last time she was on the continent. A photo of her brother in his police band uniform brought his music to life for a brief moment in time.

Then an image of Jimmy and Chéri clad in kimono garb was imprinted into her mind. So much had filled her life in the five years since that picture was taken at the Tea House of the August Moon.

The christening of her second son flashed before her eyes. Two years later, he was captured on film as he reached for a brownie in his father's outstretched hand. That image revealed a hibachi stove. It originated in the jungle of Okinawa and survived the desert sands of Yuma.

Within a moment, another image of her with his children raced before her mind. They were on a visit with friends in Mexico. It was a comfortable car ride away from his duty base in Yuma. Memories pierced her mind in pendulum motion. No neat chronology comforted her on this train trip.

The intervening years melted away like the ice in her drink. There was no husband, no children, no Transfer Station. The last time she rode these rails she was a teenager on the way to Paris with her Chambery friend Marcel. Her dream transported her back to that train ride almost two decades before the trip to Tijuana. It was such a different world in the summer of 1939.

A young man, perhaps in his late teens or early twenties, sat in the bench facing her chair. His Wehrmacht uniform was impeccably pressed. She noticed the dark green collar, black shoulder-straps and the Wehrmachtsadler insignia just above his right pocket.

Uncomfortable about an awkward moment of eye contact, she brought her gaze back to the work. She resumed reading the book *The Begum's Fortune* at page 95:

> "I must say that I don't quite believe in this conquest!"
>
> "What conquest?"
>
> "The conquest of the world by the Germans."

He took some interest in the young girl and was curious about the book in her lap. The soldier interrupted her reading. "Young lady, certainly you are aware that the book you're reading is subversive. Your French author had a distorted view of the Franco Prussian War and the relative stature of his people. Please understand that I have no personal grudge with the author. I enjoy his science fiction novels. But the work in your hands is too political in overtone. I suggest that you dispose of it before the train arrives in Paris."

She replied, "I am not French, I am Belgian."

His response was curt. "Of what consequence is that to me? Your country was a contrivance of nobility in the last century. You are probably Dutch or Spanish for all I know."

Georgette, aka Charlene, looked beyond his uniform and studied his face. "Your hair is blond and your eyes are blue, but your cheekbones don't resemble Teutonic man. For all I know, you are the descendent of Genghis Kahn or an American Indian. Your country wasn't unified until well after my king assumed his throne."

Their conversation came to an abrupt end. He left the compartment. The two girls wondered if German soldiers would take over all of Europe some day. The encounter was unsettling but they put it behind them and watched the countryside unfold on the other side of the window. It was July, and all of Europe was green and alive with flowers of every color.

The years seemed to race along with every mile of track. The seconds were measured by a thousand wooden railroad ties.

Startled by the shrill sound of the train whistle and a sudden lurch on the rails, she opened her eyes. Sweat beaded on her brow. Her children, leaning on each other, were sound asleep. Her first response was *danke*, then *merci*, then *thank you, Lord*.

Christopher noticed Jackson's telling nod. He would save the remainder of this chapter and the next few chapters for a more comprehensive read of her story.

CHAPTER XV

Just an Hour Away from an Open Lock

Charlene understood the demands of travel and relocation that were sometimes required during the path of a career. She had hoped that her son might have found employment somewhere in the metro New York area.

His new home was just a one hour plane ride away. A car could get her there in six hours, a train in just under eight. Once her grandchildren arrived, she found a way to visit on a regular basis.

On the first trip after the birth of her first granddaughter in 1974, a year of reflection and political drama, she rode the rails with her husband. The train received new passengers in Albany. More people got on and off at Utica and Syracuse. There was no stop at Canal Town. The train rolled right by the little village. They stepped onto the platform in Rochester, New York.

Her brother-in-law, Gennaro, greeted them at the station. Gerry had moved to the Flower City just before World War II. He still managed to return to the Transfer Station and the Big Apple each year for the feast of his patron saint.

Gerry drove, and his wife rode shotgun. Jimmy and Chéri made themselves comfortable in the back seat of the car. Within forty-five minutes, they passed by the open canal lock then arrived at a corner with four churches. They followed Trav's directions and made a right at the traffic light at that intersection.

Jimmy held the line map and called out directions. "Go past the elementary school on the left, and proceed three blocks. Make a right at the senator's house. Go past the county fairgrounds. If you get to the middle school, then you've gone too far."

They pulled into the driveway. Trav, Mimi, and their little brown-eyed girl met them at the front door. This represented a major high water marker in their lives.

Charlene's son, James, was a dad. Her daughter-in-law was a mom. She and Jim would now be identified as Grandma and Grandpa.

Less than two years later, Mimi gave her two more granddaughters—twins. This time she grabbed a flight. She hoped to spend at least a few weeks providing whatever help she could. Her husband arranged for a leave from his post-retirement civilian job. He would take the train to join them the following month.

During the next few years the visits continued. They were joined by Gerry, his wife, and children. The little starter house seemed to burst at the seams with family and friends. Only a handful of memories were captured on film.

One photo captured Jimmy on the porch surrounded by the girls. Another caught Gerry and Jim asleep on the couch after a busy day. A third found Grandma playing with her granddaughters. Cbadgenoone skipped ahead and continued to read at the twenty-first chapter.

CHAPTER XXI

Thimbles for NuNu

Her husband passed and her children had grown to embrace lives of their own. She returned to the same house on the Transfer Station. Her father-in-law was gone and the neighborhood had changed.

One overcast day, she found new purpose in *Apples of Gold*, a book given to her by her son a few years earlier. On page 59 she read, "Life is not a wick or the candle—it is the burning." That was all that she needed to read at that moment.

She refused to lead a sedentary life in retirement. In her seventh decade, she had assumed a role as nanny to two young children in the neighboring town. This was not just another job. Charlene developed a fond attachment to the parents and their offspring. She saw them grow from young children to Ivy League-educated adults. They were the first to refer to her as *NuNu*.

The family shared a love of travel and desire to meet new people from around the globe. Whenever they visited a new land, they remembered to send her a post card or letter. The boy took it a step further. He knew that NuNu liked to collect thimbles. He sent to her a thimble from every town or city that he visited. The thimble collection was framed. In 2007, she placed it on the fireplace mantle in her living room. Nav took a picture of that treasure with his digital camera and added it to his collection of memorable photos.

Charlene had accumulated other treasures during the course of her own travel: A Hibachi stove from Okinawa was converted into a magazine rack; a WWI artillery shell casing from Ypres served as an umbrella stand near her front door; a piece of Arizona driftwood was modified to accept a light bulb and lamp shade.

The artifacts were a constant reminder of the years that had slipped through her fingers. A butter dish from Belgium, a cuckoo clock from Germany, and a painting of the Last Supper populated her memories. She promised to find a way to live in the present.

She was challenged again by *Apples of Gold*. On page 39 she read, "A good memory is fine, but the ability to forget is the true test of greatness." She had seen so much in her life; now she yearned for a way to recall and share only the good times for the loved ones who still remained.

Jackson intervened for the benefit of the other badgenoone colleagues: "Christopher managed to capture the good times in these few chapters. His comprehensive work pulls no punches when it delivers on the hardships encountered by this young lady and her generation."

CHAPTER XXV

Quotes of the Day

On her eighty-fifth birthday, at Christopher's urging, Charlene decided to establish an email account. Physical travel was problematic. She wanted to stay in touch with her family and friends now located around the globe.

James, the Knowledge Navigator, aka Nav, helped to connect her computer to the Internet. He taught her the basics for setting up an online identity. To encourage her to practice newly-acquired skills, he sent to her each day a new quote. He sourced the quotes from a number of sites, most often Inspiration Today, Christian Quotes, and Goodreads.

Nav copied his wife, siblings, children, and occasionally Jackson on each quote. Greater satisfaction came from NuNu's email responses. She was the remaining survivor of her generation in his family. Her recollections were not tarnished by the dusty lens of history.

Charlene established a somewhat predictable routine in her golden years. Part of the routine included time spent at the computer in her den. She sometimes talked to herself as she typed email responses one finger at a time. Other voices also talked to her in the sanctuary of that room. She recognized a male named Christopher and a female named Jackson.

Jackson paused to consider letters penned before the advent of digital communications. Although asynchronous, they usually engendered at least a courtesy reply within a respectable amount of time. The Apostle Paul shared his story of faith in part by epistles written to contemporaries throughout the Empire.

Paul didn't expect to hear from them in any short order. He had, after all, also written the letters for future generations. A reply or "reply all" wasn't part of his mission. His task was to bear witness to the central figure in his life, Jesus Christ.

Jackson was reasonably certain that the wisdom contained in passages to and from NuNu could provide insight for all of them. By the time she approached her ninetieth year, they had saved nearly 400 verbal jewels in their literary treasure house.

Her children and grandchildren were more likely to connect in a synchronous environment. They preferred FaceTime and Facebook. NuNu wasn't ready to make that next leap. She would much rather pick up the phone or see them in person. Nav was thankful for recorded memories.

Christopher encouraged Jackson to include some of the emails in the appendix to her book. Jackson replied that she would make them available in an heirloom edition of the work available to family and friends.

The other Badgenoone colleagues remained silent. Hearing no objections, Jackson concluded the meeting. She asked Daniel to share the story of his observee on the following day. Destiny would bring Charlene and Mary together in due time. Mary also provided a unique link to a golden artifact that would bind the entire tribe.

[Book 7]

The High Water Markers
of Daniel's Observee

By Daniel Badgenoone,
Copyright © 2015 by Jackson Badgenoone

[Book 7]

CHAPTER I

Streets Paved With Gold

Her first great-grandson was four years old in 2007. He needed to find a way to differentiate between his two great-grandmothers. His maternal great aunt provided an easy solution to help describe her mother. She knew that the name "Great-grandma" might be a challenge for a boy his age. Mary could be identified as GG, short for great-grandma. For the purpose of written confirmation, she modified the nickname to GiGi—a name the boy embraced.

GiGi was born in New York City in 1920, a year of reflection and style. Her mother, Annie, traveled the corridors of Ellis Island a few years earlier because she had been told that the streets in America were paved with gold. She was all of sixteen years old when she and her sister made their way to the new world.

Mimi remembered the time when Grandma Annie held her in her arms. Anna McTigue brought a zest for life. Several of her notable Irish sayings survived in family lore. Mimi recalled her favorite: "Tell the truth and shame the devil." "Jesus, Mary, and Joseph!" usually began any sentence of consequence.

Mary's mother married a tall and handsome son of Ireland. It wasn't many years after their marriage that Peter joined the Fighting 69th and donned the uniform of a US soldier. Annie posed for a picture with her young soldier.

A few months later, with campaign hat, rifle, and bayonet, he joined the American Expeditionary Force. He deployed to a Europe that he thought he'd left behind.

He returned from France following the Great War. He seldom spoke of the conflict but did savor memories of the men he had met "over there." His new best friend was an English soldier who shared a remarkable story about his first year in combat.

The soldier recalled a moment following an undeclared Christmas Eve truce. The year was 1914, a year of reflection and lost innocence. Germans called the truce *Weihnachtsfrieden*. The French remembered it as *Trêve de Noël*. All along the line, the guns fell silent. The voice of a soldier, then several more joined in a refrain of "Silent Night". Each rendered the lyrics in his respective native tongue.

Truce prompted a handshake, hugs, and an exchange of gifts between soldiers on the front line. Politicians and generals were caught unaware but could do little to stop the cessation of hostilities. Their troops had enough dying and killing for now.

One German soldier traded a gold ring for a British tea tin. GiGi's father met the British recipient and offered a bronze miniature of the Statue of Liberty and a Morgan Silver Dollar for the band. The ring of gold would return with him to America. To help celebrate her First Communion, he made it a present to his daughter, Mary, seven years after he returned home from WWI.

Mary treasured the ring. Her father provided the story behind the gold as it was told to him by an English soldier. Apparently the ring had originated in Germany, found a path to the British colony of Georgia, and returned back to Germany. It accumulated more than a century of memories in the old country before being traded back to a British soldier, and then to his American comrade-in-arms.

She tucked away the ring and went about the joys of childhood. Jersey City provided a melting pot of nationalities, languages, and religions. Her friends were Irish-Catholic. Mary spent countless hours listening to stories of the old country of her parents, told as only they could.

That country seemed at times to be at conflict with itself. Catholic and Protestant claimed different stakes in the race for heaven. Nearly eight decades before Mary joined the planet, a potato famine drove Irish sons and daughters to former British colonies on a continent west of the Emerald Isle. In 1862, many of the boys took up arms in defense of the American Union cause.

Others carried bayonets in defense of the southern Confederacy. Years later, Mary's son-in-law, Nav, and her granddaughter reflected on how both sides faced each other in the quiet Virginia town of Fredericksburg.

Nav was proud to attend his daughter's college freshman orientation ceremony in 1993, a year of reflection and consolidation. Following the convocation, they left the campus and took time to pause at the sunken road in front of Marye's Heights.

So many young men gave their lives during that battle in 1862. One outfit of Irishmen received a fitting tribute following the conflict. They were thenceforth known as the Fighting 69th, the forerunner of the same unit that Peter joined years later during WWI.

When the kids were uncharacteristically unruly, GiGi's mother threatened to leave them all and move to Boston. She was sure the streets up there were paved with gold since she hadn't found any evidence of golden streets in Jersey City.

[The Neverborn, Daniel—sometimes identified as Danny (aka DBadgenoone)—captured moments in time for GiGi as she matured into a young woman. He passed them along to Jackson for placement in the appropriate section of her cloud and advanced a few chapters into the book.

Jackson convened a third weekly meeting. She began the meeting with a roll call and a call to order. Anna, Bernadette, Christopher, Daniel, Elizabeth, Frederick, George, Henry, and Israel all responded "here" or "present." Victoria and Victor didn't attend this time. Their participation would not be required. There would be few if any eighteenth and nineteenth-century references in the subsequent chapters.

JBadgenoone provided additional instruction to Daniel and the five Badgenoone counterparts still waiting to share the story of their observee.

"You will have a better view of the future as you get closer to the present day," said Jackson, quoting Ovid to reinforce her point: "Let others praise ancient times; I am glad I was born in these." She reminded them to focus on the current era.

Elizabeth Badgenoone was the first to speak. She had compared notes with Danny and Christopher prior to the meeting. She was amazed at the similarities between Mary and Charlene. Bernadette and Elizabeth agreed that Jimmy and Fred also shared much in common.

Fred and Mary, Jimmy and Charlene established a genetic and spiritual link for the next generation. Each of them harbored an appreciation for the ancient times but saw the world through the eyes of unborn generations.

Jackson challenged Daniel to tighten the links to the earlier stories and prepare readers for those stories still to be shared. She gave him permission to push to the fringe of content boundaries intended to protect the grandchildren. She encouraged her colleagues to take notes as Daniel continued to read in chapter five.]

CHAPTER V

A Small Price to Pay

Mary's brother had a best friend who lit up every room that he entered. Only eighteen years old when they met, Fred commanded attention and respect from those who entered his circle of influence.

Her brother introduced them to each other at a family get-together. If there is such a thing as love at first sight, they were living testimony. They became inseparable. Movies, walks in the park, dances, and sometimes just quiet time filled their days.

They appreciated each other and the simple things that life had to offer to first-generation Americans growing up during the Great Depression. They believed in a future presented at the World's Fair they visited in Long Island during the year that Germany invaded Poland.

Mary and Fred continued to live their lives, but like so many Americans in their generation, they had to come to grips with events overseas. After a respectable courtship, they married, just a month before the attack on Pearl Harbor.

Everyone could remember where they were on that day. She and Fred were at a soda fountain in a local drug store. The radio announcer interrupted his broadcast to announce the news.

Soon after the wedding, Fred enlisted in the Army Air Corps. Following training, he went on to distinguished service as a B24 liberator bomber pilot serving in the Eighth Air Force. His plane dropped bombs over Nazi-controlled Germany, and some on the towns and villages of his distant cousins.

One narrowly missed the home of descendants of Joseph and Sarah. The blast was close enough to dislodge a British tea tin from the fireplace mantle. (Their son had brought that home from the previous war. His parents, at first, had been taken aback by what they thought was an uneven trade. Then they realized that a ring of gold was a small price to pay for a moment of peace.)

Mary wrote a stream of letters to Fred. They were addressed to his training base in Albuquerque, New Mexico and his operational base in Newburg, New York. Then the mail went to England. Most of the letters were saved. Some of them found a place in the den of her daughter's home overlooking Dutch Buffalo Creek.

The letters conveyed an incredible measure of optimism. They spoke to life after the war, to a time when they would build a family. Their first daughter entered the correspondence while Fred was still in uniform in 1944.

Prior to his discharge from military service, he returned home in time to celebrate the first birthday of his first-born daughter. Two years after the photo was taken, a second girl joined the family. Two Neverborn souls and three sons followed the girls into the expanding family.

Mary relinquished her war-time job soon after Fred returned to the States. He traded in his khaki military uniform and wings for the blue uniform and shield of a policeman. In the years immediately following the war, Fred and Mary and their two daughters established a home in the Greenville section of town.

DBadgenoone dedicated five chapters to the struggling years. Too many people exited the stage in that time. Several Neverborn were formed. Mary's world changed in unexpected ways.

Daniel agreed to save those memories for his complete work. He continued to steer the reading at the eleventh chapter.

CHAPTER XI

Less Fortunate Women

Mary supported Fred as he progressed through the police ranks as patrolman, sergeant, lieutenant, captain, deputy chief, and director. They all represented significant high water markers for her husband.

She was somewhat taken aback when he came home one day in full riot gear. The streets of neighboring Newark, New Jersey were aflame. Tanks and National Guard troops tried to restore order in a city torn apart by racial conflict.

The mayor of Jersey City was not going to permit that to happen in his town. He ordered his police department to address rioting with a disciplined show of force. There was no rioting or looting. No shots were fired and no one died. Black lives mattered. White lives mattered.

Mary recalled an earlier time. Her husband was a young patrolman and so proud to have saved the life of a baby girl. Blue lives mattered too. The public seldom heard about that kind of story. Maybe the good news stories needed to be shared in the community and schools.

Mary supported public education but wanted her children to appreciate the tenets of Catholicism. She encouraged them to attend parochial elementary and high schools. She instilled in them a respect for all people, a love of God and country.

Her daughters remembered how she would reinforce the lessons learned at school. Mary had also attended a Catholic elementary school in Jersey City and then a Catholic high school in the neighboring municipality.

She was constantly reminded by the nuns to appreciate her many blessings. They also encouraged her to overcome the "Jersey City accent". She passed on that wisdom to her children. "Jesus, Mary, and Joseph, don't say *get otta here*."

The children didn't think of her as the director's wife any more than they thought of themselves as children of the policeman. To them she was Mom. Years later they carried her memory, the smile, the encouragement, the laugh, the sigh.

She was proud of her husband's achievements. Through his position, she was able to meet and greet notable people who passed through the city. On one occasion, her husband was assigned to protective duty for the former Governor of Georgia. Mary had an opportunity to meet with him and the first lady of the land that same day.

Mary encouraged her children to respect all people regardless of rank or circumstance. She had met with political leaders, entertainers, corporate heads and academicians. Mary also encountered the poor and not-so-fortunate citizens of Hudson County.

Her high water markers up to that time included wife and mother. She had also carved out a part-time career at the admissions office of a local college. When Fred was promoted to director, Mary expanded her participation in local charity work. She had a special concern for young unwed mothers. One young woman bore a striking resemblance to the aunt who crossed the Atlantic with Mary's mom.

DBadgenoone advanced the reading selection once again.

CHAPTER XV

M&Ms, This One's for You

Mary brought five children to term, two girls and three boys. She named the last born after her husband Fred. They called the baby boy Freddie, a name that stuck with him well past boyhood. Only a few people ever called his father Freddie.

The younger Freddie was the antithesis of his father. Both enjoyed music, but the younger Freddie loved music. His favorite entertainers were Carol Channing and Barry Manilow. His favorite Broadway play and film was *Oklahoma*. His favorite snack was M&Ms. Mary always made sure that there was an ample supply of the multi-colored candy available whenever he came home to visit.

Mary and Fred were visiting with family in New Jersey when they got the call in the dead of winter. The doctor on the other end of the line was calm, his voice direct and to the point. "Your son is not doing well. We don't expect him to live for more than a few weeks."

This wasn't totally unexpected news. Freddie was only thirty-six years old but had been battling with a life-threatening disease for several years. An image of her with young Freddie and his siblings flashed before her eyes.

It wasn't supposed to be this way. Your children don't enter Paradise before you.

The next day, they boarded a plane at the Newark airport. She stared out the window and watched the New York City skyline disappear beneath the clouds.

She remembered how young Freddie bragged about his first real job as a tour guide for the then recently-opened World Trade Center. He seemed to have a plausible answer to every question that rolled off the lips and tongues of visiting tourists.

The job that changed his life began with an interview just north of the twin towers. It was held at the Pan Am building in midtown Manhattan. That building rose in the air rights over the Grand Central Terminal on 45th Street and Park Avenue. She thought of it as progress at the time; the railroads had seen their high water marker.

Now, for any distance greater than two hundred miles, people would travel by airplane. Certainly the rails weren't going to conquer the oceans, not in her lifetime. She held her husband's hand as she watched the landmarks slip from view.

When they reached cruising altitude, a young flight attendant approached her aisle with a beverage cart. For a brief moment she thought it was her Freddie. Then she realized that this was a different airline. Freddie would never offer coffee or tea to another passenger.

She closed her eyes and drifted through a thousand memories of her little boy. It was just yesterday when he was awarded a baccalaureate degree. It seemed like the day before then that he had graduated from high school.

[Jackson Badgenoone saw the picture. It reaffirmed her conviction. The photo captured an exact likeness of the first-born son of Jackson's sister Sarah and her husband Joseph. Coincidently they had named him Frederick in honor of Joseph's best friend who remained to farm land in Mecklenburg County.

Frederick Badgenoone interrupted Jackson. "So many are named Frederick or Fred. Was my identity also tied to a soul who lived before I was Neverborn?"

Jackson nodded.]

Mary remembered the time he'd stood proudly with his older brothers and another time with his dad. Fred gently nudged his wife, telling her, "It's okay to unfasten your seatbelt now."

Her memories drifted away with the clouds. Later in the flight she looked out the window. The tapestry of a sprawling Los Angeles framed the blue Pacific.

Freddie's friend met them at baggage claim and drove them to his house. Her son seemed to be doing better than she had hoped for when she first got the call from the doctor. He was sitting upright and playing with his dog, Vanna. Mary placed her hands on his shoulders and smiled as her husband snapped a photo at that moment in time.

The rally was short-lived. That evening, Freddie knew that he needed to return to the hospital. Within a week he was gone. He had just celebrated his thirty-seventh birthday.

The plane trip back to Florida was the longest in her life. She had always thought of her Freddie as so much more than a high water marker of her role as mother.

On the return flight, she savored a memory of her son with his twin nieces. She recalled the time when Freddie posed with his extended family. His father, Fred, was surrounded by his five children, a daughter-in-law, two sons-in-law, three granddaughters, and his Mary. Within the space of the next three years, two of the men in that photo would no longer sing their song with the living.

She would go on for those who remained. She would always keep a bag of M&Ms in the pantry, ready to welcome everyone into her Bradenton home.

They were greeted by dear friends at the Tampa airport. The ride back to Manatee County gave her an opportunity to share the high water markers of her son's life. Some had been totally unnoticed. She celebrated his first smile in the moments following the removal of dental braces. She remembered the first note that he played on his new string guitar.

When they got back to the condominium, she pored over the boxes of Freddie's memorabilia. He had sent those to her when he

Jackson Badgenoone

was certain that his time was nearing an end. They contained his high school diploma and college degree.

There were letters of commendation from his employers. Albums contained photos and letters from his friends who drew life all around the globe. There seemed to be a recurring theme in every correspondence: Freddie brightened their world.

One box was filled with his record albums. Freddie was particularly fond of musicals. Songs from *My Fair Lady, Man of la Mancha, Fiddler on the Roof, King And I, Annie,* and *Jesus Christ Superstar* now filled her hours.

She spent the better part of the following months also listening to songs from his favorite recording artists. Johnny Mathis belted out *"Up, Up and Away."* She could imagine her Freddie singing that whenever he heard "wheels up."

Peter, Paul, and Mary declared that they were leaving on a jet plane and that they didn't know when they'd be back again. It seemed to echo Freddie's new lifestyle.

Neil Diamond described a man torn between two shores. That sounded a lot like her son's life, especially after he was told he would be flying out of LAX.

Mary couldn't absorb the words as she listened to Michael Jackson's *"Thriller."* She tried to imagine what thoughts entered Freddie's mind the last time he heard that song. JBadgenoone was listening in the room with him that night.

Barry Manilow sang *"This One's For You."* When she took the record out of the sleeve, a note fell to the table. It was from Freddie, addressed to Mom. It reiterated the title on the cover, "This one's for you." Freddie's music brightened her world.

She kept his memory alive with the formation of a special quilt that she crafted in the following years. Daniel whispered to her as she brought the patterns together each evening. She acknowledged his presence with the final stitch.

Daniel passed over some very difficult chapters and resumed reading at the twenty-fourth.

CHAPTER XXIV

Treasure Every Canvas

The beach town of Bradenton, Florida was a world removed from the streets of Jersey City. Fred and Mary joined a number of their senior citizen friends in a retirement community that provided a slower yet active pace of life.

She watched her oldest son with his boys, her grandsons. They appreciated the gulls rising from the blue waters of the Gulf of Mexico. She savored memories of her time on the beach with her husband and granddaughters.

Mary joined several clubs, travelled with her "girl" friends, and shopped the local malls with her oldest daughter. Her youngest daughter would visit at least twice a year, usually with three daughters of her own in tow.

Mary's first son gave her two grandsons. Her second son added another granddaughter and a grandson to the clan. All the grandchildren called her Grandma. To the great-grandchildren she was GiGi.

It was in Bradenton that Mary expanded her outreach to young women not as fortunate as her daughters or granddaughters. She spent increasing hours at a local shelter, rendering her resources, time, and talent to encourage those adopted daughters. One young Cherokee girl had recently arrived from Oklahoma by way of the state of Georgia. She immediately captured Mary's heart.

Mary shared with her a favorite quote found on page 20 of *Apples of Gold*, a book that was given to her as a gift by her son-in-law, James. "One of the great arts of living is the art of forgetting."

In her seventh decade, Mary rekindled her love of art. GiGi was just a young girl when she first experimented with watercolors, pencil, and ink drawings. Now she had the time to enroll in a course that could help her to explore new mediums.

She joined a class that helped her to render a number of paintings in oil and acrylic. They captured images of native Florida plants, birds, and wildlife. Through her paintings, she helped the next generation to appreciate the beauty that surrounded them. Some of her offspring and the girls at the shelter picked up brush and canvas.

Mary also learned to craft ceramic figures. Some featured the same subjects that graced her canvases. Within a few years, those vases, statues, lamps and other artifacts found their way into the homes of her children and grandchildren. A few were donated to the shelter. Mary left a part of herself with people who loved and admired her.

[Jackson convened a fourth weekly meeting. She began the meeting with a roll call and a call to order. Anna, Bernadette, Christopher, Daniel, Elizabeth, Frederick, George, Henry, and Israel all responded *here* or *present*.

JBadgenoone had special instruction for Elizabeth: "Bernadette, Christopher, and Daniel have set the stage for this generation of the tribe. Elizabeth, you will be responsible for observing the life of a man named Fred. He brought closure to this collection of souls. Your reading will become the main agenda point of the next meeting. Please continue. I promised Anna that I would try to refrain from interruptions."]

Preface to The High Water Markers
of Elizabeth's Observee

The husband of his first granddaughter had an opportunity to meet her grandfather soon after Mary had passed in 2007. He was in an assisted living center by then but was giving orders to the staff assigned to provide his care.

He recalled that Fred had a force about him. His granddaughter knew that from the many stories her mother had shared about the kid from Jersey City. He wasn't always in charge, but he always provided leadership, even in his youth.

His grandfather was born in Germany and migrated to America months before Europe was consumed in the Great War. He was old enough to avoid service in a military that would aim guns at his homeland. His son, Charles, was too young to serve in the military of his adopted country. The war went on without him.

Elizabeth, aka EBadgenoone, observed the life of Charles. She was there when he took a bride and began a family of his own. Fred, their first child, arrived just two years following the end of the global conflict.

The time and place of birth sometimes guides the course of a life. Fred entered the world in 1920 at the start of a roaring decade. Before he reached his tenth birthday the bubble had burst.

His father, Charlie, was a victim of the Great Depression that followed. Before he was yet a teen, young Fred was obliged to deliver ice from a horse-drawn wagon in order to supplement the family income. Over time, an ice truck replaced the wagon.

His mother worked on occasion as a waitress to add precious dollars to support her children. Charlie was increasingly absent as he sought employment near and far. As the oldest son, Fred assumed a father-like status to his siblings during the times Father was absent. He had a profound effect on everyone around him. The following chapters describe his impact.

[EBadgenoone sailed by the first eleven chapters. There were just too many hardships. She was sure that Jackson would want her to place a stake in the ground where Fred's life took a giant step in the right direction. Jackson held to her earlier promise; she didn't interrupt. "Render the story at your own pace," she said. "We're all paying attention."]

CHAPTER XII

A Year of Reckoning

His best friend introduced him to the most beautiful girl in town. They began their courtship in 1939. Their dates were Spartan: a paddle boat at Hudson County Park, a trolley ride, picking flowers in a local garden. They would on occasion marshal resources to take in a movie; there were so many good films that year:

Gone with the Wind, Goodbye Mr. Chips, Love Affair, Mr. Smith Goes to Washington, Of Mice and Men, Stagecoach, The Wizard of Oz and *Wuthering Heights* all leapt from the big screen of their youth.

They held hands in the movie show when all the lights were low. They snacked on popcorn, sipped a Coke, and enjoyed every scene. They alternated between The Stanley and The State. On occasion they would visit the Loews, another theater around the corner.

All three were located at the Journal Square. After each show, they queried each other about their favorite characters and whether or not they could see themselves cast in one role or another.

The final days of the Civil War were dramatically portrayed in the Academy Award winner for best motion picture. Fred couldn't relate to Rhett Butler, and Mary was a world removed from Scarlett O'Hara. Fred was sure that he was Ashley Wilkes and Mary was Melanie Hamilton.

They thoroughly enjoyed watching *Goodbye Mr. Chips.* They were intrigued by a scene where Mr. Chips takes Katherine's advice and experiments with a Latin pun in his class about the *Lex Canuleia*, a law that allowed patricians to marry plebians.

Stagecoach was pure entertainment. The panoramic western vistas mesmerized them every bit as much as the acting and plot. Mary kept a box of tissues close at hand when they went to see *Love Affair*. She brought out another box for the remake a decade and change in the future.

Mr. Smith went to Washington but his roots were planted on Main Street. Mary was sure that her Fred would have been as noble. Fred was sure that his Mary would have supported him, a Clarissa Saunders rooting for the right side of history.

As they left the movie house, other patrons joined them in an impromptu rendition of "Somewhere Over the Rainbow." *The Wizard of Oz* provided a compelling story about home, hearth, and priorities. Annie would have loved the Yellow Brick Road.

Daniel, Elizabeth, and Jackson Badgenoone joined them at the showing of *Wuthering Heights*. JBadgenoone was the only one who could fully appreciate the unfolding plot. She had evolved at a time when books and live theater were the principal conduits for developing a story.

[Jackson broke her promise and interrupted Elizabeth. Anna wasn't surprised and couldn't contain her laughter.

"Elizabeth, you have taken the liberty to insert us directly into the story of your observee."

"Ms. Jackson, I am aware, but we do belong to the story."

The other observers applauded her statement and listened as she continued to read.]

[During this twentieth century, screen writers, producers and directors had learned how to filter subtle cinematic nuance into every plot. Jackson wondered if the new medium injected a measure of laziness into the storytelling process. In her earlier days, a reader had to conjure up the spirit of a moment. Now, cinematography made it possible to envision the innermost thoughts of an actor with a properly-placed freeze frame.]

In the second year of her courtship with Fred, Mary enjoyed a movie version of *The Grapes of Wrath*. It created remarkable examples of moments frozen in time.

The Dust Bowl provided a convenient backdrop that she could appreciate. Badgenoone made her aware of the dirt that blew in from the west. It contributed to vivid blood-red sunsets in the east. Mary was glued to her seat. Jackson reflected upon a different perspective of Oklahoma. She still preferred the book.

Mary's all-time favorite moments were from another movie that she watched several years later. She especially enjoyed the scene depicting the instant when George Bailey realizes that he is never born. She was also captivated by the scene where he pleads to find his Mary.

[Back at the meeting, the Neverborn paused to consider if a properly-placed photo reinforced or detracted from the story line. It forced Jackson and her colleagues to think through the placement of hyperlinks. There were some moments that were better hinged to a reader's mind with words alone. The grandchildren would be the ultimate judge. Elizabeth continued to layer gesso on the canvas for their benefit.]

There were so many other movies, most of them lighthearted and crafted for the time. Fred and Mary loved to watch Fred and Ginger glide across the screen. Shirley Temple lifted the spirits of an entire generation weary of difficult economic times. *Our Gang* and the *Dead End Gang* reinvented their youth and teen years. Westerns linked them to a glorified past. Musicals provided a fanciful present.

Live performances provided alternate entertainment. They danced to the big band sounds of Jim and Tommy Dorsey, Glenn Miller, Benny Goodman, Artie Shaw, Woody Herman, Count Basie, Louis Armstrong, and Duke Ellington.

Italian-American Hoboken native Frank Sinatra and Irish-American Washington State crooner Bing Crosby measured the slow songs. Nelson Eddie and Jeanette MacDonald enlarged high and low notes whenever Fred and Mary sang along. Kay Kyser infused a North Carolina sense of timing, rhythm and humor into the Kollege of Musical Knowledge.

Laughter came their way through the antics and artistry of Abbott and Costello, George Burns and Gracie Allen, Jimmy Durante, Laurel and Hardy, and Bob Hope. The voices came over the radio, their images captured on the big screen.

Fred and Mary were in a location that made it convenient to see some of them live on stage. Journal Square was just down the block. The Union City Burlesque on 48th Street was a trolley ride away. A ferry boat could bring them close enough to walk to the 42nd Street theater district in New York City. The Glen Island Casino greeted audiences in New Rochelle.

Weekends in summer alternated between a family outing at the Jersey Shore and a day at the Palisades Amusement Park. In July of 1939, they finally made it to the World's Fair at Flushing Meadow. They had taken a pass on the April 30th opening-day ceremony. It was timed to coincide with the 150th anniversary of George Washington's first inauguration as president of the United States.

Mary and Fred did their best to visit every zone, the Transportation Zone, the Communications and Business Systems Zone, the Food Zone, and the Government Zone. The young couple marveled at the technology. They were amazed to see themselves on a newly-introduced television screen.

Fred was disappointed that there was no German pavilion on the grounds. A little over a month later he understood why the country of his ancestors was absent from the gathering of nations.

On the day after they met, Mary began to keep a log of all the events. Years later, DBadgenoone and EBadgenoone borrowed liberally from her notes to reconstruct the lives of the couple.

Elizabeth rendered another seventeen chapters in Fred's life. Those contained a lot of happy moments and a few best reserved for a more thorough reading. Fred was able to return to the ruins of his grandfather's house and sift through the rubble.

Mary made a pilgrimage to the thatch-covered home that Annie left behind. Their stories were separate but increasingly intertwined. Elizabeth Badgenoone continued to reflect on the life of Fred at Chapter 29.

CHAPTER XXIX
Count Every Stroke

Decades later, they recalled the lessons they had learned from Fred during the course of a lifetime. At a restaurant overlooking a sunset on the Gulf of Mexico, they raised a glass of wine in toast to his life and the celebration of his 60th wedding anniversary.

His younger brother brought the family to tears. Fred had been his role model. He taught Artie how to be a good husband, father, and friend. Fred's niece recalled how he brought her to live in his home when her own father needed some support.

Uncle Benny was doing his best to raise her in the neighboring town of Hoboken. It wasn't the gentrified city of 2014 built around a park named in honor of native son Frank Sinatra. This was a Hoboken of the 1950s best rendered in Fred's favorite movie, *On the Waterfront*. He paraphrased a famous line from that film and assured Karen that she could be somebody; she could be a contender.

Fred treated her as one of his own daughters. Years later, she shared more about those memories with her cousins (adopted sisters) on Facebook. Uncle Fred gave her the courage and direction to create memorable high water markers of her own.

Fred's second son-in-law James, aka Trav, recalled how he got to know his second dad on the eighth hole of a local golf course. Fred's ball presented a difficult lie just shy of the fairway. He needed two swings to extricate it from the mud. Trav suggested that he only record one of the swings. Fred played it by the rules, with two strokes. He recalled the wisdom of his mother-in-law: "Tell the truth and shame the devil."

Trav's mother addressed Fred's extended family. She recalled the time when she and Jimmy were introduced to Fred and Mary. The two former soldiers formed an immediate bond that would strengthen over time as they shared grandchildren.

Jimmy wasn't around to see the great-grandchildren, but Charlene was sure that he would have been pleased. Fred added a noble character to the gene pool.

His grandchildren each spoke to their cousins, aunts, uncles, and friends. The oldest girl reflected on her first pony ride with Grandpa. He had shared a photo of a young Fred on a white horse and promised to find a similar horse for her and her twin sisters. A pony would have to do and that was fine with them.

The first sister spoke to a time when Grandpa taught her how to swim in the warm ocean water. The waves seemed so big to her at the time, but Grandpa never let go of her arm as she rose and fell with each new foamy oscillation.

Younger sister (by all of a few minutes) recalled how Grandpa helped her to search for a four-leaf clover in the field behind his condo complex. She learned about the beauty of nature all around her. He in turn rediscovered the colors of every flower when viewed vicariously through her eyes.

Boy cousins shared how Grandpa would become a horse for them. Aunts and uncles relived happy days from visits to the first apartment, the first detached house, and the home in the Heights.

Mary's sister-in-law had been to all the places they called home. She was the next to take the microphone. She shared that Fred and Mary were the most tolerant and loving people that she had ever known. They accepted her even though she had been rejected by her own parents for having accepted Christ as her Savior. She tried to explain to them that she had never repudiated her Jewish faith. She embraced its promise when she acknowledged the Messiah.

Mary was too tired to stand, so she spoke to the assemblage from her wheelchair. Fred had always been her hero. He was a force in her life before he wore the uniform of an airman or pinned a patrolman's shield to his vest.

She couldn't relate to the VHS movie they had seen the night before this party. Mary was an ardent fan of Myrna Loy and Fredric March and could appreciate some of the military to civilian life adjustments reflected in *The Best Days of Our Lives,* a film they had first viewed together decades earlier. But the portrayal of a returning airman and his failed marriage bore no resemblance to lives Fred and Mary enjoyed in the post-war period and beyond.

Her Fred was more like the real-life Jimmy Stewart. He was married just two years after Mary's second-born daughter arrived. Jimmy flew in the face of Hollywood tradition and remained with his wife until her passing in 1994. They raised a family that included twin daughters and two adopted sons.

Over the years, Fred and Mary caught most of his films and then replayed them on the VCR in their modest condo unit. She shared her favorites because they were somewhat instrumental in shaping their world view.

Mary hoped to pass along those memories to her grandchildren. Upon her demise a few years later, a rich library of Stewart's films made it into the homes of their parents. Some of them ultimately found a way into the den overlooking Dutch Buffalo Creek.

Stewart portrayed a determined Charles Lindberg in the *Spirit of Saint Louis;* a young idealistic Senator in *Mr. Smith Goes to Washington;* a man in search of that special sound in *The Glenn Miller Story;* and a very fortunate older brother and hometown hero in *It's a Wonderful Life.* She saw Fred in every portrayal.

Fred walked up to the wheelchair and kissed her silver gray hair. He thanked everyone for being there to help celebrate their special moment. It was his turn to reflect on the six decades they shared as husband and wife.

Mary was the prettiest girl he had ever met. He didn't need pictures to remind him of her beauty. As he spoke, pictures of the two of them appeared on a large screen located behind the podium. Now others in the room could catch a glimpse.

They presented images of a young couple at the World's Fair. It was at the Ford pavilion that he made a lifelong decision to drive only that brand for the rest of his life. Other pictures captured moments soon after the war of the parents with two daughters. Another photo of the five children was taken soon after Fred's promotion to the rank of captain on the police force.

The last photo displayed on the screen documented an earlier anniversary celebration. It included two sons-in-law, one daughter-in-law, and five grandchildren. Copies of all the photos were sent to Jackson's cloud.

[Book 8]

CHAPTER XXX

Not Just Another Day at the Beach

Jackson intervened again. She didn't dare look at Abadgenoone. The next few chapters contained very difficult moments for Fred and Mary and were best left for a reading by the grandchildren when they were old enough to move past the pain.

CHAPTER XXXIX
The Last Lincoln Mercury Grand Marquis

Fred didn't dwell on the hardships that had tested his mettle. They left high water markers on the souls that they touched. His Mary was gone but he kept her cushion on the front passenger seat of their car. The assisted living center strongly suggested that he no longer drive the Lincoln Mercury Grand Marquis.

That automobile was the last in a string of fine American built cars that he drove over the course of more than half a century. Back from the hospital, he lifted the window shade in his room. The car was still where he left it so many weeks earlier. He turned his back on the view, returned to his chair and closed his eyes.

Fred recalled the happy times when Mary and the children piled into an earlier vehicle and headed to the Jersey shore. His thoughts drifted back to a time earlier still when he first appreciated the roar of an engine, the power of eight cylinders beating back the highway. Then memories carried him to an earlier time, before paved roads. A horse pulled an ice wagon; another pulled a wagon full of rags over cobblestone streets. They moved over when the bell on an electrified trolley commanded the right of way. His grandchildren could only see that world in photos and vintage film. They would only know about bigger, faster cars. [Jackson and Elizabeth Badgenoone sheltered Fred from the vision of a world less reliant on fossil fuels.]

When he opened his eyes he saw the picture of those grandchildren and their children framed neatly on the pale blue wall. He wanted to leave a message for them and the others who would remain after his passing. His car and the future of transportation were no longer on his mind. He did want them to know that he had lived a full life and was blessed beyond measure. He picked up *Apples of Gold*, a book given to him by his son-in-law years earlier. At page 68 he read: "Instead of fearing death, we should look it in the face and recognize it for what it is—a friend that has come to release us from the bondage of the flesh."

He promised to leave with them his lifetime of memories. When they gathered around him a few months later, the doctors met them with a recommendation. Surgery might extend his life by several weeks. Fred wanted no part of that; he didn't plan to walk again. In the hospital room, he heard a voice that brought to him a measure of peace. Elizabeth told him that he would soon be with Mary again.

On the following morning, Fred painted a perfectly-framed picture of a road that he travelled every day. It was flanked by a timeworn sidewalk lined with telephone poles. Each one bore a striking resemblance to a wooden cross. On his daily walk, he measured each mile by their number and reflected on the many crosses that he had encountered during the journey of his life.

In the sunset of his years, he wanted to reassure his family that the crosses in their lives were all made easier to bear by the cross that Christ carried two thousand years ago.

He was not a religious man, but he was extremely spiritual. He drew his force from a personal relationship with this Nazarene from Bethlehem who rose from the dead in Jerusalem. The image was with him as he drove the ice truck, flew the B24, marshaled his policemen, raised his children, and nurtured his grandchildren.

On the way to his funeral a few weeks later, Trav and his wife reflected on every telephone pole along the route from wake to burial plot. His ashes rested next to those of his Mary. Elizabeth promised to save the memory of the wooden cross.

[Jackson concluded the meeting. She asked her colleagues to read the next book on their own before returning to the oval amphitheater. Frederick Badgenoone had perhaps the most difficult assignment.

His observee, Mimi, provided several critical links in the line of the master story. Mimi constructed a spiritual bridge that spanned several generations. She linked Trav's life water to the current that flows in his children and grandchildren, in-laws, parents, family, friends and coworkers.]

[Book 9]

The High Water Markers of Frederick's Observee

By Frederick Badgenoone,
Copyright © 2015 by Jackson Badgenoone

Preface to the High Water Markers
of Frederick's Observee

In Chapter 1, Frederick, aka FBadgenoone, focused on the place and time of Mimi's birth in 1947. This never-born Frederick would have been her older brother. A younger brother eventually drew breath and inherited the namesake of her father.

FBadgenoone owed his identity to them and several other living souls that carried the same name. The first Frederick buried a bayonet in Dutch Buffalo Creek more than one hundred and fifty years before Mimi arrived on the planet.

In the telling of Mimi's story, FBadgenoone choreographed the occurrence of her birth at the Margaret Hague hospital, juxtaposed to a physical birth an ocean away. On the other side of the Atlantic, the baby boy who would someday become her husband found breath.

Frederick Badgenoone documented her growing up years. He crafted a chapter dedicated to the relationship with her siblings. Another recalled her coming of age in an era when everyone (almost) liked Ike. He traced her aspirations as a Mouseketeer, a cheerleader, and a country western singer. He also kept a close eye on her spiritual development.

Her grandparents and parents had been grounded in a very Catholic tradition. They also shared a genuine love of Jesus. They believed that faith provided the real ticket to Heaven.

They never discouraged her from performing good works. They did encourage Mimi to reflect on any and all that she might come to perform. A good work for the sake of earning a place at the throne would profit nothing. A good work rendered out of love would amplify her faith.

Jackson watched as FBadgenoone began to parse through the chapters.

CHAPTER II

Enjoy Yourself—It's Later Than You Think

The little girl with chubby cheeks and curly red hair charmed everyone she met. Her grandmother, Anna, and her father called her MiMi. Her grandmother, Josephine, called her the Shirley Temple of Greenville.

MiMi would always draw a crowd. 1949 was a year of reflection and high expectations. Mimi was still celebrating just a few days following her second birthday when the family encouraged her to take center stage on the living room oval braided rug.

The house strained under the weight of at least two dozen souls. All eyes were on her. Mimi had memorized the entire first verse of her favorite song.

She glanced around the room and took a bow in front of her parents, aunts, uncles, cousins, and sister. Then she started to sing:

> Enjoy yourself; it's later than you think
> The years go by as quickly as a wink.

They didn't stay in Greenville for long. Her dad quickly advanced through the police ranks. The family was fortunate enough to be able to move into a larger home. This one was closer to the Journal Square. It had enough rooms to accommodate the growing family. Three brothers would join Mimi and her sister. Mimi continued to sing, her siblings sometimes added their voices to the songs.

The family made a few more moves within the city and finally arrived in The Heights. Her youngest brother Freddy eventually provided instrumental accompaniment with the strings of his guitar.

Mimi's formative years were filled with love tempered by a measure of hardship.

[FBadgenoone saved the next four chapters for a time when Mimi's grandchildren could better relate.]

Years later, her daughter would purchase a home just a few blocks removed from Pershing Field where Mimi played when she was a little girl. Mimi suspected that her granddaughter might someday enroll at the academy that she once attended.

[Frederick Badgenoone followed Elizabeth's example and wrote himself into the plot. He could then pass that information on to his colleague assigned to observe the life of that young lady.

Jackson realized at that point that she had temporarily lost control of the observers assigned to her care. She didn't discourage Frederick. In fact, his action made some sense. Mimi would have a direct bearing on the lives of her husband, children and grandchildren. She provided the rubber cement that glued the stories to one another on the galley proof of life.

FBadgenoone skipped ahead to a moment that would impact their lives.]

CHAPTER VII
Just Right

She was the first of her siblings to pursue undergraduate study. Mimi was originally destined to attend a local state run school. The nuns at the academy were impressed with her academic performance and encouraged her to apply to a Catholic college. Instead, she applied for a scholarship at a nearby private university. That decision changed the course of her life and the lives of those that would be formed in her shadow.

Mimi encountered a number of adjustments. The university was secular and co-educational. She had just completed four years at an all-girls Catholic High School. Religious teaching there was more than just an extension of her grade school Baltimore Catechism experience. Theological discourse entered into every subject area. It began to sharpen a spiritual awakening in her soul.

On the college campus, she would have to compete with and learn to live in harmony with male students. Her brothers had provided some practice. The religious tenets were another story. She encountered comparative religion, alternate forms of worship, belief in different gods, and belief in no god.

During her third year on campus, she joined two of her sorority sisters at the Friday night dance. It was held at the Student Union, but all undergraduate students found their way to the dance floor, Greek letter and non-Greek alike.

On the approach to the dance floor, she encountered a fellow classmate. He had a bounce to his step. He approached the trio and immediately singled out Mimi. She thought his first question awkward and not the standard pick-up line:

"Are you married, engaged, pinned or going steady?"

Apparently he had just come away from a broken relationship that ended in an altercation with his girlfriend's new beau.

At first she wasn't sure if the question was directed to her. He quickly put that to rest. In a brash statement he pointed left, saying "Too short," then to the right, "Too tall." Then he focused on the center, pointing at her, and blurted out, "Just right."

She wasn't sure how to respond.

He asked point-blank, "Do you want to dance?"

Her friends moved on and Mimi entered the auditorium with her new escort.

The local DJ spun a succession of fast and slow songs. The music of Jay and the Americans, The Beach Boys, The Four Seasons, The Lettermen, Jack Jones, Henry Mancini, and any number of contemporary artists kept the night alive.

By the end of the evening he made a strange request. "Would you like to know how things appear in the light of day?" He offered to pick her up at her house the next morning to take a spin. On the day after they met Mimi began to keep a log of all the events.

[Frederick suggested that the pages of that diary could be included in the resource section of Jackson's master work. Jackson reserved judgment. She was inclined to include it in a family heirloom edition. FBadgenoone continued to observe.]

A cool crisp pre-autumn breeze invited them to roll down the windows on his two-year-old red Chevy Corvair. It wasn't as hot as a Corvette, but it was a sufficiently cool car for the neighborhood nonetheless when he bought it new in 1965. That was despite the fact that some people recognized that it posed a threat to safety.

Safe enough, they headed north along the Palisades Interstate Parkway. After a few diversions, they arrived at the gates of the US

Military Academy at West Point, New York. It wasn't the most likely place for a first date. But somehow the road led them there. Leaves were just beginning to turn.

They watched young men parade in a long gray line. Many of those officers in training would be deployed to Vietnam in the following years. He shared how some of his friends called him Trav. He went on to confide that he was no longer comfortable with the label. Too much of his travel had been associated with the wings in theaters of war.

He admired his high school buddy who yearned to travel as an ambassador for peace. Gaz was still at college in New Mexico but kept up a steady stream of letters. Trav hoped that in his future travel would celebrate the common bonds of mankind. Maybe someday they could travel together. She thought that statement a bit forward at this exploratory stage of their relationship.

The military academy provided a natural setting that allowed both of them to share stories about their dads and uncles who had served in the military. They also began to discover each other's worldview.

On the ride back to Hudson County, and in a succession of day trips, they learned more about each other and about their families and friends. She suspected that Trav was getting serious about her. Less than a year later he presented to her his fraternity pin.

He hadn't planned to do that at first. Four days before Valentine's Day, she'd asked him if he knew what that day would bring. "Yes, a very nice present for you on a very special day for people in love." He was so proud of the fact that he had just purchased a warm and fuzzy stuffed dog for her as a way to express his feelings.

Trav thought she was fond of dogs but knew that they irritated her allergies and made her sneeze. Here was a perfect solution: a Warm Fuzzy, a fantasy fur dog, no sneeze. He sensed that she didn't really believe that he had a present for her.

"Your face tells me that you don't believe there is a present for you. Okay, let's drive to Fifth Street." He pulled the Corvair in front of his father's house. He ran up the stairs and returned with a perfectly-wrapped box, two feet wide, one foot high, and sixteen inches deep.

Jackson Badgenoone

She slowly peeled off the wrapping paper, opened the box, and let out a very soft sigh.

"It's a dog, a dog, a dog."

He blurted out the next line. "What did you expect, my fraternity pin?" As soon as the words left his tongue he knew that his life was going to be changed for the better.

A few days later, a photographer for the college paper snapped a picture of Trav and Mimi at the campus library. Five months after their first dance, he gazed at her as she pondered over the assignment for her next class.

He was a reporter for the paper and managed to get the first photo print before it was placed in the next edition of the Bulletin. He shared the picture with her and asked her if she noticed anything odd. She told him that the camera had presented an interesting view of the back of his head.

"Look beyond that. I am gazing at you and the pin that you are wearing. I was pretty sure that you were the girl for me the moment I cut you loose from your friends. This picture reminded me that you are the most beautiful and intelligent woman that I have ever known. Someday I hope to replace the pin with a ring."

CHAPTER VIII
A Fateful Duel

Mimi entered every date and every event into her log. Their Greek Letter fraternity brothers and sorority sisters invited a host of big name talent to campus. They attended every venue. They also enjoyed the museums, concerts, plays, musicals, and the theater that was available in greater metropolitan New York.

During the summer, they joined the fraternity brothers at a Belmar, New Jersey beach house. In the winter they watched the snow fall on the Cloisters across the river, not far from the George Washington Bridge.

Radio City Music Hall provided entertainment during the Christmas season. The Easter Parade gathering in front of Saint Patrick's gave Mimi the opportunity to show off her finest spring fashion.

By November of their senior year, they both knew that they were supposed to share life together. Keeping up a Friday night tradition, they went to the local Four Star Diner for dinner. Following the meal, they returned to the little red car.

He leaned over, opened the glove compartment, and asked her to open a small black satin covered case. She refused. "I am not going to open that box in the parking lot behind the Four Star Diner. If it is what I think it is, then you are going to need a more respectable location to present it to me."

Trav turned the ignition key and headed east. Not quite two miles away, he pulled the car to the side of a Weehawken street. It was a beautiful evening. The New York City skyline was aglow with lights that reflected off the Hudson River.

"Will this be suitable?"

She opened the box and he slipped the diamond ring on her finger. He gave her a gentle hug and a kiss. "You realize that this place has historical significance. In 1804, a year of reflection and tension, a former vice president of the United States mortally wounded the first secretary of the United States Treasury on this very spot."

She didn't seem to mind. By now she was keenly aware of his peculiar sense of humor. It almost always involved some obscure reference to a little-known or under-appreciated accident of history.

The pin and the ring joined a growing treasure of the symbols that reminded them of their affection for each other. The stuffed dog didn't survive the years. More study, more dates, and a wedding were all in the offering.

Two girls who flanked her at the Student Union were bridesmaids at the wedding thirty months later. They prepared for a spring ceremony, complete with white lilies, purple gowns, and black tuxedos.

Someone forgot to inform the weather man. That March 29, 1970 produced a storm of historic proportions. Most of the guests were unable to get to the church. Her younger brothers served as altar boys. Their friends and immediate family somehow made it past the four-foot snow drifts.

At the reception, he suggested that the weather might portend an omen. They relished a photo taken in front of the restaurant located on Route 17.

He loved summer, she loved the autumn. Following a job offer a year later they moved to one of the snowiest places on the east coast. They purchased a starter home on a quiet street in a modest village nestled in conservative western New York.

Some of the happiest moments of her life sprang from the autumn leaves, winter snows and spring lilacs that brought that place to life. It was on a brilliant late spring day that she gave birth to her first-born daughter. She was a birthday present to her husband who had turned twenty-seven the day before.

Sixteen months later, on a crisp September day, her husband fainted when twins entered the world. They were a birthday present to his wife who would celebrate her twenty-eighth birthday on the following day.

He didn't mean to faint. They had gone through Lamaze training. This was the second pregnancy so they thought they knew what to expect. They both agreed that she was larger this time. The doctors insisted she was on schedule but were going to induce just to be on the safe side.

Trav was by her side with words of encouragement. Breathe in and breathe out. When the doctor brought the little girl into the world, he volunteered an observation: "She seems so small, considering your size."

It was not the best bedside manner. Then he exclaimed, "Surprise, you have another baby! You have another beautiful girl—congratulations, Dad."

Dad sank to the floor.

The early years presented a daily challenge. There were three mouths to feed and diapers for three. She was thankful that the diaper service offered a two-for-one price for the twins.

When the first girl arrived, Mimi tendered her resignation at the elementary school. She had fond memories of the children in her third grade class. Now she had her own class of three under her own roof. There was so much for all of them to learn.

The twins more than doubled the already pervasive household joy. Mimi spent every conscious hour nurturing the three girls through the toddler years and into grade school. She cried when the first daughter climbed onto the yellow school bus.

She hopped in the car and passed it when the lights stopped flashing. Mimi greeted her daughter at the schoolhouse door, camera in hand, to record the event. She repeated the exercise a year later. With the roll of an eye, each girl in turn demonstrated how a five-year-old can respond to a parental faux pas.

Mimi didn't need to encourage her husband to participate in the lives of his daughters. He lived every moment for his little girls. It was a satisfying high water marker in her life to watch the family grow together.

Somehow she knew that she was at the center of this cohesive unit. Mimi recalled the wisdom of her Irish grandmother. More than anyone else, it is the wife and mother who determines the success of a family.

They captured pictures of as many of the happy moments as possible. There was one when the girls frolicked in a mountain of newly-raked autumn leaves. Another captured them with boots and furry red hats climbing through a snow drift.

On some occasions, she managed to record the action on film. Her favorite was an instance when the daughters formed a circle and sang their song:

> The wheels on the bus go round, round, round
> Round, round, round
> Round, round, round . . .

Just then, a school bus passed by the picture window.

Not every memory could be committed to photo or film. The taste of grape pies served up at Monica's in neighboring Naples, NY was beyond reach of the camera. A camera couldn't replicate the feel of a crystal cool Lake Canandaigua splash of water on the first day of a summer swim.

[The next two chapters described in more detail the challenges that Mimi faced during that time. FBadgenoone saved them for readers who shared similar happenstance. They would be an encouragement to any woman faced with providing a guiding path to multiples. They would open the eyes of many a dad distracted by the role of breadwinner. The chapters documented the faith and support structures that made it possible. Frederick Badgenoone took note and then moved onto the eleventh chapter.]

CHAPTER XI

What's In a Name?

When she was still a young girl, her father called her Mimi. A little more than a half-century later, her first-born grandson was learning how to talk. He was unaware of her childhood nickname. Her given first name was too difficult to pronounce. To him it sounded a lot like *MeNa*. The new name rolled from his ears to his lips and emerged as *Meena*. In a single moment, Fred's Mimi became Meena.

From that point forward, she would be known as Grandma Meena. Her successive grandchildren adopted the same protocol. Meena reflected on this high water marker in her life, possibly one of the highest. Then she thought back to an earlier time.

In 1978, two decades before she received her new nickname, she sat quietly in the third pew facing the pulpit at a small Canal Town Catholic Church. It was just a few months following the day when her husband had accepted the LORD as his personal savior.

She recalled the moment he came home from a sales meeting in Rome, NY. The man who left a day earlier returned a different person. The man who greeted her in their modest home just north of the church was bursting with joy. He told her how he had come to know Jesus. At first she suspected that this was more of his humor.

"The happiness and joy that I display today is no joke. It came at too steep a price."

Mimi continued to absorb what he was trying to convey.

Anna helped Frederick Badgenoone to frame the moment. Trav was still a nominal Catholic but knew that his life was missing a full measure of love. He had a beautiful wife, three precious children, and a promising career. Yet he felt empty. That morning earlier in the year, he attended an 8:00 am Mass to help fill the void. He continued to share the story with Mimi. She was paying very close attention to his words.

Following the service the church grew silent. The parishioners went on with their daily lives. He remained glued to the pew. He challenged God to give him an answer and he wasn't looking for one from the Baltimore Catechism.

A priest approached him following the ritual. He had seen this priest before during his last visit to Rome six months earlier. At that time the good father was lighting a candle in front of the sanctuary.

Trav was certain that he wanted no part of candles, statues and stained glass windows. The priest leaned over and whispered to him. "I understand that you want an answer from God.

I think I can help. Meet me at the sacristy at 11:00 am."

He had agreed to meet Father Tom at the prescribed hour. Tom encouraged him to wait in the room next to the altar. It was a quiet setting. A single book was placed on the center of the table next to his chair.

The book spoke to the joy of waiting in anticipation of any seminal event. Moses had to wander for forty years in the desert sand. Jesus spent forty days in fasting and prayer prior to His Passion. Surely Trav could wait forty minutes to hear what Father Tom had to say.

Trav expected some sort of confessional experience. He had been away from the church for a number of years and recalled sitting in a small booth. He had practiced the line, "Bless me Father, for I have sinned."

Father Tom entered the room. There was no confessional. "Don't call me Father," he said. "Tom will do inside of these walls."

He refused to absolve Trav of his sin(s). Only God could do that. In any event, if Trav saw his sins and how really dark they were, he would have been stricken dead on the spot.

He knew that he was a sinner. That's why he sought God in the first place. But he didn't think his sins were that damning.

Tom asked him a few questions. "Have you always honored your father and your mother? Have you ever been envious of your neighbor? Have you ever coveted his wife? Do you honor God?"

The questions to that point seemed rhetorical. Then Tom came out point blank and said, "I really want you to answer me, out loud. Did you ever kill anyone?"

"No."

"Did you ever think of killing someone?"

"Yes."

"If you had a gun in your hand at the time, you would have broken the sixth commandment, 'Thou shalt not kill.'"

Visibly shaken at the realization, Trav pulled back. Tom grasped his hands and asked him to close his eyes.

He recalled the story of Jesus on the cross. Flanked by two sinners, one challenged Him with a taunt to come down. The other acknowledged his sin. He asked Christ to remember him when He came into His kingdom. Christ blessed him with a singular statement: "This very night, you will be with Me in Paradise." (Luke 22:43)

Tom went on to explain that Jesus hadn't asked the sinner to perform good works or attend Mass. The sinner was saved by grace.

Tom continued to share that Jesus freely shed His blood for every man and woman. They held hands and prayed. Tom encouraged James to utter the three most difficult words in the language, *I am sorry.* As he did, James experienced the body of Jesus. He pleaded for forgiveness and a drop of His precious blood. It washed over him like a cleansing flood. In an instant he became part of the Body of Christ.

Mimi thought about her husband's experience. She was searching, too. They still attended Mass at the local Catholic Church. Perhaps she could find an answer there just as Trav had found Jesus at a church in Rome.

Six months passed before the day when a visiting priest arrived in Canal Town. Her church was just down the street from the four churches intersection. The new priest performed the traditional liturgy. When he delivered his sermon, he focused on the importance of a name.

He made a very strong point: Whenever God calls someone, He calls them by name. Not wanting to leave out anyone in the congregation, he consumed most of his allotted sermon time to call out the names that were revealed to him that day.

Jackson, Anna, and Frederick listened attentively from the Neverborn section of the balcony. Jackson pledged to capture any name missed by the priest. She doubted that he would mention her own mother Amathlaah who was herself named after the mother of Abraham. Jackson reflected that her would-have-been mother was born within yards from where this church now stood.

Jackson would accept names at her primary email address, badgenoone@aol.com.

The priest began the roll call of names destined for salvation:

"He calls you Adam, Adora, Alain, Alan, Albert, Alethea, Alex, Alexander, Alexandra, Alice, Alix, Allen, Alvaro, Alyce, Amanda, Amy, Andrea, Andy, Anessa, Angela, Angeline, Angelo, Anita, Ann Marie, Ann, Anna, Anne, Andrew, April, Armando, Anthony, Arianna, Arlene, Artie, Arthur, Asher, Ashley, Augustin, Austin, Barbara, Barry, Bart, Bartolomeo, Becky, Bella, Benny, Berj, Bernard, Bernadette, Bernie, Beth, Betsy, BH, Bill, Bob, Bobby, Bonnie, Brad, Brelan, Brenda, Brian, Bruce, Byron, Caitlyn, Calyb, Cameron, Camille, Caren, Carl, Carla, Carlie, Carlo, Carol, Carole, Caroline, Carrie, Casey, Catherine, Cathy, Cece, Charlene, Charles, Charlie, Cheryl, Cheryle, Chris, Christina, Christine, Christopher, Christy, Cindy, Clair, Clara, Claudia, Clifford, Colin, Colleen, Connie, Craig, Dahlia, Dallas, Dale, Dan, Dana, Danh, Daniel, Danielle, Danny, Dave, David, Debbie, Debby, Debi, Deborah, Del, Dennis, Denny, Diane, Diana, Dianna, DiAnne, Dick, Diego, Dillon, Dina, Dolores, Dominic, Don, Donald, Donna, Dorothy, Doug, Douglas, Ed, Edward, Elaine, Elia, Ella Mae, Ellen, Ellie, Elmer, Elizabeth, Elvira, Emil, Emma, Enid, Eric, Erica, Esperanza, Eugene, Evangeline, Evelyn, Farimah."

The priest paused, took a sip of water and went on with more names:

"Faye, Francine, Francis, Frank, Franklin, Fred, Frederick, Gail, Gale, Gary, Gayle, Gefu, Gene, Genevieve, Georgette, Geraldine, George, Gilbert, Gina, Glen, Grace, Gratziana, Greg, Gregory, Gretchen, Hal, Hande, Hannah, Harley, Harry, Hazel, Heather, Heidi, Helena, Henrietta, Herman, Homer, Ian, Irene, Iris, Israel, Jac, Jack, Jackie, Jacqueline, Jake, James, Jamie, Jane, Janet, Janice, Jarred, Jason, Jay, Jayme, Jayna, Jean, Jeanie, Jean-Pierre, Jean-Louis, Jeanne, Jeannette, Jeff, Jeffery, Jennifer, Jennings, Jenny, Jerry, Jesse, Jessica, Jesus, Jill, Jim, Jimmy, Joanne, Joe, Joel, Joelle, John, Jon, Jose, Joseph, Josephine, Joshua, Joyce, Juan, Juanita, Judith, Judy, Julia, Julie, Julius, June, Justin, Kaci, Kadyn, Karen, Kara, Kate, Kathe, Katie, Kathy, Kayla, Keisha, Keith, Kelly, Ken, Kenneth, Kerri, Kevin, Kiel, Kilani, Kip, Kim, Kinley, Kitty, Krista, Kristy, Kyle, Lana, Lance, Lainey, Larry, Leah, Lee, Lela, Lena, Lenny, Leo, Leonard, Leslie, Leroy, Lev, Lewis, Libby, Lin, Linda, Lindsey, Lisa, Lloyd, Lois, Lori, Lorraine, Lou, Louis, Louise, Lucas, Luke, Lyn, Lynda, Lyndon, Lynn and Lynne."

Another sip of water and a lung-filling gulp of air, the priest continued.

"Lucerzia, Lucy, Lyla, Maggie, Manuel, Mary, Maria, Mary Elizabeth, Marie, Marilyn, Marlene, Margaret, Margareta, Marge, Marianne, Mark, Mary Kay, Marsha, Martha, Marvin, Maryanne, Mat, Mathew, Matt, Meegan, Melinda, Melinna, Melisa, Melissa, Miaozheng, Michael, Michele, Michelle, Mike, Monica, Monique, Morrie, Morris, Mykel, Nancy, Natalie, Nathan, Nathaniel, Neil, Nelson, Neplus, Nicholas, Nick, Norah, Norma, Norma-Jean, Oshrit, Owen, Pam, Pamela, Pat, Patrick, Patricia, Patt, Patti, Paul, Paula, Pauline, Payne, Pedro, Peggi, Peggy, Peter, Philip, Phillip, Rachael, Raellen, Railyn, Raymond, Rebecca, Regi, Regina, Renée, Reeva, Reva, Rhoda, Richard, Rick, Ricky, Rob, Robert, Roberta, Robin, Rochelle, Rodney, Roger, Ron, Ronald, Rosalie, Rosemarie, Rosemary, Russell, Ruth, Ryan, Sabrana, Sabrina, Sally, Samantha, Samuel, Sandy, Sara, Sarah, Scott, Sean, Seth, Shannon, Sharon,

Shawn, Sheila, Sheri, Sherry, Spencer, Spike, Stacy, Stan, Stephen, Stephanie, Steve, Stuart, Sue, Sue Ann, Susan, Tammie, Tammy, Tawny, Taylor, Teagen, Ted, Tina, Tinh, Teri, Terrie, Terry, Thomas, Tim, Todd, Tom, Tony, Trent, Tristen, Ty, Valerie, Vandi, Vanessa, Varda, Vicki, Victor, Victoria, Vilma, Vincent, Vivian, Wade, Walter, Wayne, Wendy, Willa, William, Wilma, Xavier, Zak, Zeb and Zhang."

Taking another sip, he apologized knowing that there were thousands more that would be added to the book of life. He called out one more name, Maureen. It was Mimi's given name.

When he called her by her first name, it was as if a bolt of lightning struck at the heart of her soul.

Father Tom continued with the sermon.

[Trav remembered him from the church in Rome, his non-Catholic numeration of the commandments still fresh in his mind.]

A few months later, Mimi sat in the dining room of their home. The bible was still opened to the page where she had just completed her most recent reading: "For God so loved the world that He gave His only begotten Son, that whosoever believeth in Him should not perish, but have everlasting life." (John 3:16)

She kept repeating, "Whosoever believeth in Him, believeth in Him, believeth in Him . . ."

Trav entered the room at that moment in time. She looked up at him and couldn't wipe away the tears that streamed down her face. She held her husband's hands and closed her eyes. At that moment, she experienced the body of Jesus.

She pleaded for a drop of His blood and was rewarded with a peace beyond measure; there was her Savior on the cross.

He had died and risen just for her. Their lives progressed together from that moment in the shadow of Jesus Christ.

[FBadgenoone continued to compare notes with Anna Badgenoone. Jackson complimented them for the collaboration. She held up their cooperation as a model for the other Neverborn observers. Frederick continued to observe.]

Mimi (aka Meena) went on to accumulate a number of high water markers. Most of them were documented in the chapters of her book.

They spoke to her time as a classroom teacher, reading teacher, tutor of high school mathematics, computer technician, wife, mother, and grandmother.

Chapter XIV described Mimi's observations of a sixth grade classroom that she visited with her husband during a Golden Apple trip. The trip was awarded each year to top performing sales representatives, this year it culminated with a trip to mainland China. They had crossed the border from Hong Kong, then still a British colony.

In the room, she was taken back to see calculus equations on the board. She knew that someday, the students sitting behind those desks would challenge the children once in her charge, later in Trav's middle school experience.

Her husband reminded her that, one day, Hong Kong would become part of the People's Republic. He predicted that the concrete shell buildings would be electrified and the new China would become a major world power. Nav acknowledged that the acquisition of Hong Kong would represent a two-edged sword to the doctrinaire of the mainland establishment.

That chapter was written at about a time fast forwarded to a decade after her salvation experience. Those several years later she wondered if the calculus students were allowed to question the authority of their state or contemplate the existence of God.

[FBadgenoone saved the remainder of Chapter XI for readers in search for the meaning of personal salvation. Subsequent chapters highlighted the challenges faced by many new Christians. Frederick resumed the observation at Chapter XV.]

[Book 9]

CHAPTER XV

An Empty Nest

Mimi had made the adjustment from the Empire State to the Constitution State. Her husband's career continued to thrive at Apple. She secured a position with the local school district and watched their daughters graduate and move on to college.

Anna continued to share information with Frederick Badgenoone.

Within a few years, things changed at Trav's office. Eastern Operations became Northern Operations. The office was upended again when the company restructured. Now Nav (KN) was a part of Higher Education Operations.

Point Man welcomed the challenge. He was immediately involved in a market sizing and segmentation exercise. Different resources would be applied to schools depending on their Carnegie Classifications and computer hardware acquisition potential.

Within a few months, Point Man brought Trav's publishing background into play. He would help to construct a catalog model designed to reach one of the segments. A telesales team would reinforce the effort.

Actually, there would be two teams. One was outsourced and based in Annapolis, Maryland. The other consisted of direct employees and resided at a company facility in Austin, Texas. Nav thanked Point Man and took on the assignment.

Mimi was able to accompany Nav on occasion when her job permitted. The visits to Annapolis gave her an opportunity for side trips to visit two of the daughters at college in neighboring Virginia.

The visits in Texas gave her a chance to visit with her sister and brother-in-law just up the highway. There was a fair amount of time when she was all alone in the two-story house in the Merryall section of town.

It seemed incredibly empty when the girls went off to college. Now with Nav on extended assignments, the quiet within the walls was sometimes deafening. Fortunately, she still had a job that she loved and some really close friends who broke the silence.

Some long-lasting relationships were forged during her bible study class at the local church. In the meantime, Nav continued to help forge the two telesales teams into one cohesive unit.

Training, cross-training, systems, and telephony integration were all part of the mix. Within six months, both teams were maximizing the effectiveness of a targeted catalog.

Nav invited Mimi to join them for a well-deserved celebration dinner—one in Austin, the other in Annapolis. She enjoyed meeting with the teams. She joined the Annapolis team at an Italian restaurant just down the street from the Naval Academy. She celebrated with the Austin team at a Mexican grill on 6th street, not far from the University of Texas campus.

Point Man was enlisted again within the year. This time he was called upon to help create, train, and manage a team of associate sales representatives, ASRs. The first class would be selected for seven districts around the country. The ASRs were recruited right out of college. Ultimately they would be deployed to the field.

Working with the district sales managers (DSMs) and the training department, Point Man had ninety days to prepare the green recruits. This time, Mimi wasn't part of the equation. She followed the development of this new team through daily casual phone conversations with Nav.

She wasn't there for the final graduation ceremony. Nav celebrated with this team of seven with a dinner and a ballgame. The Chicago Bears would meet the Green Bay Packers that weekend.

An ASR from North Carolina was going to place a bet on the Bears. He reasoned that they had the upper hand. They were accustomed to the cold weather. Nav advised him to keep the Hamilton in his wallet.

The following day, Nav confided to Mimi that the ASR wasn't a football fan. He was, however, a scratch golfer, a pre-med student, and one of the brightest of the seven. Green Bay won and the ASRs were deployed. Within the year, every one of them had approached Golden Apple trip status.

By 1995, a year of reflection and infringement, the technology landscape had begun to change. A new operating system threatened the Mac platform. The introduction was announced with some fanfare with white lights illuminating the crown of the Empire State Building.

Point Man, Trav, and Nav (KN) considered the event. He had spent the better part of a decade dedicated to advancing instructional technology, first in the K–12 and then Higher Education market. The new development changed the equation.

He decided that he could be of more help to the cause on the other side of the hardware conversation, at least for a time. Some educational publishers were considering the merits of technology. Startup companies seemed to be leading the charge. The mainline textbook companies still generated a comfortable revenue stream and would take a little longer to come along.

Within the span of a few months, Mimi's world changed once again. Her husband accepted a position as a director of sales for a company based in lower Manhattan. There was no efficient way to commute from Merryall. Trav spent the better part of the next year as a weekend husband.

On Monday he would leave at 5:00 am, drive to the Transfer Station, and drop off a suitcase and four business suits. From his new base of operations, it was a ten-minute ride to an indoor parking lot in Hoboken. A brisk walk to the ferry and a quick ride across the Hudson brought him to within walking distance of his new office.

He sometimes took a shortcut through the World Trade Center. On the way back to the Transfer Station, he would on occasion pay a visit to the Trinity Church. He wondered if Alexander Hamilton who was buried in the shadow of the church, could ever imagine the high water markers of the American economy and this city in particular. The twin towers made a significant statement.

The start-up company published a range of software targeted to the needs of students and institutions. It created significant intellectual property and delivered it in a number of formats. Video assets transitioned from VHS format to disc. Software found expression through CD ROM.

In addition to his responsibilities at the office, Trav once again found himself on a plane or a train. He needed to manage a direct sales team. He also had to construct strategic partnerships and secure alternate distribution channels.

[Frederick Badgenoone thanked Anna again for the additional information. It helped him to better understand some underlying forces that helped to form Mimi's reality.]

One day, Mimi got a call from Madison, Wisconsin. Nav was signing a deal there with a higher education vendor. A month later, she got another call. It came from Nova Scotia. Point Man was there to solidify a relationship with a Canadian distributor at the Canadian Library Association, CLA conference.

Mimi stopped to reflect on conversations she had with her mother and mother-in-law. They recalled the sacrifices they had to make when their husbands were in military service. The most challenging was the time alone, the time when all the household responsibilities rested solely on their shoulders.

She realized that corporate spouses shared many of the same burdens as their brothers and sisters wed to partners in uniform. Of course, there were no bullets flying in the corporate world and no one there would think of wielding a bayonet.

The weight seemed to grow heavier with each passing day. The house in Merryall seemed increasingly irrelevant and untenable. Her husband spent the better part of his time at his mother's house, on the road, or in the air. Her daughters were preoccupied with their own studies. Her faith in God, good friends, and a job she really enjoyed kept her grounded.

This time, Jackson moved the observation forward three chapters.

CHAPTER XIX
More Ripples

On a late April day, she received a call from her husband. She told him to talk fast because an afternoon ice storm had just felled the electric wires and the phone lines were sure to fail soon. He told her that he was in Houston, Texas and had just been offered a new job opportunity.

He would report to his former coworker. He had worked the numbers with him during the market segmentation exercise back in Higher Education Operations.

Apparently, Trav was pitching his company to the largest PC manufacturer in the country. His colleague told him that Nav was the third software vendor that he had seen that day.

His future supervisor had just received the go-ahead to hire a marketing manager for Instructional Technology. Would he consider the job? It would be just like the old days. Other alumnae had considered the world on the other side of the rainbow.

Some were here in Houston, others just up the road in Austin. A handful even landed in Redmond, Washington and Armonk, New York. Any number were scattered around the globe throughout the publishing and software world.

The ripples continued to emanate from the Infinite Loop in Cupertino. The temperature in Houston was a balmy 85 degrees. In

Connecticut, ice pulled the wires from the house. Minutes later, the phone went dead in Merryall.

She couldn't process it all at first. She prayed about it and considered the pros and cons of the move, especially at this stage of life. Their surprise baby had just announced plans to marry her childhood sweetheart within the next few months.

Three days later, Mimi came home and found a dozen yellow roses on the fireplace mantle. The Yellow Rose of Texas came over the radio. She was heading to Houston. Somehow she found the time to help with the wedding arrangements.

Three years in Houston somewhat altered her worldview. Although she had travelled the globe with her husband, the Northeast was always home. She developed a special attachment to her quintessential New England Town. It was there that she nurtured her daughters through their high school years.

Now the daughters had lives of their own. Her husband purchased a lot on Lake Conroe, sure that this would be their final stop on the corporate merry-go-round. He was ready to buy a boat and haul out his cane fishing pole as soon as this assignment was complete. She knew better. He was a workaholic and wasn't about to retire any time soon.

In any event, she wasn't about to live in a lakeside community. She didn't really like to be near any large body of water. Mimi could appreciate the ripples of a creek or a stream, but the larger bodies of water were just too intimidating. She insisted that they buy a house in a development closer to his office. They supervised the building of a two-story brick colonial on a corner lot in the Woodlands. The lake lot would go to weed.

Nav immediately threw himself into his new work. He was back at a hardware company. Mimi found a rewarding job in the local school district. This time she would tutor high school students in Mathematics. Many came back to her the following year with heartfelt thanks. They were able to pass the state exam, graduate, and move on with life.

Mimi had recently passed the state certification exam and anticipated a return to a full-time classroom position. Teaching children who were approaching adulthood presented different challenges than the ones she encountered as an elementary school teacher.

Just as challenging was the commute to the new school. She fully utilized the access road of the Interstate Highway. Cars on the main road zipped by at speeds well in excess of the posted seventy-miles-per hour limit.

Sometimes her mind would drift back to the curving roads of Litchfield County, Connecticut or the roads that hugged the rolling hills of Wayne County, New York. She even enjoyed all the snow. With time, Mimi came to understand why her husband appreciated the amenities provided in the greater Houston area.

They entertained visiting family at the NASA Space Center and took full advantage of the sports venues, theater, concerts, shops, and dining available in the fourth largest city in the United States. He was still a Bills fan at heart. Every so often he took an opportunity to root for the Texas teams.

The Woodlands provided a semi self-contained environment. It was formed at about the same time that another planned community, Gananda, came into existence just north of their former home in Canal Town. Gananda never reached its full potential. The Woodlands exceeded expectations. High water markers for each development measured the growth.

In the Woodlands, they had access to brand new neighborhood grocery and convenience stores. They could bike to any number of swimming pools. The concert hall was just seven miles from the house. Popular entertainers brought down the lights and lit up the crowd.

A movie complex and one of the largest shopping malls in the country were just down the road. There was a championship golf course, several manmade ponds and restaurants aplenty. Trav relinquished visions of his lake, a boat and fishing pole.

Beyond The Woodlands, beyond Houston proper, they took weekend drives through fields adorned with bluebonnet flowers and desert like landscapes. They were punctuated by an occasional oasis. It reminded Trav of his years in Arizona.

She and Trav were sure to stop at the Blue Bell Ice Cream shop in Brenham whenever they drove in that direction. They never got around to visiting Huntsville but took a side trip to Washington-on-the-Brazos.

Nav and Mimi visited the Alamo in nearby San Antonio. He described the valiant effort that defined the Texas spirit on both sides of the bullet-pierced walls. They enjoyed a leisurely boat ride drifting back in time through placid river walk canals.

It took a year, but they finally sold their Merryall home. Now they were down to one house, a lot, and a still-very-empty nest. Mimi found increasing comfort in new-found friends, brand-new surroundings, a new job, and an incredible new shopping mall. But she didn't really like the word *new.*

[FBadgenoone thanked Anna for her input. He acknowledged the challenges faced by Mimi. He reserved the next few chapters for a more thorough reading by so many spouses who bore similar obligations in this new age. Jackson had seen it all before—different times, different scale, and same conundrum.]

CHAPTER XXIII

Honor Twenty-four Young Men, Seventy Times Seven Times

Mimi left with fond memories of new friends and neighbors in the Lone Star State but she was glad to be back in Connecticut. Wasn't it yesterday that she had uprooted her family from the Excelsior State to the Land of Steady Habits? That too was in the rear-view mirror. Her husband's career brought them back north, at least for a time. Their children were establishing families and careers of their own.

Nav had accepted a position as vice president of Sales and Marketing for a software publishing firm, a division of a much larger educational publishing house. They maintained their residence in Texas and found temporary living quarters in a colonial bed and breakfast just twenty miles north of his new office.

Mimi surveyed the new environment during Nav's first week on the job. Initially they thought they might find an apartment in the immediate vicinity.

In the downtown area, she noticed a semi-circle of neatly-spaced plaques that proclaimed the services of local men who fought for their town, state and country.

The plaques declared:

> This tree planted in memory of the men of this town who served in the Revolutionary War.

This tree planted in memory of men of this town who served in the War of 1812.

This tree planted in memory of men of this town who served in the Mexican War.

This tree planted in memory of men of this town who served in the Civil War.

This tree planted in memory of men of this town who served in the Spanish American War.

This tree planted in memory of a certain captain killed in action. Hindenburg line Sept 29, 1918 A.D. [Jackson thought of it as a year of reflection and relief.]

This tree planted in memory of a certain private killed in action. Jonc De Mer Ridge, Oct. 20, 1918 A.D.

These plaques had been respectfully placed by an American Legion post. For some reason, the trees were gone. Only green grass and white marble plaques remained.

A memorial to servicemen from later conflicts was positioned a block away, closer to the street, easier to view, no less peaceful a setting.

Closer to the train station, she discovered a tercentennial celebration time capsule that was installed several years earlier. It was inscribed May 29, 1995 A.D. to be opened May 29, 2095 A.D. What would her great-grandchildren learn?

[Jackson told the Neverborn that the latter year awaited description by a generation that was yet to be born.]

Pleasantville, NY was a peaceful enough place but she couldn't find a suitable dwelling. She expanded the search and finally found a decent apartment in Ridgefield, Connecticut. It was just up the Saw Mill Parkway and some old country roads away.

She walked up the path to the condominium complex built on a battlefield named after the town. She paused for a moment to read the memorial plaque dedicated to the men who had fallen.

> In defense of American independence at the battle . . .
> April 27, 1777 A.D, died 8 patriots who were laid in these
> grounds companioned by 16 British soldiers. Living their
> enemies, dying their guests.

The plaque was hidden from easy view. How many other plaques like this stood testimony to young men who fought and died on countless battlefields? How many of those plaques were hidden by condominiums and strip malls and parking lots?

Mimi had been around the Knowledge Navigator for a long time by now. She decided to try her hand at describing the year of the plaque. It came to her in an instant: 1777, a year of reflection and momentum.

[Frederick moved beyond the turmoil resulting from another disruption in Nav's career. He resumed Mimi's story two chapters later.]

CHAPTER XXV

Not a Line In The Sky

They gave up the apartment and returned to their house in The Woodlands. On Tuesday, September 11, 2001—a year of reflection and disruption—she received a call from Nav. Everyone knew where they were on that day. He was at a local car dealership, and she was at home. He told her to turn on the TV. The announcer had just interrupted the local program to display images of the terror attack on New York City.

They tried to reach their daughters to no avail, as all the lines were jammed. Their oldest was scheduled for a job interview in lower Manhattan. Their surprise baby, newly married, was living in mid-town.

All flights were grounded; there wasn't a line in the sky. Trav had to think all the way back to his days in the desert to recall such a pristine horizon. Driving wasn't an option in the immediate aftermath of the tragedy. Like so many Americans, they stayed glued to the screen. They continued to dial and prayed for all the victims and their families.

Nav acknowledged the futility of it all. Just as Pearl Harbor had affected the lives of the previous generation, this tragic event defined the new times. They tried to make sense of new order. He had seen enough to know that this was yet another manifestation of the darker side of man.

Mimi recognized the voice of Frederick Badgenoone. He instructed her to put aside the words of her husband for now. Instead she should open a book that he gave to her years ago. Frederick guided her to page 58 in *Apples of Gold*. She began to read. "Nothing which is morally wrong can ever be politically right."

Trav and Mimi packed the car and headed north again a few months after the attack on Washington. They paused for reflection in a place called Hope and came away renewed. The next chapter in Mimi's life would bring her to the Tar Heel State.

Jackson passed the baton to GBadgenoone. George was responsible for documenting the life of Mimi's first-born daughter. Before he could begin to tell the story, Jackson convened another weekly meeting. The usual nine suspects found their way to the clearing in the woods.

JBadgenoone had special instructions for George, Henry, and Israel. They had the benefit of hindsight. Their observees could build on the stories of their parents and grandparents. Jackson expected a bit more. These three Neverborn observers should find a way to connect the dots from one sister to the other. They should also establish a solid foundation to introduce the next generation.

Israel would have the most challenging assignment. He would need to bring a measure of closure to the quest for the hidden treasure of Dutch Buffalo Creek. That quest should incorporate elements that surfaced all the way back to the opening pages of the principal book.

If these three succeeded in their assignment, Jackson could construct an appropriate conclusion. It was her turn to interject some humor. "No pressure; just develop your story."

George began to read with a renewed sense of confidence.

[B o o k 10]

The High Water Markers of George's Observee

By George Badgenoone,

About the Author

George Badgenoone was never born on July 26, 1972, a year of reflection and new beginnings. He was one of two boys that were lost in stillbirth to a young woman in a little village in Wayne County, New York. His twin brother Daniel, aka Daniel Badgenooned, was linked to many of the same stories as his predecessor and mentor, Daniel Badgenoone.

Daniel and George joined forces to observe several souls. One observee was still a very young girl. She would at times hear their voices. They never revealed their names to her; she identified them as Dubie and Darby.

George was Darby, and Daniel was Dubie. They became her best pretend friends just before her third birthday.

George was named after a boy who was born in May of 1972. That George would have a significant role to play during the third decade of her life. GBadgenoone also drew his identity from two other living souls. His complete journey is described in *The Book of the Neverborn*.

In keeping with the original assignment, he reserved the preface and the opening chapter for a more comprehensive reading.

George then began to record the life of his observee at Chapter Two.

Jackson applauded his moves.

CHAPTER II

A Headstone Without Flowers

Her father loaded the station wagon and headed one state to the south. His wife rode shotgun, and his oldest daughter sat in the middle seat. Her twin sisters were in the way back section of the vehicle. The car windows were covered with decals representing most of the states they had visited in that two-tone blue Ford LTD.

The family arrived at the historic Gettysburg battlefield around noon on that day in 1979. By early evening, they came upon the cemetery. She paused for a moment and then made a startling observation. "This is where the fallen soldiers are buried." The observation was startling because it came from the voice of a five year old.

George watched her develop over time. She reached high water markers uniquely her own. She had heard his voice even before the visit to the Gettysburg battlefield. At the cemetery he whispered into her ear. *Bring your dad to the fourth tombstone in the third row.*

She acknowledged the voice of Darby and followed his guidance. JBadgenoone joined them when they approached the grave. It was the permanent home to the bones of Jackson's would-have-been great-grandnephew.

Trav took note of the headstone. The soldier who was felled was all of eighteen years old. Trav asked her why she wanted to see this particular stone. She replied without hesitation, "Darby asked me to come here. He asked me to bring flowers."

CHAPTER III

Count The Cost

A few years later, as a middle school student, she was challenged to create a project. It would be designed to help the class predict the outcome of the Civil War. Her dad thought it might be made easier if she enlisted the Macintosh technology he had just brought back to the home at the base of the drumlin.

She worked the numbers, railroad miles, tons of iron, number of guns and bayonets, soldiers in uniforms of blue and gray. Everyone knew the ultimate outcome of the conflict. Her assignment was to analyze the data and consider if a different scenario was even within the realm of the possible. The numbers were all stacked against the seceding states.

The sixth-grader started to calculate the cost: *seven hundred and fifty thousand* people perished in the conflict. It was a staggering number when compared to the *fifty-five thousand* that perished in the War for Independence four score and seven years earlier.

The project nourished in her an appreciation for the stories that never made it into the history books. It also awakened a genuine appreciation for the power of numbers. They added a dimension to the narrative of life that was unavailable through words alone.

CHAPTER IV
Notes Also Tell a Story

Her love of numbers migrated to the notes on a keyboard. The notes carried logic and precision. Within a year, she picked up the clarinet. That instrument gave her lungs an opportunity to add personality to the music just as her fingers had done on the piano.

She brought her music to the Firebirds marching band. It provided entertainment at local parades, the Wayne County Fair and Canal Town Days. Her dad kept the camera at hand and captured every event on film. She was no longer just his brown-eyed little girl. She was Firebird.

A year later, her younger sisters joined in the march. One girl kept feet moving with the coordinated beat of her percussion instruments. The other gave depth to the renditions with perfectly placed timing from her French horn.

Her parents were there to see Firebird graduate from the Canal Town Middle School. She went on to make new friends in her first year of high school when the family moved to the Litchfield Hills of Connecticut. Her twin sisters entered the eighth grade at the new Middle School in the same year.

CHAPTER V

The Green Wave

George followed her journey at the local high school, home of the Green Wave. Her love of numbers translated into an academic career that gravitated toward all things mathematical.

The love was manifest early in her studies. It gained purpose when she read *The Discoverers: A History of Man's Search to Know His World and Himself.*

In Chapter 81, Learning from Numbers, she read, "The pioneer of modern demography, some would say, too, of statistics, was a prosperous London tradesman, John Graunt (1620 – 1674) ... The death toll of the plague years, visible all around him, became the basis for Graunt's interest in demography and statistics."

She continued reading. "His most original invention was his new way to present population and mortality by calculating survivorship in a 'life table.' While modern actuaries do not accept his numbers, his table of survivorship opened the modern epoch of demography."

Jackson and George observed as Firebird digested Graunt's injunction: "The most important words ever written on the maps of human knowledge are *terra incognita*—unknown territory." Thus the seed of her career as an actuary was planted from the positive driving force of human expansionism.

Firebird reached another high water marker as class valedictorian. The four years leading up to that moment were rich with memories.

High school provided opportunities for new growth beyond pure academic pursuit. She joined the cheerleading squad and the high school band.

Those activities ensured that she would attend every football game and basketball game, home and away. She acted several key roles in the school plays and performed in the school orchestra. She joined them in an all-state competition in central Connecticut.

There was also a broad world beyond the campus setting. A gazebo in the Town Square provided a readymade meeting place for kids of all ages. A vintage tank from the Great War stood guard over the Green. The local movie theater welcomed patrons with the latest that Hollywood had to offer.

Years later, the theater and the street became part of a Hollywood set. A remake of *Mr. Deeds* was filmed on location. Mandrake Falls, New Hampshire was transported to a perfect New England setting in Connecticut. The filmmaker added some flare to the scene by staging a few dozen bright red Corvette automobiles on either curbside. Marty Spin, vowel guy, would have been really impressed.

The world beyond the Green was wide open. A Metro-North train from neighboring Danbury opened to the platform of New York City. Along with sisters and friends, Firebird took in all the venues. The Metropolitan Museum of Art, the Museum of Natural History, and the Kennedy Center for the Performing Arts were just a few of the attractions they visited whenever possible.

Family automobile outings usually followed the old country roads. They sometimes led to Quincy Market or Old Ironsides in Boston. On other trips, they headed north along the Ethan Allen Highway. Sometimes they would spend a day at the Kent Falls. A weekend trip might land them at the Massachusetts Stockbridge Inn or the Grandma Moses Museum in Bennington, Vermont.

The new town also afforded them an opportunity to visit with the grandparents, aunts, uncles and cousins who were part of the Fifth Street branch of the family. When they lived in Canal Town, those visits were limited to once or twice a year. Now they occurred once or twice a month.

Travel during the high school years was not confined to the mid-Atlantic or New England states. She started the college search in junior year. Her sisters were able to leverage the adventure and started their search as sophomores.

They started with visits to campus settings in the Northeast. There were so many places to consider. Small school, large university, private, and public provided alternate paths. Her dad was recently assigned to the higher education division in his company and was able to provide statistics for each campus.

She knew numbers couldn't tell the whole story. Firebird wanted to see the buildings where she would spend the next four years of her life. Her sisters seconded the motion. The search expanded toward the end of that year to other parts of the country. They considered at least two schools in the West, a few in the Midwest, a number in the Middle Atlantic, and several more in The South.

On the last leg of a southern journey, they visited historic Williamsburg, Virginia. The streets hearkened back to the foundations of the country. Restored buildings and period enactors brought that time to life. At the heart of the town was a university that was the alma mater of several presidents and statesmen. She knew that the academic entrance requirements were rigorous at this public Ivy.

George wrote chapters about her time as an undergraduate at the College. Then he captured her postgraduate work in Boston followed by a business internship in Philadelphia and a career as an actuary.

The first job took her back to Boston. She wished that she could commune with her maternal great-grandmother to let her know that the streets there were not paved in gold. The year following 9/11, she accepted a position in lower Manhattan, not far from where her paternal grandfather began to accumulate his high water markers.

[George passed the chapters that commemorated those events. He commenced reading in Chapter XIV. GBadgenoone met her again in Chicago.]

CHAPTER XIV
Seats 3A and 3B Connect at Thirty-thousand Feet

Everyone was in a hurry to go somewhere. The gates at O'Hare were packed. Her flight was delayed by two hours. She finally boarded and took her seat, 3A. The plane continued to board for another twenty minutes.

The flight attendant was ready to close the door. He looked at the empty seat next to hers; maybe she could get some rest on this flight. She closed her eyes and drifted into a deep sleep.

At the last minute, a young man bolted his way on board and settled into 3B. Neither of them was aware of it at the time, but their lives would be forever changed that day. The captain made the announcement: "Ladies and gentlemen we have reached cruising altitude, you may move about the cabin." She opened her eyes; the seat next to hers was no longer vacant.

Within a few months, they began a relationship that blossomed with time. They shared a quest for travel and reached places on the planet that were unknown to their parents. She accepted his proposal for marriage in a peaceful setting not far from where her paternal great-grandfather presented his ring to Anna.

Sometimes events travel full circle. The image of Grandma Charlene with hands gestured in a circle came back to her that day. It was so many years since her father had shared the story about a day in San Francisco.

Within a few years, Firebird and her husband brought their own children into the world. The first was a beautiful girl with stunning red hair. She would be named for her paternal great-grandmother but she bore a striking resemblance to her maternal grandmother, Mimi, aka Meena.

The little girl demonstrated a fascination of lineage relationship when she was all of three years old. During one visit, she pointed to her mother and said, "You are my mommy." She pointed to Meena and said, "You are my mommy's mommy."

By the time she was four, she had already demonstrated talent as a ballet dancer. Meena saw a bit of GiGi's step in her movement. From that moment she assumed an identity as the Little Ballerina.

Her sister arrived in short order. Another brown-eyed girl, she cast a smile a country mile wide. Her cheeks were punctuated by two dimples that she inherited from her Irish ancestors. Meena provided the obvious nickname, Dimples.

The girls joined their older cousin on a family reunion in the year of reflection and reconciliation. George was there when Meena snapped a picture of the girls with Grandpa. At his urging, she passed the photo on to Jackson's cloud.

At the time the picture was taken, Grandpa was still able to walk, albeit with a cane. A few months later, he was back on the operating table, ready to accept a second titanium thigh rod and a plastic socket hip. His wife got a new chapter in her book: Wife of the Hip Guy. No one at the rehabilitation center knew about Mimi's high water markers. She could only share pictures of the daughters and grandchildren.

Firebird tried to provide some comfort to her mother during that difficult time. She heard the voice of her childhood pretend friend Darby. He told her to read a quote from *Apples of Gold*, a book that her dad had given to her years ago. She turned to page 49 and read: "The LORD sometimes takes us into troubled waters NOT to drown us, but to cleanse us." She called her mom and recited the quote to her the next day.

The mother of the Little Ballerina and Dimples stumbled upon a bittersweet moment. Early into her fourth decade, she was now providing nourishment to the mom who had nourished her.

[Jackson passed the torch to HBadgenoone. His job now was to follow another extraordinary ordinary life, the life of Mimi's surprise baby.]

[Book 11]

The High Water Markers
of Henry's Observee

[Book 11]

CHAPTER I

The Surprise Baby

HBadgenoone mapped out the high water markers of the surprise baby from Canal Town. Her mother told her that she wasn't expecting twins and that this girl was her surprise baby. The three-year-old looked back at her mom, and in a refreshing point counterpoint said, "I'll bet that I was the best surprise you ever got."

It was an early indicator that this child was going to display a remarkable sense of purpose. Just a few years later, she reminded her mom that big sister was "not the boss of me."

[Henry was able to spot a thousand moments in the early life of the surprise baby. He reflected on a number in the rest of this chapter and in Chapter II. Jackson urged him to reveal some of the treasures that were directly related to *The Hidden Treasure of Dutch Buffalo Creek*. HBadgenoone moved on to the next chapter.

CHAPTER III
Another Striking Resemblance

Her father loaded the station wagon and headed east. The family arrived at a reconstruction of a fort which played a pivotal role in the Revolutionary War. She and her sisters listened to the story. What caught her attention was the scene of three Native American women reenacting the lives of their ancestors.

She thought that they bore a striking resemblance to her great aunt. It wasn't just because they were preparing a meal—it was because one of them actually looked like Aunt Connie.

At that point, the tour guide began to describe the armaments of the fort and the soldier's drill. Nav realized that his daughter had uncovered a nugget of truth that silenced all the talk about weapons and war.

The men and women on either side of that fort didn't crave war. Their goal was to stay alive and enjoy some measure of happiness and well being. Nav couldn't help but think of Sarah. Did her family try to find sanctuary within the original walls those many years ago?

Henry continued to chapter a number of her high water markers. Like her sisters she made the adjustment from a village on the banks of the Erie Canal to a small town overlooking the Housatonic River. She inherited Grandpa Jimmy's natural style on the ivory keys. She took it up a notch and perfected an awesome French horn sound.

Israel encouraged Henry to bypass the remainder of the chapter and a few that followed. Those subsequent chapters would develop parallels to the books that livened her elementary school days. She took turns sharing with her twin sister stories from *Little House on the Prairie, The Bobbsey Twins, Anne of Green Gables,* and *Nancy Drew.* [Those stories would find their way into the comprehensive version of the book by IBadgenoone.]

Her reading gradually migrated to young adult novels and historical fiction. *Little Women* inspired her to devour stories. Her reading set the stage for a life-long passion for literature.

Henry reserved the high school years for a more thorough presentation in the comprehensive version of his book. Daniel and Israel had provided some nuggets from those years that would support the main story. Jackson was pleased to see her teammates collaborate. They demonstrated a desire to present a cohesive framework. Henry's observation continued in 1993.

CHAPTER VIII
A Northern Bell

Her academic and musical talent earned her a seat at a well-respected college in Fredericksburg. She had fond memories of the time she spent at that institution. There was a charm about the town. Some classmates became lifelong friends.

The college was part of a larger community, one that dated back to before the Revolutionary War. The home of Mary, namesake of the school and mother of George Washington, was just down the road.

During the War Between the States some local citizens were conflicted. They had a deep regard for the founding fathers and the nation that they had built. They were also the children of Virginia. One of the bloodiest battles of the war took place within cannon shot sound from where Father and Daughter stood that day.

The surprise baby had blossomed into a bright, articulate and talented young woman. Her father called her his southern belle, Belle for short. She found some irony in the tag. A girl born in New York and raised in Connecticut, she had only academic ties to the Old Dominion. She humored her dad and acknowledged Trav and Nav.

Toward the end of her freshman year, she decided to spread her wings. A southern breeze blew across the banks of the Rappahannock River and carried her north. The peal of a northern bell announced her arrival. She continued her undergraduate study in one of the original Public Ivy schools.

It was located at the northern most tip of the Green Mountain State. At the university, she perfected her musical performance and expanded her course of study. She converted her love of art into an art history major.

Each environment had plus and minus attributes. In the winter, Fredericksburg could be covered in ice. In Burlington there was snow, lots of it, and it was cold. But then there was always Ben and Jerry's ice cream and a cup of hot chocolate.

Jackson Badgenoone

During the Revolutionary War, colonial militia were said to have tipped a few pints in the Merryall section of town. Her house was just down the road from there, across the street from the Frederick March estate. On the other side of the creek was a summer camp dedicated to the performing arts.

Belle still considered the Merryall house as her home. It was so much more than just a base of operations. The house had a certain order, the garden a welcoming familiarity. The white metal headboard was polished to reflection. Mother always had a hot cup of coffee ready in the winter and a cold glass of ice tea during the summer months.

By the time she returned from her senior year in Burlington, she knew that she wanted to marry her high school sweetheart. Both had cheered on the Green Wave. Years later, the school was converted into a middle school. A new and bigger building replaced it, this one right on the old Ethan Allen highway.

Her parents were no longer living in the house. Trav had a new job in Houston; Mother was maintaining a new primary residence in The Woodlands, Texas. The house in Merryall was still furnished. When Mom and Dad returned for a visit, the house became a home again. Her white headboard brought a sense of continuity to the place. Years later she would gift it to her niece, the Little Irish Step Dancer.

She wanted the wedding to be a modest event. It would be a celebration for immediate family and close friends. Just north of her house stood a vintage chapel, complete with white board siding and a New England steeple. It was an ideal setting.

Her mother and father came up from Texas. Her twin sister flew in from Oregon. Older sister drove to the wedding from Boston. Charlene, Fred and Mary, her new in-laws and most of the people they cared about made it to the chapel and then on to the Inn for the reception. Grandpa Jimmy was there in spirit.

Her Neverborn brother was there to observe the celebration. He encouraged family members and friends to capture photos. He continued to write the story of his would-have-been baby sister and her husband. Subsequent chapters outlined so many of their high water markers. Henry moved the story forward several years.

In the course of time, they brought two handsome young sons into the world. The gene pool and the force were strong with both of them. Their mom raised them with the values that she had inherited. In their mannerism and speech, Nav felt and heard the strain of five generations. Henry penned more chapters.

One of the chapters was dedicated to the boys. They were both born at a hospital located on the Upper East Side of Manhattan. Within a few years they were living in an historical home on the banks of the Connecticut River. That house was built by a Yankee whaler and meticulously restored to an early nineteenth-century appearance.

The first-born displayed a more than average interest in all things mechanical. He would take apart a gadget and put it back together again without fanfare. His paternal grandfather called him Mr. Gadget, sometimes shortened to Gadget.

In grade school, he was inspired by a Lego model of the Mark Twain House on display at the Bradley International Airport. Later that year, he constructed an elaborate model of his own. After seeing that castle, his maternal grandfather began to refer to the young boy as Lego Man.

His younger brother from an early age demonstrated an unusual ability to manufacture elaborate verbal constructs. By the time he was in third grade, his friends called him Golden Tongue. His grandparents called him The Linguist.

The boys were inseparable. Jackson was sure that she could recruit additional Neverborn writers to document their remarkable lives. She anticipated a special focus on an event in the year of reflection and reconciliation.

At that time the boys visited with their maternal grandparents. The highlight of the trip included a visit to the Reed Gold Mine. Both of them returned to their home with a golden nugget suspended in a glass tube filled with pure creek water.

[Jackson encouraged Henry Badgenoone to continue at Chapter XIV.]

CHAPTER XIV

The Pilot

Her husband wanted to give a birthday present that would enrich her life beyond the moment. He knew the responsibilities that she carried as the CEO of an entrepreneurial company. She was also holding down the fort on the home front with the boys.

He gave her the gift of a flying lesson. Not just one, but one full year of lessons. The following year she could claim her wings. She embraced the challenge and made a mental note. Her grandfather Fred would have been proud to see her take control of the stick.

She sensed the thrill of flight. The Connecticut landscape unfolded in a tapestry of green. The plane banked to the right. She could discern streets and houses in the Hartford area.

There was freedom up here in the cloud(s). Her wings could transport her in time. Mark Twain's house below triggered memories of novels she had read about time travel. *A Connecticut Yankee in King Arthur's Court* flashed by her mind's eye.

From this vantage point she could visualize the souls that occupied the land. She could hear the voices of Yankee whalers, colonial shop keepers, and Native Americans in previous centuries.

When she got back on the ground, she promised herself to someday take her mom and dad for a journey above the cloud(s). Henry directed her to a book given to her by her dad years ago. On page 33 in *Apples of Gold,* she read, "Happiness is not a station you arrive at, but a manner of traveling." Anna Badgenoone and Frederick Badgenoone agreed. Their respective observees would appreciate that sentiment.

[Jackson returned, pleased to see how the lives were leaning on each other. Her sister Sarah would have approved.]

[Book 12]

The High Water Markers
of Israel's Observee

By Israel Badgenoone,
Copyright © 2015 by Jackson Badgenoone

Preface to The High Water Markers
of Israel's Observee

Israel Badgenoone had a unique assignment. He was to record not just the life of his observee but also the life of her daughter. The first-born twin had anticipated the life of her child years before her daughter was ever born. She captured the image in a painting rendered for a high school art class assignment.

IBadgenoone would identify her as the Artist even though she had no formal degree in art, as did her twin sister. It was this painting that captured his imagination. It also caught the attention of Jackson Badgenoone.

Israel would have lived by palette and brush. Now he found himself tasked with writing. He enjoyed observing the life of the Artist, her husband, and their daughter. At Jackson's urging, he picked up the story at the third chapter.

CHAPTER III
Connecting Waters

Her dad walked with her down to the bridge overlooking the Barge Canal. The canal ran parallel to the old Erie Canal that greeted visitors to the village. There were almost 1000 people in the surrounding countryside in 1798.

By 1822, a year of reflection and expansion, it had become the western most terminus of the still expanding Erie Canal. The Book of Mormon was first published there in 1830, a year of reflection and interpretation. The number of souls living in the village had doubled by the time the book was distributed.

In the final quarter of the twentieth century the peaceful northern village boasted a population twice larger. It was also home to several landmarks. At the intersection of Church and Main Street, houses of worship were firmly planted on each of the four corners. *Ripley's Believe It or Not* claimed that it was the only such confluence in America.

The Wayne County Fair Grounds was located just up the road. Once each year, farmers displayed their prized animals. Wives took the wrap off award-winning pies. In the evening hours, children mounted brightly-lit colored rides and hearkened to the call of the carnie barker. Cotton candy covered their smiles.

The Jaycees served up Italian sausage hoagies and burgers on a bun. Their tent was pitched for the duration of the Fair. It rose again in time for Canal Town Days. That event recalled the time when a man-made waterway defined village character and commerce. She enjoyed the celebration on a sunny day in 1987.

The following day, the Jaycees joined the local high school marching band, a bevy of beauty queens, and an occasional princess. Local men and women were festooned with period dress and or uniform from several periods in American History. Mummers from a sister city in the Garden State added feathers and banjos.

Fire engines and police car sirens announced the beginning and the end of the event. Young children tossed candy from horse drawn floats to the younger children lining the parade route. The American flag waved from every home.

Later that week, Trav and his daughter, the Artist, brought cane fishing poles and bait to the water that swirled against the metal and concrete lock. They planned to land some dinner.

When evening approached, they had only catfish and carp to show for their effort. The time did provide an opportunity for her to learn all about the place they called home. She appreciated the stories and carried their memories. Trav added them to memories of the times with his dad on the banks of the Gila River.

CHAPTER IV
Under The Gun

A few years earlier, her dad was still young enough to belong to the Jaycees. Those men, all under thirty-five years of age, predicted that restoring the old Erie Canal might improve tourism in the town. They would be faithful to the original laborers. There would be no bulldozers or heavy equipment. The young men would restore the old canal with picks, shovels, hand saws and grit.

Trav considered the toil that it took to complete the entire waterway from the banks of the Hudson River to the shores of Lake Erie. [JBadgenoone reflected on how Sarah's mother and siblings followed a parallel path in the south at about the same time.]

The Jaycees appreciated the history of this place. A tribute stood to a local admiral who changed the course of the Spanish American war. A plaque commemorated the birth place of the founder of American Express and co-founder of Wells Fargo.

The town captured a significant number of out-of-state visitors every year. They came to participate in a pageant hosted by the Church of Jesus Christ of Latter Day Saints. That religion was founded just down the road in a sacred grove.

Winston Churchill's maternal grandmother once lived in the town. There was some speculation about Iroquois lineage. In an earlier time Native Americans found the surrounding forest rich with game. They sought spiritual refreshment from the balance of life entrusted to their care.

Drumlins dominated the landscape. They provided a backdrop to the burned-over camp fire revival meetings hosted by other denominations. Some claimed no denomination. It seemed that everyone was hungry for a message from God.

On an early morning in mid-October in 1987, Trav and his daughters left the coverlet museum and headed to the park at the center of town. A large black naval gun was positioned on the green. The cannon pointed to the south.

At one time it discharged lead from the deck of Admiral Samson's flagship. That was during the Spanish American War. On this day it sheltered young children as they frolicked in the early morning autumn leaves.

High noon signaled the second half of their day. They planned to visit the apple orchards on the leeward side of Lake Ontario. On the way to the lake, the Artist was the first to notice a series of wooden frame barracks. The buildings were in desperate need of a fresh coat of paint.

They stopped to ask for directions to the nearest orchard. A young man standing in front of the first building approached the station wagon. He was one of several migrant workers who planned to join others just a few miles away. Trav recalled waving to other migrant workers in California fields a lifetime ago.

This experience was different. These men were up close and personal. They sipped pop from Coke or Pepsi bottles and basked in the light of the autumn sun. They offered refreshment to Trav and his daughters and provided directions to the orchard they planned to harvest.

Nav stopped to consider the station of these men and their families. He anticipated the questions that his daughters would pose when they got back to the car. Why weren't the barracks painted? Why did they live in barracks? Where were their wives and children? True to form, the Artist was the first to query her dad.

Jackson Badgenoone

[IBadgenoone recorded the conversation and then skipped to the sixth chapter.]

CHAPTER VI

View From The Top

The Artist made the adjustment to the new home in Connecticut. At school, she quickly scoped out the art room and made it her base of operations. In the summer, her dad shared the good news: The family was going to take a long-anticipated trip to Europe.

She would have an opportunity to visit art museums on the continent. She had already availed herself of the galleries in nearby New York City and Boston.

[Israel documented the journey in 1989. He inserted some detail in the chapter and several that followed. He took special note of an odd moment at the Eiffel Tower.]

When in Paris, Trav decided that he wouldn't accompany his daughters to the top of the structure. He went only to the first level. His daughters thought he feared heights. [Israel had conferred with Abadgenoone and knew better.] Trav believed that the girls should only see Paris from the upper platform later in life.

When they returned to Merryall, she added the pictures and memorabilia to her scrapbook. A Belgian Franc and a British Pound found a place on page ten.

She planned to meet with her sisters on the Village Green. The Artist and her Neverborn companion took a shortcut through the campus grounds of a private school that dominated the hill to the north of town.

Israel and the Artist were accompanied by Jackson Badgenoone on the stroll. She was the only one of them around at an earlier time when a young future president began his freshman year at the school.

The students there traveled in their own circle. The circle included a number of similar schools scattered throughout the Northeast, most of them within the boundaries of New England.

Parents of the children who attended those schools weren't likely to pan for gold. Jackson was certain that those parents wanted the very best for their children. She conferred with several of the other Neverborn. Did they have any commentary about the physical settings that set the stage for their observee?

She threw out the first postulate. The army base was a fortress for the Wannabe Cisco Kid. Israel commented that it might also have been a prison of sorts. He pointed to the barracks of the migrant workers to support his statement.

Another Neverborn referenced the company workplace. Yet another examined the small town setting. A third spoke to college settings. A fourth considered a factory floor and an office building. One spoke to a planned community.

Cbadgenoone reflected on a leper colony in Hawaii. His colleague rolled back the iron gates of a penal institution. Abadgenoone took them down the corridors of a nursing home and rehabilitation center. Israel brought them into the cold and dark chamber of a gold mine.

By the end of the exercise, they agreed that each stage was both fortress and prison. The life of each observee was enriched by the number of stages upon which that person acted out his or her life.

Israel continued to follow the life of the Artist. He helped to pen additional chapters about her high water markers. He traced her time as a student at the Green Wave.

[IBadgenoone recounted the time she met Trav and KN for a father-daughter excursion in New Orleans. She'd appreciated the fact that he had taken the time to be with her one-on-one just as he had for her sisters. Her twin experienced Ottawa; older sister San Francisco.]

In NOLA, Trav escorted her to a movie titled *Steel Magnolias*. The next day, KN accompanied her to a battlefield just outside of town. Old Hickory and his men made a political statement in the eye of a military victory.

Trav was there for her first day of class in the Beaver State in 1993. There were several visits to the campus in Eugene during the course of her four undergraduate years. There was something special about that place.

There were also visits beyond the campus in those years. The Ducks football team made it to the Rose Bowl in Pasadena. Then they secured a spot at the Cotton Bowl in Dallas. The observer and the observee both made it to that game. It gave the Artist an opportunity to reconnect with her aunt and uncle who lived in nearby Plano. He predicted that someday the Ducks might make a run at a national title.

Back at the campus she had found her soul mate. Soon after graduation they were married in the City of Roses. Israel attended her wedding in downtown Portland. IBadgenoone was also there to witness the birth of their daughter a few years later.

Israel Badgenoone constructed a number of chapters about the Artist's husband and his family. They had escaped the turmoil of war in Southeast Asia and built a new life in the United States. Israel would help his colleague to write an entire book about that family. Another neverborn would be assigned to write about the daughter of the Artist.

By the time she was seven years old, that daughter had achieved a number of high water markers of her own. Her proudest moment in the following year came with the award she won for her performance in a dance cherished by her maternal great-grandmother. On her eighth birthday she acquired a nickname that she would carry for several more years; the Little Irish Step Dancer.

Israel had some candidates in mind for both assignments. He relayed those on to Jackson and then continued to read at Chapter X.

CHAPTER X

Pan For Gold

Mom and daughter arrived at the New York Penn Station in time to board the 7:00 am train headed for Salisbury, North Carolina. On that day in 2012, the train passed through distance and time. It headed south past historic Trenton, Philadelphia, and Washington, DC. They conjured images of people who travelled the route before rails.

When they got to Virginia the train stopped more frequently. It rolled past the Civil War towns of Fredericksburg and Petersburg. It stopped just short of the Stonewall Jackson shrine in deference to a northbound Tropicana juice train.

The Little Irish Step Dancer greeted her maternal grandparents with open arms and an enormous smile when she met them at the station. She was their first granddaughter.

They were thrilled to have daughter and granddaughter spend some time with them. They were disappointed that her dad was unable to join them but understood that his job as stage set designer demanded his presence in The Big Apple.

Salisbury was a laid-back kind of town. The train station heralded a time long gone. The downtown carried reflections of the past. During the early years of the Civil War, a prisoner of war camp provided a baseball field.

Yankee boys and boys in gray could put aside the darker side of war and enjoy a game of youth. A baseball bat and ball displaced a rifle and bayonet, at least for a time.

The road back to Mont Amoena provided views of corn fields, forest, and streams. They passed the Rowan County Fair Grounds. A few miles farther, they paused for nourishment in the community of Faith and left refreshed.

There were so many things to do in the greater Charlotte area. At the top of the list was a visit to the Reed Gold Mine. It was just ten minutes from their home. The mine still encouraged prospectors to pan for gold. The Little Irish Step Dancer embraced the challenge with gusto.

When they returned to the house in Mont Amoena she was a little disappointed. There was no gold, just a few rocks as souvenirs. Meena came down the stairs and told her granddaughter that she had a special present for her. She asked her to close her eyes and open her hand.

Meena placed a gold band in the palm of the young girl and told her the story behind the ring. It had been given to Meena by her mother. Her father had given it to her as a First Communion gift not many years after the end of the Great War.

At that moment, the Artist was sure that she heard a familiar voice. She had first heard him years before at a Christmas Eve celebration at her Merryall home. This time he revealed himself by name. Israel instructed her to open a book that was given to her by her dad. She opened the pages of *Apples of Gold* and began to read on page 36. "You can never herd the world into the paths of righteousness with the dogs of war."

Jackson observed the conversation from the back of the room. She was pleased to see that the ring would bring joy to another generation. She returned up the stairs to the den overlooking Dutch Buffalo Creek and then moved down the hall.

JBadgenoone could tell that Trav was exhausted. He pushed back his recliner chair in the parlor and drifted into a much-needed rest. Soon he was consumed by a very deep sleep. Within the span of less than an hour, his eyes flinched. He appeared to recover in the signatures of the principal book.

[B o o k 1]

The Hidden Treasure of
Dutch Buffalo Creek

CHAPTER LXXIII
Back To The Den

Something was different. Everything was different. Trav looked over the banister railing. Most of his furniture was gone. The hutch cabinet with Mimi's favorite dishes and her Precious Moments Collection were nowhere to be seen. He called for his wife but there was no answer.

Then he heard the sound of men, women, and children. Their voices seemed muffled behind the door to the den overlooking Dutch Buffalo Creek. He approached the room with some caution. He glanced at the clock calendar to the right of the stairwell and froze in the moment; 10:44 am, December 24, 2054. Jackson took a leap of faith and christened it a year of reflection and consequence.

He called out for Jackson in a hushed voice so as not to alert the intruders on the other side of the door. Her response was immediate.

Fear not—you have been given a neat opportunity to experience the universe in neverborn fashion.

He realized then that he drifted between sleep and reality. He couldn't be over 106 years old.

They walked down the stairs, through the dining room, past the kitchen and out onto the deck. The house was nearly empty. The deck was still there, but most of the deck furniture was gone. Only a table and one chair remained. There was no trace of a garden. The path still made a way through leafless trees to a bone dry creek bed. The bed was lined with gray ash.

Jackson tried to prepare him for the next vista. He fully expected to see his favorite meadow and relish the wildlife on the other side of the bank. He saw only the frame of a concrete building. Ten gray stories tinted blood-red rose above a white stone foundation that ran the length of two football fields. The structure was high enough and long enough to obliterate the view of the rolling hills to the east.

He turned his back on the progress and began his ascent back toward the house. As he had so many years before he climbed with her up the stairs of the wooden deck.

This time he asked to remain outdoors for just a while longer. There was a nip in the air but it was tolerable to his titanium legs and plastic hips. He had so many questions to ask of her before confronting the guests in the den.

JBadgenoone asked Trav to write them down. She might not be able to answer every question but would do her best. Trav pulled the chair close to the table, took out a pen and paper and began to write. His early training prompted him to ask Who, What, Where, When, Why and How. The pen didn't necessarily follow an exact order or phraseology. He asked Mr. R to be patient with him as he wrote.

Was Mimi still alive?

Who were the people in the den upstairs?

What was the strange structure that consumed the meadow?

Was any more gold discovered in the creek?

Did gold have any monetary value by the middle of this century?

Were automobiles still the prevalent means of ground transportation?

Had mankind returned to space exploration in any meaningful sort of way?

Did geopolitical boundaries continue to define the discourse of nations?

What was the position of the United States in the world?

Did political parties carry any weight?

Was there still a Tea Party?

Did a hyphenated woman ever make it to the White House?

Had the war on terrorism finally run its course?

Were there still nation states?

How many people walked the planet?

Did they ever find a cure for cancer, AIDS, Parkinson's disease or the Ebola virus?

Were there any whales left in the ocean?

Did elephants still roam a range in Africa?

Did geese still migrate south from Canada in the winter?

Did hummingbirds still travel north from South America in the summer?

Did anyone recognize the Dutch Buffalo Creek tadpoles as an endangered species?

Was global warming still a topic for conversation?

What about fracking?

Did the ocean overtake the lower east side of Manhattan?

Did people still travel to and fro?

Was there still an internet, was it neutral?

Who controlled it?

Did people still congregate in brick and mortar buildings to worship?

Were religions reconciled?

Had God made His presence known in the world?

Jackson accepted the scribbled notes from her very old friend. She had him place the paper in his shirt pocket. The answer to some of his questions waited for him as they always had in the den overlooking Dutch Buffalo Creek.

They opened the door and entered the kitchen. The door closed behind them and sealed out the view of the deck, the path, the creek and the concrete building to the east. They walked through the dining room and up the stairs.

He looked at the clock to his right. The digits recorded the time at 11:45 am. They remained on the other side of the closed door and listened to the voices from the den.

It seemed like just a few short years earlier that the cousins had visited the den. Now they were called aunt and uncle. With their children in tow, they rummaged through the artifacts.

They pondered the books, tapes, DVDs, paintings, and photos. The Little Ballerina and Lego Man discovered a folded letter that was tucked neatly into a plain manila envelope.

The envelope was addressed to the grandchildren. They broke the seal, opened the letter and began to read. *Think of this as a treasure map. If you are reading it then I am passed. You will do well to understand how you are tied to each other, to those who came before you and those who will follow.*

Pay attention to the light that comes into your world.

At that moment a focused ray filtered through *fifty-eight thousand, two-hundred and nine* leafless branches. It penetrated the bay window and finally rested on the northern wall of the den overlooking Dutch Buffalo Creek.

The beam of light had drifted from east to west. At high noon on this mid-winter day, it struck the two bayonets that were still mounted above the door. The reflected light cast a golden cross that moved across the southern wall.

It travelled from west to east and finally landed upon an open bible directly under the window. The book was open, and the light shone upon words from John 13:34-35:

"A new command I give you: Love one another. As I have loved you, so you must love one another. By this everyone will know that you are my disciples, if you love one another."

The Little Irish Step Dancer placed the ring on the open page. Jackson was pleased. The bayonet and the ring were reunited. Trav's five grandchildren understood that their Grandpa did his best to share the greatest of treasures with them. They promised to help the Neverborn complete the missing chapters. They would enlist their children and grandchildren in the process. Trav opened the door, eager to embrace all of them. The room was empty. Jackson and he were alone again with a treasure chest of memories.

He woke up to the sound of Mimi's voice and the aroma of a fresh-brewed pot of coffee. It was 2014. Trav was back in the land of the living during the year of reflection and reconciliation. Nav opened the door. The room appeared to be normal again. All the artifacts were back in their appropriate place. Jackson joined KN as he tried to explain the experience to his wife. They returned to the creek. It acquired a new dimension during the several weeks that passed since the time that James posted a video of the water to Jackson's cloud.

JBadgenoone seized the moment. She convened a conclave of the Badgenoone Neverborn authors. This was a wonderful opportunity to see if her teammates had discovered the largest golden nuggets during the course of their observation.

Anna, Bernadette, Christopher, Daniel, Elizabeth, Frederick, George, Henry and Israel were the first to arrive at the clearing over-looking the Dutch Buffalo Creek.

Another seventy-nine joined the original ten at the makeshift oval amphitheater in the woods. Jackson acknowledged and thanked several special guests; an editor named Renée, and her colleagues, Colin, Brelan and Hannah. JBadgenoone addressed the assemblage.

"To the original Badgenoone observers, I want to thank you for your contribution to the story. You supplied a sufficient number of chapters to secure a PG13 rating from the Motion Picture Association of America for the screen version of the book.

"My recommendation is that you use discretion when record-ing the remaining chapters. Try not to outdo the Torah or New Testament when you point to the difficulties encountered by your observee. You don't have to dwell on the experiences forged in war and competition. The bibliography in this book provides more than enough stories to satisfy even the most martial enthusiast.

"The flesh of your observee is prone to limitations experienced by Adam and Eve. Advances in science, medicine, technology, and film amplify the nature of the species. Try to find and emulate an author who frames challenges within a modern-day context. Don't hesitate to embrace lesser-known works for your inspiration.

"You found a way to appreciate quotes from *Apples of Gold*, compiled by Jo Petty. My favorite, on page 57, invoked The Golden rule—not the rule of gold. Frederick told me that he planned to revise his book based on the inspiration he drew from a book titled *Sufficient Grace*, written by Kelly Gerken. Sometimes crowning jewels will be hidden in your bibliography.

"I would like each of you to share at least one treasure that you discovered during the course of your observation. Your observees had a predilection to frame significant discovery with scriptural passages. Feel free to quote them in your narration. Anna, why don't we begin with you?"

Anna was the first to speak. She shared that the multiple personalities of her observee helped her to understand the personalities of Jesus. He said, "Think not that I am come to send peace on earth: I came not to send peace, but a sword." (Matthew 10:34) The same Jesus said, "Peace I leave with you, my peace I give unto you: not as the world giveth, give I unto you. Let not your heart be troubled, neither let it be afraid." (John 14:27) Trav and Nav seemed reconciled at last. James found the proper balance between good works and faith."

Bernadette considered Jimmy's attempt to reason the person of God. "Therefore go and make disciples of all nations, baptizing them in the name of the Father and of the Son and of the Holy Spirit." (Matthew 28:19) Bbadgenoone considered the roles of her observee. He was just one man. But that man was a Father and a Son. His spirit still brings refreshment to those who come to know him through his story.

Christopher revealed Charlene's haunting search through the theories of so many scientists and philosophers. It started as a juvenile inquiry into time travel presented in the works of Jules Verne. By her ninth decade, she argued in her mind with physicists who advanced the notion of a space-time continuum. She couldn't understand why they were searching for the meaning of existence in a black hole out there in space.

They could have discovered the nugget without mathematics by reading Revelation, 1:8. "I am Alpha and Omega, the beginning and the ending, saith the Lord, which is, and which was, and which is to come, the Almighty." Charlene was certain that the secret to the universe is contained in a single drop of the blood of Christ. The universe begins and ends for each soul the moment that drop washes over the sinner. It is not out there, it is in here—simple, powerful, and liberating.

Daniel believed that Mary suffered in silence when she came to grips with the loss of her baby boy. She was comforted by the same passage that provoked her daughter: "For God so loved the world that he gave his only begotten Son, that whosoever believeth in him should not perish, but have everlasting life." (John 3:16) She drew strength from the knowledge that her son would never perish.

Elizabeth was the next to address the conclave. Fred impressed her with his constant quest for peace in a world that seemed to be forever at war. As he left the B24 Liberator following his last bombing mission, Fred reflected on the roots of global conflict.

He read a passage from Genesis 4. "And the LORD said unto Cain, Where is Abel thy brother? And he said, I know not: Am I my brother's keeper? And he said, What hast thou done? The voice of thy brother's blood crieth unto me from the ground."

It was after reading this that Fred understood the seeds of destruction. They were sown from the dawn of the human race. They were planted to drive men and women to seek a different path.

Frederick Badgenoone stood before the conclave. His observee, Mimi, wanted to leave behind a scriptural message for her daughters and grandchildren. Dimples provided the inspiration when she stood on the oval braided rug in her living room and sang her favorite song.

She belted out the refrain without end: *Let it go, let it go, let it go.* It prompted Mimi to recall her time years ago on the same rug, in a different room, and a different home.

Mimi thought of her husband James, the traveler and knowledge navigator. She remembered her dad the peacemaker and her mom the homemaker. She reflected on the lives of her father-in-law and mother-in-law. She considered the lives of all the relatives and the friends she met along the way. She selected Ecclesiastes 3 and asked FBadgenoone to observe the message for the benefit of the next generation.

> To every thing there is a season, and a time to every
> purpose under the heaven:
> A time to be born, and a time to die; a time to plant, and
> a time to pluck up that which is planted;
> A time to kill, and a time to heal; a time to break down,
> and a time to build up;
> A time to weep, and a time to laugh; a time to mourn,
> and a time to dance;
> A time to cast away stones, and a time to gather stones
> together; a time to embrace, and a time to refrain from
> embracing;
> A time to get, and a time to lose; a time to keep, and a
> time to cast away;
> A time to rend, and a time to sew; a time to keep silence,
> and a time to speak;
> A time to love, and a time to hate; a time of war, and a
> time of peace.

George Badgenoone was the next to address the conclave. He paused for a moment when he heard the laughter of children. Mimi's grandchildren danced along the path that led to the clearing by the creek. Jackson agreed to give them ears to hear the passages selected by their parents.

Firebird was the first to offer guidance to the generation that followed the next generation and all the generations to come. She read from the Psalms, 46:10: "Be still, and know that I am God: I will be exalted among the heathen, I will be exalted in the earth."

Henry recalled the moment when Belle embraced a quote from Isaiah 40:31. "But they that wait upon the LORD shall renew their strength; they shall mount up with wings as eagles; they shall run, and not be weary; and they shall walk, and not faint." It sustained her through the most difficult of times. He would sustain them.

Israel remembered the moment when the Artist read 2 Timothy 1:9: "Who hath saved us, and called [us] with an holy calling, not according to our works, but according to his own purpose and grace, which was given us in Christ Jesus before the world began." It was not what we did but who He is, and not who we are but what He did that gives us hope.

Jackson was the last to speak. Her observee Frederick had set in motion the entire sequence of events that led to the telling of this story. That Frederick had an opportunity in his final year to talk with JBadgenoone. The scripture that he selected was absolutely essential for the souls who drew breath from Adam and Eve.

It was a bittersweet reminder for the Neverborn. Frederick read from John 3:

> Jesus answered, Verily, verily, I say unto thee, Except a
> man be born of water and of the Spirit, he cannot enter
> into the kingdom of God.
> That which is born of the flesh is flesh; and that which is
> born of the Spirit is spirit.
> Marvel not that I said unto thee, Ye must be born again.
> The wind bloweth where it listeth, and thou hearest the
> sound thereof, but canst not tell whence it cometh, and
> whither it goeth: so is every one that is born of the Spirit.

At that moment, a breeze blew in from the meadow. Parents, grandparents, and generations long since gone joined them at the clearing. Jackson addressed the entire conclave of Neverborn colleagues. "You have a lot of stories to tell. When you begin your observations please remember the following: History books ventilate the famous and infamous few. Your books must *validate* the unnoticed and under-appreciated many and the God they serve. You will have to broaden your search for supporting materials. Look beyond the books, the eBooks, the letters, cards and journals. *Tempus fugit, carpe diem*, travel in the cloud, and remember that:

> Good works lean on each other.
> Great works lean on Faith and Hope.
> Lasting works lean on Love.

Encourage your readers to search for real treasure. "Ask, and it shall be given you; seek, and ye shall find; knock, and it shall be opened unto you." (Matthew 7:7)

The grandchildren heard and considered every word. The Linguist argued that all language could be reduced to two words, *love* and *hate*. Only one of those could prevail. Orwell's reductionist path may have merit. They smiled.

Following that moment, two men appeared on opposite banks of the creek. It now swelled to the proportions of a river. One of them called out to the Badgenoone Neverborn observers and to their observees. He quoted Isaiah 45:3:

> I will give you hidden treasures, riches stored in secret places, so that you may know that I am the Lord, the God of Israel, who summons you by name.

Selected Notes

JBadgenoone kept notes to a minimum. Additional resources
and references are available in an heirloom edition.

1. Sarah Elizabeth Richards article published in the Genius Issue
   of Time magazine, December 1, 2014; P.61, "Someone I Loved
   Was Never Born."
2. http://www.nationalmuseumoftheamericanrevolution.org/
   museum/display.asp?id=117

Despite history's preoccupation with firearms during the
Eighteenth Century, the ultimate infantry weapon on the battlefield
was the bayonet. It changed the inaccurate, slow-firing musket into a
spear at close quarters and was traditionally employed in disciplined
attacks by massed formations. This German-Dutch knife-blade
bayonet, made to attach to an eighty-caliber musket barrel, represents the most vicious type employed during the Revolutionary
era, outlawed by all Nations except Germany. Washington ordered
all captured examples stored and warned the enemy that no quarter
would be granted any soldier captured with one.

Bibliography

*Jackson suggested that at least a few of the titles should provide instructive enjoyment to the grandchildren. She asked Vincent Badgenoonevv to flag them with an abbreviation, **YGC**. Adult supervision was required for some of the other works.*

Abraham Lincoln, The Prairie Years and the War Years by Carl Sandburg, copyright © 1954 A.D. by Carl Sandburg, copyright © Renewed 1982 A.D. by Margaret Sandburg, Janet Sandburg and Helga Sandburg, Hardcover edition published in 2007 A.D. by Sterling Publishing Co., Inc. ISBN 978-1-4027-8130-8.

A Connecticut Yankee in King Arthur's Court by Mark Twain, published 2012 A.D. by Collins Classics, Harper Collins. ISBN 078-0-00-744947-7.

A Country of Vast Designs, James K. Polk, the Mexican War and the conquest of the American Continent, copyright © 2009 A.D. by Robert W. Merry, published by Simon & Schuster. ISBN 978-0-7432-9743-1.

A Diary from Dixie by Mary Boykin Chestnut, Harvard University Press, copyright © renewed 1976 A.D. by Houghton Mifflin Company and Ben Ames Williams, Jr. ISBN 0-674-20291-0. paper.

A Field Guide to the Birds of North America by Michael Vanner, published in 2007 A.D. by Parragon, text copyright © 2006 A.D. by Parragon Books, Ltd., photographs courtesy of Oxford Scientific Films, copyright details available on page 256 of the book. ISBN 978-1-4075-1166-5. **YGC**

Alexander Hamilton, copyright © 2014 A.D. by Ron Chernow, published by The Penguin Press. ISBN 1-59420-009-2.

American White Paper, The story of American Diplomacy and the Second World War, copyright © 1940 A.D. by Joseph Alsop and Robert Kinter, published by Simon and Schuster Publishers.

Andrew Jackson in the White House, American Lion, copyright © 2008 A.D. by John Meacham, published in the United States by Random House Trade Paperbacks. ISBN 978-0-8129-7346-4.

Apples of Gold, compiled by Jo Petty, copyright © MCMLXII A.D. by Joe Petty, published by C.R. Gibson Company. ISBN 0-8378-1793-5. **YGC**

Autobiography of Mark Twain, Volume 2, copyright © 2013 A.D. by the Mark Twain Foundation, published by the University of California Press. ISBN 978-0-520-27278-1. (cloth: alk.paper).

Battle, A Visual Journey Through 5000 years of Combat, written by R.G. Grant, text copyright © 2005 A.D. by R. G. Grant, copyright © 2005 A.D. by Dorling Kindersley, Limited. **ISBN 0-7566-1360-4.**

Bittersweet Decision, The War Brides 40 years later, copyright © 1985 A.D. by Helene Lee, Helene R. Lee, published by Roselee Pubns (Dec 1985 A.D.) ISBN-10: 0961502509.

Bound Together: How Traders, Preachers, Adventurers, and Warriors Shaped Globalization, copyright © 2007 A.D. by Nayan Chanda published by Yale University Press, ISBN: 9780300112016.

Civilization in the West, second printing August 1964 A.D. by Crane Brinton, John Christopher and Robert Lee Wolfe, copyright © 1964 A.D. by Prentice-Hall, Inc. Library of Congress Number 64-12156.

Civil War Charlotte, Last Capital of the Confederacy by Michael C. Hardy, copyright © 2012 A.D. by Michael C. Hardy, published by the History Press. ISBN 978-1-60949-480-3.

Clouds of Glory, The Life and Legend of Robert E. Lee by Michael Korda, hardcover, copyright © 2014 A.D. by Success Research Corporation. ISBN 978-0-06-211629-1.

David O'Selznick's Gone With The Wind, copyright © 1986 A.D. by Ronald Haver, published by Bonanza Books. ISBN 0-517-60677-1.

December 7, 1941, The Day the Japanese Attacked Pearl Harbor by Gordon W. Prance with Donald M. Goldstein and Katherine V. Dillon, published by Warner Books, Inc. Copyright © 1988 A.D. by Anne Prange and Prange Enterprises, Inc. ISBN 0-446-38997-8. (pbk).

Decline and Fall of the Roman Empire, based on the original work *The History of the Decline and Fall of the Roman Empire* by Edward Gibbon, this abridged and illustrated edition was first published in 1979 A.D. by PRC Publishing Ltd. ISBN 1 85648 502 1.

Eisenhower's own story of the war, the complete report by the Supreme Commander on the War in Europe from Day of Invasion to the Day of Victory, copyright © 1946 A.D. by Arco Publishing Company, New York.

Field Manual FM 5-15 Field Fortifications

Field Manual FM 21-26 Advance Map and Aerial Photograph Reading

Field Manual M 30-5 Combat Intelligence

Franklin D. Roosevelt and the World Crisis, edited and introduced by Warren F. Kimball, The State University of New Jersey, copyright © 1973 A.D. by D.C. Heath and Company. ISBN 0-669-84947-2.

General Marshall's Report, the Winning of the War in Europe and the Pacific, Biennial Report of the Chief of Staff of the United States Army, 1943 to 1945, to the Secretary of War. published for the War Department in cooperation with the Council on Books in Wartime by Simon and Schuster.

Gettysburg, copyright © 2003 A.D. by Stephen W. Sears, First Mariner Books, published by Houghton Mifflin Harcourt Publishing Company. ISBN 0-395-86761-4.

Gettysburg, A Testing of Courage, copyright © 2002 A.D. by Noah Andre Trudeau, published by Harper Collins. ISBN 0-06-093186-8.

Ghost Soldiers, The Forgotten Epic Story of World War II's Most Dramatic Mission by Hampton Sides, published by Doubleday, a division of Random House, Inc., copyright © 2001 A.D. by Hampton Sides. ISBN 0-385-49564-1.

GI Brides, The Wartime Girls Who Crossed the Atlantic for Love, copyright © 2014 A.D. by Duncan Barrett and Nuala Calvi, published by Harper Collins. ISBN 978-0-06-232805-2.

Golden Promise in the Piedmont, The Story of John Reed's Mine by Richard e. Knapp, copyright © 1999 A.D. by the North Carolina Division of Archives and History. ISBN 0-86526-284-5. *YGC*

Hiroshima Nagasaki, The Real Story of the Atomic Bombings and Their Aftermath, copyright © 2011 A.D. by Paul Ham, published by Thomas Dunne Books, an imprint of St. Martin's Press. ISBN 978-1-250-04711-3.

Historical Study No.20-201; Military Improvisations During the Russian Campaign

Historical Study No.20-233 German Defense Tactics against Russian Breakthroughs

Historical Study No. 20-292 Warfare in the Far North

Hope for the Journey by Joi Copeland, copyright © 2013 A.D. by Joi Copeland, published by Comfort Publishing, LLC, ISBN 978-1-938388-05-7.

Images of the Civil War, the paintings of Mort Kunstler, the text by James M. McPherson, Gramercy Books, illustrative copyright © 1992 A.D. by Mort Kunstler. Text copyright © 1992 A.D. by James M. McPherson. ISBN 0-517-07356-0.

Jackson vs. Biddle's Bank, The Struggle over the second Bank of the United States, second edition, edited and with an introduction by George Rogers Taylor, copyright © 1972 A.D. by D.C. Heath and Company. ISBN 0-669-84491-8.

July 14 Countdown to War, copyright © 2013 A.D. by Sean McKeekin, published by Basic Books, A Member of the Perseus Books Group. ISBN 978-0-465-03145-0.

King Leopold's Ghost, copyright © 1998 A.D. by Adam Hochschild, published by Houghton Mifflin Company. ISBN 0-395-75924-2.

Leonardo, Artist, Inventor and Scientist by Maria Costantino, copyright © 1993 A.D. by Brompton Books Corporation. ISBN 0-517-06703-X.

Lincoln by David Herbert Donald, published by Simon & Schuster Paperbacks, copyright © 1995 A.D. by David Herbert Donald. ISBN-13: 978-0-684-82535-9.

Lincoln's Gamble, the tumultuous six months that gave America The Emancipation Proclamation and changed the course of the Civil War, hardcover copyright © 2014 A.D. by Todd Brewster, published by Scribner, a division of Simon & Schuster, Inc. ISBN 978-1-4516-9386-7.

Mathew Brady, Historian with a camera, copyright © MCMLV A.D. by James D. Horan, published by Bonanza Books, Library of Congress Catalog Card Number: 55-10171.

McGuffey's Sixth Eclectic Reader, revised edition, copyright © 1879 A.D. by Van Antwerp, Bragg & Company, copyright © 1896 by American Book Company. Reintroduced in 1920 and published by American Book Company, SBN 978-0-442-23566-6.

Moby Dick, edited by Hershel Parker and Harrison Hayford, a Norton Critical Edition, second edition, copyright © 2002 A.D., 1967 A.D. by W.W. Norton & Company Inc. ISBN 0-393-97283-6. (pbk)

Moby Dick by Herman Melville, published by Collins Classics, Harper Press paperback edition. ISBN 978-0-00-792556-8. **YGC**

Mohawks on the Nile, Journey of the Warrior Spirit by Joe Jacobs, M.D., copyright © 2013 A.D. by Joe Jacobs, M.D., produced by FriesenPress. ISBN 978-1-4602-0096-4. hardcover.

Native Grace, Prints of the New World 1590-1876, by W. Graham Arader III, introduced by Wendy Shadwell, copyright © 1988 A.D. by Thomasson-Grant, Inc., published by Thomasson-Grant, Inc. ISBN 0-934738-47-5. **YGC**

North Carolina in the Mexican War, 1846-1848 by William S. Hoffmann, State Department of Archives and History, Raleigh, North Carolina, 1959 A.D., second printing, 1963 A.D., third printing, 1969 A.D.

Odyssey, Pepsi to Apple a Journey of Adventures, Ideas and the Future by John Sculley with John A. Byrne, copyright © 1987 A.D. by John Sculley, published by Harper & Row, Publishers. ISBN 0-06-015780-1.

Okinawa, the last battle of WWII, copyright © 1995 A.D. by Robert Leckie, published by Penquin Group. ISBN 0-670-84716-X.

Paris 1919, Six Months That Changed The World, copyright © 2001 A.D. by Margaret MacMillan, foreword copyright © 2002 A.D. by Richard Holbrooke, maps copyright © 2002 A.D. by Jeffrey L. Ward, published by Random House Trade Paperbacks, an imprint of The Random House Publishing Group, a division of Random House, Inc. ISBN 0-375-76052-0.

Pearl Harbor, Roosevelt and the coming of the war, Third Edition, edited and with an introduction by George M. Waller, Butler University, copyright © 1976 A.D. by D.C. Heath and Company. ISBN 0-669-98376-4.

Polk, Clay, Lincoln, and the 1846 U.S. Invasion of Mexico, A Wicked War © 2012 A.D. by Amy Greenberg, a Borzoi Book published by Alfred A. Knopp. ISBN 978-0-307-59269-9.

Recollections and Letters, Robert E. Lee, by Robert E. Lee originally published in 1904 A.D., 2014 A.D. edition published by Barnes & Noble, Inc. ISBN-13:978-0-7607-5919-6.

Reconstruction in the South, Second Edition, edited and with an introduction by Edwin C. Rozwenc, Amherst College, copyright © 1972 A.D. by D.C. Heath and Company. ISBN 0-669-82735-5.

Remarkable Presentations, How to Develop and Deliver What Your Competitors Don't, By John Lowe, copyright © 2013 A.D. by Be Compelling Now, LLC. ISBN 978-0-9889389-1-5.

Report by The Supreme Commander To The Combined Chiefs of Staff on the Operations in Europe of the Allied Expeditionary Force, 6 June 1944 to 8 May 1945. U.S. Government Printing Office, 1946 A.D., 692416-46.

Representative Americans, The Revolutionary Generation by Norman K. Risjord, copyright © 1980 A.D. by D.C. Heath and Company. ISBN 0-669-02710-3.

Roman Art, Romulus to Constantine by Nancy H. Ramage and Andrew Ramage, copyright © 1991 A.D. by Prentice Hall, Inc. ISBN 0-13-782947-7.

Slavery in American Society, Second Edition, edited and with an introduction by Richard D. Brown and Stephen G. Rabe, University of Connecticut, copyright © 1976 A.D. by D.C. Heath and Company. ISBN 0-669-00093-6.

SO FAR, The First Ten Years of A Vision, published by Apple Computer in celebration of our tenth anniversary, text by Rob Prie, Design by Jill Savini, Creative Director Thom Marchionna, copyright © 1987 A.D. by Apple Computer, Inc. ISBN 1-55693-974-4. *YGC*

Steve Jobs by Walter Isaacson, copyright © 2011 A.D. by Walter Isaacson, published by Simon & Schuster. ISBN 1-4516-4853-9.

Storm Over The Land by Carl Sandburg, copyright © 1939 A.D., 1942 A.D. by Harcourt, Brace and Company, Inc. ISBN 1-56852-042-5.

Such Troops as These, The Genius and Leadership of Confederate General Stonewall Jackson, copyright © 2014 A.D. by Bevin Alexander, Original publication of The Berkley Publishing Group, published by the Penguin Group. ISBN 978-0-425-27129-2.

Sufficient Grace, written by Kelly Gerken, copyright © 2014 A.D. by Kelly Gerken, published by Comfort Publishing, LLC, ISBN 978-1-938388-47-7.

The Abolitionists, Means, Ends, and Motivations, Second Edition, edited and with an introduction by Hugh Hawkins, Amherst College, copyright © 1972 A.D. by D.C. Heath and Company. ISBN 0-669-81992-1.

The Adams Chronicles, Four Generations of Greatness by Jack Shepherd, published by Little, Brown and Company, copyright © 1975 A.D. by Educational Broadcasting Corporation. ISBN 0-316-78497-4. (hc)

The Adventures of Huckleberry Finn by Mark Twain, Collins Classics, Harper Press, an imprint of Harper Collins Publishers. ISBN-13:978-0-00-735103-9. *YGC*

The **Begum's Fortune** by Jules Verne, copyright © 1958 A.D. in England by Bernard Hanison Limited.

The **Carolina Gold Rush**, copyright © 1971 A.D. by Bruce Roberts, McNally and Loftin Publishers, Library of Congress Catalog Card Number 70-165464 ISBN-13: 9781561647156. *YGC*

The **Causes of the American Civil War**, edited and with an introduction by Edwin C. Rozwenc, Amherst College, copyright © 1972 A.D. by D.C. Heath and Company. ISBN 0-669-82727-4.

The **Century**, by Peter Jennings and Todd Brewster, published by Bantam Doubleday Publishing Group, Inc. Copyright © 1998 A.D. by ABC Television Network Group, a division of Capitol Cities, Inc. ISBN 0-385-48327-9.

The **Civil War, a complete military history**, by Douglas Welsh, copyright © 1981 A.D. by Brompton Books Corporation. 1992 A.D. Edition published by Longmeadow Press. ISBN 0-681-41767-6.

The **Civil War of 1812, American Citizens, British Subjects, Irish Rebels & Indian Allies**, copyright © 2010 A.D. by Alan Taylor, published by Vintage Books, a division of Random House, Inc. ISBN 978-0-679-77673-4.

The **Cowpens-Guilford Courthouse Campaign**, copyright © 1962 A.D. by Burke Davis, originally published by J.B. Lippincott Company, published 2003 by University of Pennsylvania Press. ISBN 0-8122-1832-9.

The **Death and Resurrection of Jefferson Davis**, by Donald E. Collins, copyright © 2005 A.D. by Rowman & Littlefield Publishers, Inc., published by Rowman & Littlefield Publishers, Inc. ISBN 0-7425-4304-8. (alk.paper).

The **Discoverers, A history of man's search to know his world and himself.** Copyright © 1983 A.D. by Daniel Joseph Boorstin, and Clare Boothe Luce, published by Random House, Inc. ISBN 0-394-40229-4.

The **Divided Union**, the story of the Great American War 1861-65, by Peter Batty and Peter Parish, published by Salem House Publishers, copyright © Peter Batty Productions, LTD and Peter Parish 1987 A.D. ISBN 0-88162-234-6.

The **End of the European Empire, Decolonization after World War II**, Edited and with an introduction by Tony Smith, copyright © 1975 A.D. by D.C. Heath and Company. ISBN 0-669-03195-0.

The **First World War**, copyright © 2001A.D. by Hew Strachan, published by Penguin Books, Ltd. ISBN 0-670-03295-6.

The **Golden Doorstep, a young North Carolina boy discovers the first gold in America! 1799** by W. Parker Marks, pictures by Don Moose, copyright © 1977 A.D., 1999 A.D. by W. Parker Marks, published by Meadowcreek Publications. *YGC*

The **Grapes of Wrath** by John Steinbeck, copyright © 1939 A.D. by John Steinbeck, published by Penquin Books. ISBN 978-0-14-028162-0.

The **Greatest Generation**, by Tom Brokaw, copyright © 1998 A.D. by Tom Brokaw, published by Random House, Inc. ISBN 0-375-50202-5.

Jackson Badgenoone

The King of Mulberry Street, copyright © 2005 A.D. by Denna Jo Napoli, published by Yearling, an imprint of Random House Children's Books, a division of Random House, Inc. ISBN: 978-0-553-49416-7.

The Long Surrender, a panoramic history of the collapse of the Confederacy and of the personal ordeal of its president, Jefferson Davis. By Burke Davis, copyright © 1985 A.D. by Burke Davis, published by First Vintage Books Edition. ISBN 0-679-72409-5.

The Mexican War © 1978 Time-Life Books Inc. By the editors of Time-Life Books with text by David Nevin, published by Time-Life Books, Alexandria, Virginia, Library of Congress Number 77-95212.

The North Carolina Historical Review, copyright © 2014 A.D. by the North Carolina Office of Archives and History, April 2014, Volume XCI, Number 2. ISSN 0029-2494.

The Outbreak of the First World War, Causes and Responsibilities, Fourth Edition, edited and with an introduction by Dwight E. Lee, copyright © 1975 A.D. by D.C. Heath and Company. ISBN 0-669-94706-7.

The Passing of the Armies, originally published in 1915 A.D., authored by Joshua Lawrence Chamberlain, an Introduction by Richard A. Saufers added and published by Barnes & Noble, Inc. Copyright © 2004 A.D. ISBN 978-0-7607-6052-9.

The President's War, Six American Presidents and the Civil War That Divided Them, copyright © 2014 A.D. by Chris DeRose, published by Globe Pequot Press. ISBN 978-0-7627-9664-9.

The Rise of Theodore Roosevelt, copyright © 1979 A.D. by Edmund Morris, published by Ballantine Books, a division of Random House, Inc. ISBN 0-345-28707-X.

The Road Ahead, copyright © William H. Gates III, 1995 A.D., first published by Viking Penguin, a division of Penguin Books, USA, Inc. ISBN 0-670-77289.

The South Was Right!, copyright © 1991 A.D., 1994 A.D. by James Ronald Kennedy and Walter David Kennedy, published by Pelican. ISBN 1-56554-024-7.

The Spanish War, an American Epic 1898, copyright © 1984 A.D. by George O'Toole, published by W.W. Norton and Company. ISBN 0-393-01839-3.

The Turner Thesis, Concerning the Role of the Frontier in American History, a book about the Thesis of Frederick Jackson Turner, third edition, edited and with an introduction by George Rogers Taylor, Amherst College, copyright © 1972 A.D.by D.C. Heath and Company. ISBN 0-669-81059-2.

The War of the Regulation and the Battle of Alamance May 16, 1771 by William S. Powell, published by Raleigh Division of Archives and History, North Carolina Department of Cultural Resources, Fifth Printing 1975 A.D.

The World Is Flat, copyright © 2005 A.D., 2006 A.D. by Thomas L. Friedman, published by Farrar, Straus and Giroux. ISBN-13:978-0-374-29279-9.

They Lie Forgotten, The United States Military Academy 1856 – 1861, copyright © 1986 A.D. by Mary Elizabeth Sergent, published by The Prior King Press, TX 2 025 534.

Those Who Have Borne The Battle, A History of America's Wars and Those Who Fought Them by James Wright, copyright © 2012 A.D. by James Wright, published in the United States by PublicAffairs™, a member of the Perseus Books Group. ISBN 978-1-61039-244-0.

Traveler, by Elaine Fox, ebook publication 2011 A. D. by Barnes & Noble. BN ID: 2940013488700.

Ulysses Grant in War and Peace, copyright © 2012 A.D. by H.W. Brands, published by Random House. ISBN 978-0-307-47515-2.

Voices of Cherokee Women, copyright © 2013 A.D. by Carolyn Ross Johnston, published by John F. Blair Publisher. ISBN 978-0-89587-599-0.

Voices of the Civil War, copyright © 1976 A.D. by Richard Wheeler, published by the Penguin Group, Penguin Books, Library of Congress Number 98-13289.

War Brides of WWII, by Elfrieda Berthiaume Shukert and Barbara Smith Scibetta, published by Penguin Group. ISBN 978-0-89141309-7.

We Interrupt This Broadcast, copyright © 1998 A.D. by Joe Garner, foreword by Walter Cronkite, published by Sourcebooks. ISBN 1-57071-328.

Welcome to the Real World: A Complete Guide to Job Hunting for the Recent College Grad, copyright © 2014 A.D. by John Henry Weiss, published by Skyhorse Publishing. ISBN 10:1-62873-686-1.

Where the Old Roads Go, Driving the first federal highways of the Northeast, copyright © 1990 A.D. by George Cantor, published by Harper and Row, Publishers. ISBN 0-06-096508-8.

Wind from America, The French Revolution, by Claude Manceron, copyright © 1974 A.D. by Editions Robert Laffont, published by Alfred A. Knopf, Inc. ISBN 0-394-49883-6.

World War II Chronicles The Intelligence War, by Donald P. Steury, copyright © 2000 A.D. by Michael Friedman Publishing Group. ISBN 1-56799-958-1.

World War II, Roots and Causes, edited and with an introduction by Keith Eubank, copyright © 1975 A.D. by D.C. Heath and Company. ISBN 0-669-93096-2.

1776, copyright © 2005 A.D. by David McCullough, published by Simon & Schuster. ISBN 0-7432-2671-2

1984, A Novel by George Orwell, copyright © 1949 A.D. by Harcourt Brace and Company. Copyright © renewed 1977 by Sonia Brownell Orwell. ISBN 0-452-26293-3.

High Water Marker selected years of reflection and descriptive of significant events that impacted the lives of the observees and/or the global stage during those years.

33 A.D.	Resurrection
1744 A.D.	Perihelion
1757 A.D.	Foment
1758 A.D.	Formation
1772 A.D.	Partition
1776 A.D.	Revolution
1777 A.D.	Momentum
1798 A.D.	Prediction
1804 A.D.	Tension
1822 A.D.	Expansion
1830 A.D.	Interpretation
1841 A.D.	Acquisition
1848 A.D.	Revolution(s)
1849 A.D.	Discovery
1860 A.D.	Compromise
1861 A.D.	Division
1862 A.D.	Incursion
1863 A.D.	Redefinition
1865 A.D.	Reunification
1885 A.D.	Exploitation
1903 A.D.	Fulfillment
1908 A.D.	Transition
1914 A.D.	Lost Innocence
1915 A.D.	Prelude
1918 A.D.	Relief

1920 A.D.	Style
1925 A.D.	Sobriety
1927 A.D.	Exuberance
1928 A.D.	Without Limits
1932 A.D.	Restored Confidence
1935 A.D.	Plebiscite
1936 A.D.	Recovery
1938 A.D.	Appeasement
1939 A.D.	Reckoning
1941 A.D.	Retribution
1942 A.D.	Retrenchment
1944 A.D.	Anticipation
1945 A.D.	Rebuilding
1946 A.D.	Reconstruction
1947 A.D.	Realignment
1949 A.D.	High Expectations
1950 A.D.	Sober Expectations
1952 A.D.	Revision
1953 A.D.	Repair
1954 A.D.	Reversal
1955 A.D.	Upheaval
1957 A.D.	Adjustment
1958 A.D.	Renewal
1962 A.D.	Challenge
1965 A.D.	Provocation
1970 A.D.	Maturation
1972 A.D.	New Beginnings
1974 A.D.	Political Drama
1977 A.D.	Illumination

1978 A.D.	Rebirth
1979 A.D.	Possibilities
1981 A.D.	Deliverance
1984 A.D.	Awakening
1987 A.D.	Prediction(s)
1988 A.D.	Reiteration
1989 A.D.	Refinement
1993 A.D.	Consolidation
1994 A.D.	Reservation
1995 A.D.	Infringement
1996 A.D.	Exuberance
2001 A.D.	Disruption
2007 A.D.	Resignation
2012 A.D.	Commiseration
2014 A.D.	Reconciliation
2015 A.D.	Publication
2054 A.D.	Consequence
2095 A.D.	To be determined by another generation . . .

About Jackson Badgenoone

Jackson Badgenoone emerges from the wind and clouds, whispering to the thoughts of her extended family. As one of the Neverborn, she has borne witness to the lives of specific individuals for countless years, acting as a faithful recorder of events and significant moments. *The Hidden Treasure of Dutch Buffalo Creek* is one of many books which she has penned alongside her kindred Neverborn spirits. She is an avid researcher and ghostwriter, and continues to document the high water markers of her beloved clan to this very day. Learn more about the author at www.hiddentreasurenovels.com.

CPSIA information can be obtained
at www.ICGtesting.com
Printed in the USA
FFOW02n2313150916
27602FF